Landscapes of Desire

Metaphors in Modern Women's Fiction

Avril Horner

Lecturer in English, University of Salford

Sue Zlosnik

Senior Lecturer in English
Liverpool Institute of Higher Education

HARVESTER WHEATSHEAF

New York London Toronto Sydney Tokyo Singapore

First published 1990 by
Harvester Wheatsheaf
66 Wood Lane End, Hemel Hempstead
Hertfordshire HP2 4RG
A division of
Simon & Schuster International Group

Typeset in 11/12 pt Baskerville
by Photoprint, Torquay

Printed and bound in Great Britain by
Billing and Sons Ltd, Worcester

British Library Cataloguing in Publication Data

Horner, Avril, *1947–*
Landscapes of desire: metaphors in modern women's fiction.
1. English fiction Women authors History and Criticism
I. Title II. Zlosnik, Sue, *1949–*
823.912099287

ISBN 0–7108–1228–0

1 2 3 4 5 94 93 92 91 90

For Howard and John, and our six sons, Laurie, Joel, Daniel, James, Sam and Tom

Contents

Preface

We first thought of writing this book when we were teaching courses on women writers in the Extra-Mural Department of Manchester University. We both wish to record our gratitude not only to the students of that Department, but also to students we have taught at the University of Salford, De La Salle College and the Liverpool Institute of Higher Education. Their enthusiastic responses to these women writers provided the first impetus for this book; their contributions to discussions continued to sharpen and enliven our ideas while *Landscapes of Desire* slowly took form. This book is intended to be helpful to students like them and to anyone interested in exploring feminist readings of women's writing.

We would also like to thank Jackie Jones of Harvester Wheatsheaf for her constant encouragement and support.

A.H.
S.Z.
1990

Introduction

This is a book about reading women's writing. It is particularly concerned with how women writers of the past came to terms in their work with contemporary social constructs of 'woman'; how, in effect, their work deconstructed cultural paradigms of womanhood delineating the serene mother, the beautiful siren, the devoted wife, the eccentric artist. Reading these novels and short stories many years later, we need to have some sense of the historical context of each work (in order to understand these paradigms more clearly) and an awareness of the values we bring with us to these texts. We celebrate, with Patrocinio P. Schweickart, the notion of a 'community of women readers'[1] as a community which, through fresh reading strategies, has recreated and revalued the work of women writers. At the same time, we are aware that it is all too easy to be tempted into glossing over any aspect of a woman writer's life and work which would seem to contradict a reading of them as politically correct. Our view is that, rather than desperately trying to redeem all women's writing as radical, feminist critics must develop reading strategies that come to terms with the contradictions and ambivalences of women writers.

The works we discuss are all drawn from the rich tradition of women's writing which has come into its own only in the last twenty years or so. That the discovery of this tradition has coincided with the resurgence of feminism is, of course, no accident. Texts such as Kate Chopin's *The Awakening* and Charlotte Perkins Gilman's *The Yellow Wallpaper*, which are now part of the literary canon of women's writing, were not widely available until women entered the world of publishing and academia and gained the power to shape that canon. Further, as Jean Kennard pointed out in 1981 in an article entitled 'Convention coverage or how to read your own life', even texts which *were* easily available could not lend themselves to feminist interpretations until women readers developed the critical concepts which make those readings possible. Such concepts, Kennard argued, crystallised in 'a series of conventions available to readers of the 1970s which were not available to those of 1892'.[2] Since the 1970s, however, feminist criticism has become increasingly sophisticated; in so far as this has brought it academic credibility that is all to the good. We must recognise, however, that it thereby risks the danger of being intelligible to an ever-decreasing part of that 'community of women readers' to which Schweickart refers. We do not wish to intimidate our readers by assuming extensive knowledge of theory; nor do we wish to patronise them by adopting the rather simplistic reading model of authentic realism, since this model embraces an unproblematic notion concerning the 'real' nature of women.[3] We have therefore chosen a middle path, keeping the close reading of texts at the centre of our method and drawing only lightly on the surrounding fields of psychoanalysis, feminist theory and cultural studies. Inevitably the selection of certain episodes and passages betrays our own interests and liberal feminist values but we have tried to resist 'raiding' texts in a way that seems to distort or simplify what might well be a position of ambiguity or compromise on the part of the writer.

Moreover, we are concerned at the way in which any highly theorised critique necessarily subordinates the literary text to another discipline or disciplines. This does not mean that we inevitably reject concepts that other disciplines have to offer. For example, it is clear that however uneasy we might feel at French feminism's heavy reliance on Lacanian psychoanalysis, it gives us abstractions which are conceptually rich and provocative. The concept of *écriture féminine* allows us to perceive women's writing as offering an alternative discourse to that of patriarchy. It is also clear, however, that much French feminist theory has moved further and further away from the actual and the historical and closer to the vatic and the mystical. For the feminist reader of literature such a mode of understanding brings with it the danger that Janet Todd has described as theory's tendency 'to mystify history into the timeless model of psychoanalysis'.[4] We should surely heed her concern that the historical dimension of women's writing is an important part of the complexity of women's experience:

> The psychoanalytic approach emphasizing language opens up much. With Freud's help we have seen the difficulty of the relationship of identity to sex, with Lacan's the difficulty of relationship when no fixed essences exist. Such insights must unsettle criticism, but, to me, the psychoanalytic method forecloses on the final elusiveness of a text, which is precisely the presence of history. Literary works give images of women that are not absolutely identical, and the differences among them must be significant. Historical flux and change should not be prematurely ended in symbolic stasis so that women can suffer once and for all an identity fixation on the level of style, releasing action only to the 'woman' of the semiotic. Ultimately the psychoanalytic woman is another reification and the reading taken to preserve her is an erasing of the history of women which we have only just begun to glimpse.[5]

In her introduction to number 55/6 of *Yale French Studies*, Shoshana Felman discusses the subordination of literary texts to psychoanalysis and defends literature as a way of knowing. She argues that, in taking literature as a body of language to be interpreted, psychoanalysis seeks power and authority over the literary text, using it to satisfy its own desire. She comments that this often leaves the literary critic dissatisfied, feeling that:

> literature is in effect not *recognized* as such by psychoanalysis; that the psychoanalytical reading of literary texts precisely *misrecognizes* (overlooks, leaves out) their literary specificity; that literature could perhaps even be defined as that which remains in a text precisely *unaccounted for* by the traditional psychoanalytical approach to literature.[6]

Noting that psychoanalysis draws on literature for many of its key concepts (the Oedipus complex and Narcissism, for example) and therefore uses fiction 'in order *to speak of itself*, in order to *name itself*', she concludes that 'in the same way that psychoanalysis points to the unconscious of literature, *literature, in its turn, is the unconscious of psychoanalysis*.'[7] She therefore demands a relationship of dialogue between the two areas, in which implication might replace mastery as an interpretative mode. Indeed, she offers irony – a vital dimension of literary writing usually missing from the discourse of psychoanalysis – as a means by which literature is able to deconstruct the fantasy of authority:

> Psychoanalysis tells us that the fantasy is a fiction, and that consciousness is itself, in a sense, a fantasy-effect. In the same way, literature tells us that authority is a *language effect*, the product or the creation of its own *rhetorical* power: that authority is the *power of fiction*; that authority, therefore, is likewise a fiction.[8]

We agree with Felman that a relationship of dialogue, rather than mastery, should exist between the two areas and state here our particular interest in metaphor which, we would suggest, can speak in a text of a concern only half recognised, or completely repressed, by the author's conscious mind. Further, we have chosen to work with metaphor partly because it is a familiar literary concept and one which is therefore meaningful to a wide audience. Inevitably informing all discourses and all narratives, metaphor is foregrounded in literary texts. In so far as the meaning of metaphor can shift with reader response, metaphor also foregrounds ambiguity and ambivalence; it is perhaps for this reason that literary writing often seems reduced by theoretical or polemical appropriation which seeks to banish ambiguity. Metaphor has, moreover, a subversiveness of its own: it can threaten the stability of the dominant discourse by its ability to disrupt the threshold of meaning. Metaphor, Alan Singer suggests, challenges the dominant culture since 'insofar as it purports new meaning (metaphor) always entails a radical suspension of the thematic grids that locate the threshold of meaningfulness in language and inscribes us in the familiar texts of our culture.'[9] Metaphor, claims Don Cupitt

> is the device by which we can evade the Law of the signifier. *Verdichtung* becomes *Dichtung*: metaphor is subversive, innovative, creative. It makes language flexible and allows us to break out of the prison of the code. The manifest signifier, the term substituted, by its very novelty and unexpectedness alludes to as well as veils the latent or repressed signifier that it has replaced.[10]

Also writing theoretically on metaphor, Patricia Parker, in her essay 'The metaphorical plot', refutes Wallace Stevens's view that there is no metaphor for metaphor; there is, she argues, no dearth of metaphors for metaphor. From classical times, writing about metaphor has been dominated by the notion of 'place' – 'of territory already staked out, of the tropological as inseparable from the topological'. Metaphor itself is seen as the crossing of boundaries, as a transgressive act. She goes on to suggest that the multiplicity of plots associated with metaphor – transference, transport, transgression, alienation, impropriety, identity – suggests why metaphor can be at work in so many genres not just as a figure of speech or rhetorical ornament but as 'a structuring principle'.[11] We have adopted this way of reading metaphor in the texts we examine and have attempted to relate it to the way in which women might read women's writing. We have deliberately avoided using the term 'symbol' which, with its Romantic connotations, suggests a metaphysical essentialism avoided by the writers we examine in this study. The works under scrutiny in *Landscapes of Desire* all implicitly acknowledge the power of metaphor: metaphor can structure, rather than merely ornament a text; its chimerical nature unsettles thresholds of meaning and can be used to challenge the fixity of the dominant discourse.

In *Landscapes of Desire*, we have chosen to discuss work by Charlotte Perkins Gilman, Kate Chopin, Edith Wharton, Virginia Woolf, Jean Rhys and Margaret Atwood. What prompted this particular selection was our recognition that many novels by women writers of the late nineteenth and early twentieth century have certain configurations of metaphor in common. What are these configurations? We noticed repeated use of a dynamic relationship between room, house, land and sea and we began to realise that this relationship carried a significance which went beyond plot. Our first aim is to offer a reading of these works which interprets such configurations in a fresh way; our second is to ask whether similar metaphorical writing in later twentieth-century novels may be read in the same way – suggesting, perhaps, a continuing tradition of alternative quest and vision in women's writing. We are aware of the dangers of making all women seem to tell the same story. Nevertheless, it is an historical fact that women have long held a politically marginal position in Western culture; we wish to argue that the works we consider, which evolve from discrete and separate historical moments, all question that marginality by querying, *through metaphor*, the fixity of the dominant discourse of their time. The fact that male writers as diverse as Blake and Kafka have adopted a similar strategy in order to query the dominant values of their culture does not invalidate our argument. It suggests that rather than being an exclusively female way of writing, such a method describes a state of alienation which can be felt by both sexes. Being positioned on the margin of the dominant discourse seems to express itself in a preoccupation with boundaries, space and occupation.

We are not, of course, the first readers to notice the opposition between house/room and sea as a structuring principle in women's fiction. Our own understanding of the metaphorical implications of this opposition owes much to the work of Anglo-American feminist literary critics such as Ellen Moers, Elaine Showalter, Sandra Gilbert and Susan Gubar. The room has often been used as a metaphor for the physical and psychological constriction of women. Gilbert and Gubar's massive work, *The Madwoman in the Attic: The woman writer and the nineteenth-century literary imagination* (1979), deserves much credit for having traced so carefully images of enclosure in the work of nineteenth-century women writers; Elaine Showalter has written of the red room in *Jane Eyre* as representing 'a paradigm of female inner space'; Jennifer Gribble has examined the way in which the room as image in Tennyson's 'The Lady of Shalott' recurs in nineteenth-century fiction.[12] When, however, the image of the room is associated with women's economic independence and the fulfilment of artistic desire – as it is in Woolf's *A Room of One's Own* (1928) and her 'Professions for women' (written as a speech in 1931 and first published in essay form in *The Death of the Moth* in 1942) – its value changes and it becomes associated with autonomy, choice and freedom.

Unfortunately, sixty years on from Woolf's essay, only a small minority of women possess their own space and have fulfilled their potential; consequently the room is still often used to suggest negative feelings of constraint, or is used with some ambiguity, as it is in Marilyn French's *The Women's Room* (1977). At the opposite extreme from this we have a sense of space, envisaged in wide sweeps of open land and uncharted tracts of sea. The moors of *Wuthering Heights* (1847), the veldt of Schreiner's *Story of an African Farm* (1883), the sea in the work of Chopin, Woolf and Rhys are all examples of landscape used not just to give a sense of place but to suggest, sometimes with ambivalence, the possibilities for self that lie beyond society, outside patriarchy, and within the future. These possibilities, many of which are to do with rejecting the cultural construction of gender, must inevitably be connected with forces of wildness, fluidity and the unknown. This is not because woman herself is wild and unknowable, a conclusion which would drive us dangerously towards the essentialist position which sees woman as the embodiment of nature, instinct and intuition. It is because articulating the desire for woman's sexual, social and artistic freedom depends on suggesting what is not known, what is not acceptable, what lies beyond the civil boundaries of culture at the moment of writing and even beyond the words in which a culture inscribes itself. Drawing on the work of anthropologists Edwin and Shirley Ardener, Elaine Showalter describes women's culture as a 'wild zone' which exists in the realms of metaphysics or consciousness rather than in actuality.[13] In the same essay, Showalter refers to Myra Jehlen's definition of women's literary estate as suggesting:

> a more fluid imagery of interacting juxtapositions, the point of which would be to represent not so much the territory, as its defining borders. Indeed, the female territory might well be envisioned as one long border, and independence for women, not as a separate country, but as open access to the sea.[14]

The notion of a border giving physical presence to a state of marginality is recurrent in women's writing and thinking in terms of a 'landscape of desire' is well embedded in feminist literary critical practice. In so far as the texts we examine all query the social construction of 'femininity', they are poised on the border between the dominant culture and the 'wild zone'. However, we would suggest that the metaphorical configuration of room, house, land and sea is not simply an archetype of women's writing but that its use is inflected by the contemporary possibilities offered by feminism; we have tried to bear in mind what Janet Todd calls 'the presence of history' for both author and text. Thus the works we examine are placed in a particular historicised relation in such a way, we hope as to subject this mode of enquiry to a closer and more intensive scrutiny than it has formerly sustained.

The work of Gilman, Chopin and Wharton coincided with what can now be seen as the beginnings of modernism. Virginia Woolf was the contemporary of male writers such as Eliot and Joyce who have, until recently, dominated our understanding of modernism as a movement. Modernism involved a rejection of traditional forms in all the arts; writers, like painters and musicians, began to question the adequacy of existing conventions for representing feeling and experience. The novelist writing in the realist manner deals with the social and the knowable, a fact which the internal logic of the plot confirms; 'truths' are demonstrated through the stories of people's lives told in largely chronological fashion; the conventional closure of death or marriage reaffirms the validity of those 'truths'. Loss of faith in the realist novel to represent the complex and subjective nature of experience led to experiments in the form of the novel which included disrupting linear time, abandoning sequential plotting and jettisoning causality. In modernist works, the discourses of society, through which ideology operates, are fragmented and made strange; the lack of causality queries historical and cultural inevitability; death as closure becomes problematical and is no longer simply understood. Such texts are not concerned with 'truths' but with inviting the most uncomfortable questions about what we term 'reality'. Boundaries between the objective and the subjective dissolve alarmingly and as readers we are forced to reconsider what forces constitute the self, often with disturbing implications for our sense of autonomy.

It is only now, however, that the relationship between feminism and modernism is beginning to be explored.[15] From a feminist point of view, the kind of formal challenges to the realist novel which Woolf makes may be seen as a perception of the inadequacy of existing discourse for the woman writer. There is, in all the works we examine, a sense of the author pushing at the boundaries of realism, as if the exploration of psycho-sexual oppression demands a rejection of conventional narration as well as conventional values. It is perhaps not surprising that two of the American works discussed here – Kate Chopin's *The Awakening* (1899) and Charlotte Perkins Gilman's *The Yellow Wallpaper* (1892) – make tentative moves towards modernism; it is a development in fiction that coincides with the American and English cry for universal suffrage. Even the most orthodox, in terms of narrative presentation, of the novels we examine – Edith Wharton's *The House of Mirth* (1905) – departs from the techniques of realism in its concluding pages and renders its narrative and subject through dream, fantasy and vision. Closure is problematical in all the texts we discuss, especially in Chopin's *The Awakening*, Virginia Woolf's *The Voyage Out* (1915) and Jean Rhys's *Good Morning, Midnight* (1939). By the 1930s, however, when Rhys was producing her early work, both modernism and feminism were in decline. Significantly, then, Rhys uses the techniques of modernism to convey the repression of woman's desire.

For the woman writer, modernism, which dissolves boundaries, allows a particularly potent manner of expression; for her, the body itself may be a site of conflict in which the concepts of what is 'natural' within society play themselves out. Many of these concepts are not of her own making if she lives, as most women do, in a patriarchal society. The quest for an alternative, more valid sense of sexual self and how that might relate to the creative self is the quest that informs much women's writing. The frequency with which madness appears in the plot is an indication that within existing discourse, such desire and discontent must be unfocused; they can be socially contained only through categorisation as madness, a pathological condition. The shifting meaning of that emotive word, 'madness', and its role within the power structures of society, have recently been subject to much scrutiny: Foucault's *Madness and Civilization* (1961), Elaine Showalter's *The Female Malady: Women, madness and English culture, 1830–1980* (1985) and Don Cupitt's *The Long-Legged Fly: A theology of language and desire* (1987) have all contributed to a fuller understanding of the political and historical dimension which a diagnosis of madness must involve. In terms of biographical re-assessment, Stephen Trombley's book, *'All That Summer She Was Mad': Virginia Woolf and her doctors* (1981), has drawn attention to the cultural instability of the term 'madness'. Modernism itself, of course, was subject to early accusations of madness and derangement. Quentin Bell informs us in his biography of his aunt that 'It was Leonard's duty to deal with the indignant art-lovers who exploded with mirth or rage before the works of Picasso and Matisse.'[16] For many years the power of Woolf's vision has been relegated to the margins of meaning within our culture through the claim that her work is eccentric. The meaning of 'madness', both in art and life, is always volatile since it is defined in relation to what is culturally unacceptable; what is culturally unacceptable changes with history and so, therefore, does the meaning of 'madness'. The state of madness in these novels is therefore itself a metaphor for what is not culturally assimilable. In this way, madness becomes a double signifier: it is both the mental anguish suffered by women such as Charlotte Perkins Gilman, Virginia

Woolf and Jean Rhys in their real lives but it is also a metaphor for what cannot be contained within culture. The fact that madness, vision and delusion occur in conjunction with the sea in *The Awakening* (1899), *The Voyage Out* (1915), *To the Lighthouse* (1927) and *Wide Sargasso Sea* (1966) suggests that freedom from the boundaries of discourse and culture – which the sea metaphorically represents in these works – is a source of terror. This terror, however, is the foundation of a future freedom. Patricia Waugh points out in *Feminine Fictions: Revisiting the postmodern* (1989) that an historical perspective allows us to qualify the Freudian and Lacanian premise that women speaking against the symbolic order will inevitably be heard as insane; she uses the words of Janet Sayers to make her point:

> It is because the obstacles to women realizing the individual freedom promised by capitalist society are not eternal but are historical and social that the struggles of feminists over the last three hundred years to overcome these obstacles in order to realize their needs as individuals have not been as futile as Lacan's theory of the mirror stage implies them to be.[17]

In *Landscapes of Desire* we are concerned, then, with works that negotiate the psycho-sexual terrain between cultural definitions of gender and what can be imagined beyond those definitions. In the novels and short stories we have chosen for analysis, contemporary society is therefore never simply abandoned, but is always present as a carefully observed point of reference for a critique of woman's place within it. Further, all these works implicitly acknowledge that boundaries are both actual and psychological. The writers we examine are all concerned with two kinds of boundaries: those effected by society, often through the law, as walls of resistance to women's equality or power and those less obvious, but more insidiously powerful boundaries, which lie within the female psyche as a result of her socialisation. The first kind can be likened to a wall which can be overcome through protest and subsequent change of law; the suffragettes who chained themselves to railings were expressing, unconsciously or not, their imprisonment by boundaries which were unacceptable to intelligent, twentieth-century women. Such walls can be climbed over, demolished or dismantled; the law itself can be changed and used as a crude battering ram, as has recently happened with the Equal Opportunities Act. The other kind of boundary is much more impervious to attack because it cannot be easily seen; it exists in the unconscious and functions to determine perception before the rational, conscious mind even knows what has happened. In this, it may be likened to the ha-ha, a boundary to a garden or park so designed that it does not interrupt the view because it exists as a *sunken* wall, fence or trench. This is the type of boundary Jane Austen implicitly recognises in *Mansfield Park* (1814) when she describes Maria's feelings of constraint, faced with the prospect of marriage to Rushworth and the boundaries of the Sotherton estate. 'You have' says Henry Crawford, 'a very smiling scene before you'; Maria, however, is not cheered: '"Do you mean literally or figuratively? Literally I conclude. Yes, certainly, the sun shines and the park looks very cheerful. But unluckily that iron gate, that ha-ha, give me a feeling of restraint and hardship. I cannot get out, as the starling said."'[18]

Maria's flight across the ha-ha, which anticipates her elopement with Crawford, is not condoned by Jane Austen. Her condemnation of Maria's conduct, as well as her harsh treatment of the lively, albeit selfish, Mary Crawford suggests a rather conservative imagination. It is, however, an imagination which is fully aware of the ways in which a culture constrains the intellectual, artistic and moral development of its women and prevents their self-expression: '"Men have had every advantage of us in telling their own story. Education has been theirs in so much higher a degree; the pen has been in their hands"' says Anne Elliot in *Persuasion* (1818).[19] It could be argued that Jane Austen's novels chart, with wit and irony, the cost to her heroines of choosing to live within the confines of the ha-ha. Perhaps *Mansfield Park*, with its heroine, aptly surnamed Price, who marries a decidedly unimpressive hero, is her most ambivalent expression of that cost and consolation. In all Austen's novels, marriage as closure is an expression of desire domesticated and merged with economic destiny. Many years later, Jennifer Dawson in her novel *The Ha-Ha* (1961) was to present a heroine who, 'slightly bothered about the nature of reality'[20], finds herself confined to an asylum which is surrounded by both a wall and a ha-ha. The wall, which can easily be scrambled over, presents no problem to this young woman, but her inability to subscribe to what she sees as the unreal game of society's rules, represented by the ha-ha, leads to a diagnosis of schizophrenia.

The importance of the unseen boundary, or ha-ha, is one explored by Virginia Woolf in her essay 'Professions for women' (1931). In that essay she accepts that many visible and legal obstacles to women's economic equality with men have already been overcome: 'You have won rooms of your own in the house hitherto exclusively owned by men.'[21] She realises, however, that these obstacles have not constituted the most important boundary and attempts to show, through her own development as a writer, how other less obvious boundaries are, in fact, more potent in inhibiting women's creative potential. Later, in *Three Guineas*, she was to describe these less tangible constraints as 'mystic boundaries'. Recent feminist theory has contributed much to our understanding of the nature of these boundaries, seen and unseen. We would argue, however, that this theoretical work was anticipated in the creative writing of the novelists discussed in *Landscapes of Desire*. An implicit recognition of the power of discursive formations to constrain and restrict is expressed in metaphors of enclosure; a sense of the self as existing beyond those constraints is expressed in metaphors of fluidity and freedom from boundaries.

In selecting certain works for discussion, we have necessarily landscaped our own text. Any author who wishes to prove a thesis is forced to do this and we make no apology for not producing a comprehensive survey of women's fiction; we have not aimed at an encyclopaedic inclusiveness. We hope, instead, to demonstrate that the women writers whose work we discuss were intuitively aware of how 'woman' is constituted by and within discourse; and that the recurring configurations of metaphor in their fiction subtly articulate the constraints that the construct 'woman' places on the woman writer. It is a measure of how discourse itself has shifted since these works were written that we are now able to read these metaphors afresh. As women readers in the late twentieth century, we can construct anew the creative conflicts of women writers of several generations ago and can reconstitute the meaning of their metaphors in accordance with our own recent history and the insights that feminism has given us.

1
Awakenings

> She began to look with her own eyes; to see and to apprehend the deeper undercurrents of life.
>
> Kate Chopin, *The Awakening*, p.151.[1]

The three novels examined in this chapter, Edith Wharton's *The House of Mirth*, Charlotte Perkins Gilman's *The Yellow Wallpaper* and Kate Chopin's *The Awakening*, all concern women of artistic sensibility whose potential is not fulfilled. The stifling of this creative desire is connected with constraints imposed on the central character. The most powerfully inhibiting of these constraints are not monetary or legal but psychological: each heroine is surrounded by cultural paradigms of woman that speak of what it means to be 'feminine' at a particular historical moment. The suffocating nature of these social constraints and their withering effect on the development of the artistic mind are conveyed by images of enclosure in the three works. In this sense, all three novels conform to what Susan J. Rosowski, in an essay entitled 'The novel of awakening', has described as 'the female *Bildungsroman*'. In the hands of the male author, the *Bildungsroman* charts the hero's emotional, moral and intellectual apprenticeship and his acquisition of a philosophy of life; the female *Bildungsroman*, however, is primarily about an awakening to limitations:

> The novel of awakening is similar to the apprenticeship novel in some ways: it also recounts the attempts of a sensitive protagonist to learn the nature of the world, discover its meaning and pattern,

> and acquire a philosophy of life, but she must learn these lessons as a woman. This difference results in other differences between the novel of awakening and the apprenticeship novel. The subject and action of the novel of awakening characteristically consist of a protagonist who attempts to find value in a world defined by love and marriage. The direction of awakening follows what is becoming a pattern in literature by and about women: movement is inward, toward greater self-knowledge that leads in turn to a revelation of the disparity between that self-knowledge and the nature of the world. The protagonist's growth results typically not with 'an art of living', as for her male counterpart, but instead with a realization that for a woman such an art of living is difficult or impossible: it is an awakening to limitations.[2]

In our Introduction, we drew attention to the dynamic relationship between room, house, land and sea in women's writing and the complex meanings that this relationship can evoke when it is seen to refer metaphorically to the boundaries effected by culture and discourse and what lies beyond them. In this chapter we construct that configuration of metaphor across three works in the hope that such an intertextual reading will illumine further the metaphorical dimension of each text. Our reading of Edith Wharton's novel thus stresses its emphasis on rooms and interiors; we choose to focus on the notion of threshold in Charlotte Perkins Gilman's short story; we see Edna Pontellier's final swim in Kate Chopin's novella as a crossing of that threshold and boundary and as an act which metaphorically dissolves the social and linguistic construction of the self. It is, however, only in *writing* that this metamorphosis can be achieved in any positive sense. In the realm of real life such reconstitution is impossible; but writing, as Mary Jacobus has pointed out, is another realm and 'as the subject "I" is dissolved in writing, so boundaries themselves are called into question; rendered, not terra firma, but fiction too.'[3] Edna Pontellier does not, therefore, simply return to nature; rather her act is the rejection of a cultural inscription of womanhood, the political and linguistic constraints of which are metaphorically represented by the rooms and houses through which she moves.

Edith Wharton's *The House of Mirth*

Our first glimpse of Lily Bart is through the eyes of Lawrence Selden and it is one that emphasises the nature of Lily as artefact and product of polite New York society at the turn of the century:

> Selden was conscious of taking a luxurious pleasure in her nearness: in the modelling of her little ear, the crisp upward wave of her hair – was it ever so slightly brightened by art? – and the thick planting of her straight black lashes. Everything about her was at once vigorous and exquisite, at once so strong and fine. He had a confused sense that she must have cost a great deal to make, that a great many dull and ugly people must, in some mysterious way, have been sacrificed to produce her.[4]

This analogy leads him to speculate on the possibility that the material of Lily's inner being may be fine, 'but that circumstances had fashioned it into a futile shape' (p.5). However, his words, while they give voice to his belief in Lily's potential, betray his own limitations: his is a way of seeing which can realise women only as objects of the male gaze. The company which Lily keeps has strict notions about what constitutes acceptable and feminine behaviour; there is thus no way in which Lily can use the fine material of her artistic sensibility in order to support herself in the *nouveau riche* society of New York. The problem for Lily, then, is that which later faces Ned Silverton's sisters who are ruined by their brother's card-playing debts: she is unable to support herself financially. Dreams of autonomy and independence remain mere dreams because the social system in which Lily moves provides no way for a single woman to support herself in American polite society at the turn of the century. The novel presents only two alternatives to Lily's parasitic life-style: the admirable but impoverished state of independence that Gerty Farish has embraced or the physically exhausting life of the 'work girls' (p.315) of whom Nettie Struther is one. For Lily Bart, both alternatives are unthinkable. She is a 'lady'; she has not been trained to work, but to look beautiful and to marry:

> Inherited tendencies had combined with early training to make her the highly specialized product she was: an organism as helpless out of its narrow range as the sea-anemone torn from the rock. She had been fashioned to adorn and delight; to what other end does nature round the rose-leaf and paint the humming-bird's breast? And was it her fault that the purely decorative mission is less easily and harmoniously fulfilled among social beings than in the world of nature? That it is apt to be hampered by material necessities or complicated by moral scruples? (p.301)

The narrator's language expressing Lily's perception here gives an ironic edge to their naive fatalism. Further, the polished rhetoric of the passage presents the reader not only with a series of questions concerning social determinism but also undermines the validity of the answers that the questions seem to invite.

The reality of financial dependency is, in Lily's case, exacerbated by a taste for expensive and beautiful clothes. Her vanity and materialism, encouraged by social notions concerning the 'feminine', are the major flaws in her character and they result in her undoing. They are flaws she recognises in herself when she confesses to Gerty Farish that she wants admiration, excitement and money above everything else (p.166). When, through a series of unfortunate circumstances, she is forced to work for her living she can do so only inadequately. Like Amelia Osborne in Thackeray's *Vanity Fair*, she has 'been brought up to look ornamental' (p.297); her artistic talent has been encouraged only as a feminine accomplishment and is therefore not marketable. Wharton's novel, like Thackeray's, asks the question how far the tragic situation of one talented and utterly conventional woman can be attributed to the society which has formed her expectations, and how far to her own misjudgement and foolishness; how far, in fact, she is a 'highly specialized product' and how far she is an autonomous social being.

The novel takes its title from 'The vanity of fame' section in Ecclesiastes:

> A good name is better than precious ointment; and the day of death than the day of one's birth. It is better to go to the house

of mourning, than to go to the house of feasting: for that is the end of all men; and the living will lay it to his heart. Sorrow is better than laughter: for by the sadness of the countenance the heart is made better. The heart of the wise is in the house of mourning; but the heart of fools is in the house of mirth. (Ecc. 7:1–4)

This section is followed by one entitled 'The quest for wisdom'; for the reader who cares to refer Wharton's quotation to its source, there is ironic interplay between these subsequent verses which describe as 'more bitter than death the woman, whose heart is snares and nets, and her hands as bands' (Ecc. 7:26) and the pathetic failure of Lily's schemes and plans. Wharton's use of the biblical phrase as title is not meant to enforce a simple moral didacticism, but to draw attention to the way in which the social and linguistic construction of reality is a 'house' in which we all live. Lily's tragedy is that she is unable to move beyond the 'house' of New York society and this no doubt reflects Wharton's earlier capitulation to convention and respectability; as Sandra Gilbert and Susan Gubar have pointed out, 'where Schreiner, Gilman, and Chopin had each struggled to find ways out of the Hisland that so degraded and diminished women – "*sorties*", to use Hélène Cixous's phrase, into a Utopian Herland – Wharton mostly saw signs that said NO EXIT.'[5] Indeed, Lily whole-heartedly adapts herself and her energies to living within the confines of this house. It is a house of conservatism, shallowness and materialism – a house of vanity and mirth. Such a 'frivolous society', wrote Wharton,

> can acquire dramatic significance only through what its frivolity destroys. Its tragic implication lies in its power of debasing people and ideals. The answer [to the puzzle of portraying 'old woe of the world' through the medium of a vain pleasure-seeking society] was my heroine, Lily Bart.
>
> Once I had understood that, the tale rushed on toward its climax.[6]

Within the boundaries of this shallow society, certain roles are played out in rituals of significance. In order to earn their place in such a building and have some share in that wealth and power, ambitious men and women have to barter with society as Lily's surname suggests. A woman who wishes to succeed in this way, as Lily explains to Gerty Farish, has to develop the social skills of card-playing and small talk, and have 'just the right dress for every occasion' (p. 266). Part of Lily's foolishness is to overestimate the power and position that such collusion gives her. She also mistakes the nature of her hold over men; by the end of the novel the reader can see that such sexual power, which is temporary and intangible, is as nothing compared to the material power held by wealthy men and women. The narrator recognises early on, even if her heroine does not, that Lily's power over men derives from a sexual game in which her victories can only ever be temporary:

> letting Trenor, as they drove homeward, lean a little nearer and rest his hand reassuringly on hers, cost her only a momentary shiver of reluctance . . . the renewed sense of power in handling men, while it consoled her wounded vanity, helped also to obscure the thought of the claim at which his manner hinted. (p.85)

Lily realises too late that this 'sense of power' is illusory. She deludes herself into thinking that she has complete power over Gus Trenor and George Dorset; that as Rosedale's wife she will be able to transform him into 'the Rosedale she felt it in her power to create' (p. 253). Finally, however, her aunt's will teaches her 'the powerlessness of beauty and charm against the unfeeling processes of the law' (p. 230) and she comes to see what Sim Rosedale has recognised all along – that in the House of Mirth, reputation and power have everything to do with money and nothing to do with integrity:

> She had, in short, failed to make herself indispensable; or rather, her attempt to do so had been thwarted by an influence stronger than any she could exert. That influence, in its last analysis, was simply the power of money: Bertha Dorset's social credit was based on an impregnable bank-account. (p.261)

Lily, however, has her own peculiar brand of integrity: when Sim Rosedale suggests a rather murky strategy involving Bertha Dorset's letters to Lawrence Selden, Lily rejects it although it would offer her power of a sort, because 'she saw that the essential baseness of the act lay in its freedom from risk' (p.260). Lily is very much drawn to risk: playing cards with the Trenor set, 'she knew that the gambling passion was upon her' (p.27); her shady liaison with Gus Trenor results from a desire to gamble in the Wall Street world 'of "tips" and "deals"' – a world which seems to offer 'the means of escape from her dreary predicament' (p.82); she briefly joins the gambling set at the Casino in Monte Carlo; even her death, as Rachel Blau DuPlessis has pointed out, is something of a gamble with chloral, the odds against a lethal side-effect being stacked a hundred to one.[7] Like George Eliot's Gwendolen Harleth, Lily seems to gamble herself away in a series of small acts of miscalculation and self-destruction. The prize the House of Mirth offers is high for a woman with no prospects beyond marriage: comfort and luxury for the rest of her life. The stake, however, is correspondingly high: it is Lily's 'real self', an elusive phenomenon which Selden claims always to be glimpsing yet Lily never finds. Ironically, Selden thinks he sees 'before him the real Lily Bart' (p.135) when she is most disguised – as Mrs Lloyd in the *tableau vivant* episode. Further, he finds her most appealing when she appears helpless, 'like a hurt or frightened child' (p.95). She is never able to develop fully as an adult because the world of New York society is interested in her only as an object of beauty and amusement. Moreover, Lily colludes with this world which disapproves of women who want to create artistically, to think seriously and to move beyond mental childhood.

Wharton herself had close knowledge of the suffocating limitations such a society placed upon its clever women, as Cynthia Griffin Wolff has pointed out:

> Edith's family felt that a career as an artist would certainly be undesirable even for a young man – though it would have been quite suitable for a young man to dabble in a little desultory writing or painting. For a *woman* to pursue the life of a professional artist was something akin to harlotry.[8]

Unlike Wharton, who finally struggled through such boundaries, Lily capitulates to the demands of her society; like

George Eliot's tale of Maggie Tulliver, *The House of Mirth* deals with the fate of many talented women rather than with the success of the extraordinary few. It is interesting in this connection to note that one of Wharton's own nicknames was 'Lily';[9] it would seem that just as Virginia Woolf had to slay the Angel in the House to allow the artist in her to survive (see pages 68–9), so Edith Wharton murdered her pretty and conventional self in the character of Lily Bart and thereby allowed the writer in her to emerge. Her heroine, however, never finds another 'self'. A huge part of Lily lies undiscovered and unexpressed; with Lily's gradual betrayal of her talents, the Muses turn into Furies who hound her towards death. They also express her own repressed rage at her fate – 'She was trembling with fear and anger – the rush of the furies' wings was in her ears' (p.173) – and her fear of those more powerful than herself: 'More and more, with every fresh mischance befalling her, did the pursuing furies seem to take the shape of Bertha Dorset' (p.296). Finally they become indistinguishable from life itself, which by this time is a miserable existence in a seedy rented room: 'Perspective had disappeared – the next day pressed close upon her, and on its heels came the days that were to follow – they swarmed about her like a shrieking mob' (p.322).

Lily's slow and tragic slide into poverty and death is charted by her progression through a number of rooms and houses. These rooms and houses are emblematic of the House of Mirth; the rituals and entertainments which go on within their walls enact various aspects of the wider society to which the title of the novel alludes. It is presumably no accident that the first two buildings through which Lily passes obliquely allude to plays by Shakespeare in which masculine control of property and marriage is a major theme. 'The Benedick', which is owned by Sim Rosedale, recalls the confirmed bachelor hero of *Much Ado About Nothing*, a play which scrutinises the relationship between love and power and the power of love itself; Sim Rosedale comments on the building's name, 'I believe it's an old word for bachelor, isn't it? I happen to own the building – that's the way I know' (p.15).

Similarly, Gus Trenor's house, 'Bellomont', recalls Portia's father's house at Belmont in *The Merchant of Venice* where the stern dictates of her father's will are enacted. However, unlike Portia, who manipulates the situation to her advantage, neither Lily nor her suitor meets the terms of her aunt's will. Unlike Portia, Selden does not give a dazzling court performance in the service of his loved one even though he is a lawyer; instead he maintains his usual role as a passive observer of spectacle. Lily spends some time in her aunt's house, but 'contrasted with the light tints and luxurious appointments of the guest-rooms where so many weeks of Lily's existence were spent, it seemed as dreary as a prison' (p.109). What Lily has not yet realised, of course, is the more subtle imprisonment that these opulent houses effect. The ostentatious architectural nature of houses like the Wellington Brys' – which is modelled on the *Trianon* of Versailles – and the Trenors', built in the Corinthian style, suggests a shallow society peopled by materialists of the worst order. Lily passes through such houses and buildings in the novel in a downward social spiral: we see her set within the Casino at Monte Carlo, the Trenors' Fifth Avenue home, Gerty Farish's apartment, the 'unfinished' house at Roslyn which the Gormers have rented from Van Alstyne, Mrs Hatch's house, and Mme Regina's 'millinery establishment'. As her fortunes decline, she is reduced to living in rented rooms; at one stage she lives in a 'few square feet' in a hotel 'on the edge of a fashionable neighbourhood' (p.246). Her circumstances here are a sharp reminder of her failure to support herself:

> Her rooms, with their cramped outlook down a sallow vista of brickwalls and fire-escapes, her lonely meals in the dark restaurant with its surcharged ceiling and haunting smell of coffee – all these material discomforts, which were yet to be accounted as so many privileges soon to be withdrawn, kept constantly before her the disadvantages of her state. (p.247)

Later, when briefly employed by Mrs Hatch, she moves to the Emporium Hotel. Her final lodging-place, whilst she is working at Mme Regina's, is a 'narrow room, with . . . blotched wallpaper and shabby paint' (p.287) in a seedy boarding-house; it is here that she dies.

Always we see Lily within the confines of walls of houses or gardens; nowhere in the novel docs she simply escape into landscape. We learn early that she 'had no real intimacy with nature, but she had a passion for the appropriate and could be keenly sensitive to a scene which was the fitting background of her own sensations' (p.64). Lily thus allows herself to be defined by the social situation in which she moves, despite her recognition that the society of which she is part is a 'great gilt cage in which they were all huddled' (p.54). Her quest takes her from New York to Long Island, Monte Carlo and Sicily but nowhere do we have any sense of changing natural landscape. This is at once a recognition of her vulnerability and a condemnation of her lack of imagination; she has accepted the social boundaries and constraints set up by polite American society and has no vision of what 'self' might be construed beyond the House of Mirth. She is simply unable to imagine existing in another element. The fluidity of water, used by many women novelists to suggest the possibility of freedom and transformation, works in this novel only to suggest metaphorically the fear of insolvency, the fear of being engulfed by a 'mounting tide of indebtedness' (p.77). Ironically, the brief, manipulative note which Lily writes to Selden after the *tableau vivant* entertainment at the Brys's, is sent in an envelope fastened with 'a grey seal with *Beyond*! beneath a flying ship' (p.154). Selden thinks to himself that 'he would take her beyond – beyond the ugliness, the pettiness, the attrition and corrosion of the soul –' (p.154). His failure to do so is a betrayal both of what he sees in Lily and of his own visionary 'republic of the spirit' (p.68); her failure to envisage another realm beyond that of New York society is equally a betrayal of her own talent and potential.

That talent Lily uses wholly to present herself to her best advantage in a world of drawing-rooms and gardens. The occasional feeling of dissatisfaction results in nothing more than a *frisson* of *ennui*:

There were moments when she longed blindly for anything

> different, anything strange, remote and untried; but the utmost reach of her imagination did not go beyond picturing her usual life in a new setting. She could not figure herself as anywhere but in a drawing-room, diffusing elegance as a flower sheds perfume. (p.100)

She is, indeed, as the narrator later remarks, 'like some rare flower grown for exhibition, a flower from which every bud had been nipped except the crowning blossom of her beauty' (p.316). This reification of femininity is to be found reflected in the art of the period, particularly in the work of Alphons Mucha, whose use of flowers to represent the 'feminine' is, as Judith Fryer has pointed out, very distinctive:

> His barefoot, flowering goddesses in their diaphanous gowns become part of decorative motifs or frames that cannot contain them: the image spills from its boundaries in sensual triumph. In illustrations with titles like *Profile of a Woman with Orchids in a Decorative Frame* and *Woman with Lilies*, the lines of the woman's body, her costume, her jewels, her hair become the shapes of petals and leaves and stems: the woman herself is a flower.[10]

An exotic and cultivated specimen of this species, Lily is unable to survive in the cold blast of poverty where she withers away into misery and oblivion. Her name therefore stands in oblique and ironic contrast to the lilies of the Book of St Matthew who 'toil not, neither do they spin' (6:28–30). Before her decline into incompetent millinery, Lily 'toils' in a socially acceptable way by making herself a delightful ornament for the society in which she moves. Her major triumph in this respect is her appearance in a *tableau vivant* at the Welly Brys'. Carry Fisher, who has organised the entertainment, persuades 'a dozen fashionable women to exhibit themselves in a series of pictures' (p.131). The nature of Lily's triumph, however, exposes both the values of New York society and her collusion with them. The *tableaux vivants* designed by 'the distinguished portrait painter, Paul Morpeth' (p.131) require that a number of women dress themselves as the subjects of famous paintings and then recreate those scenes on stage. Beneath the respectability of interest in art lies a more suspect voyeurism; the women are not required to speak or think, merely to pose and look graceful while the men feast on their beauty. As in Wharton's novel, *The Reef* (1912), sexuality is a dark and powerful presence beneath sparkling waves of polite social intercourse. Van Alstyne comments to Selden after the entertainment, '"what's a woman want with jewels when she's got herself to show? The trouble is that all these fal-bals they wear cover up their figures when they've got 'em. I never knew till tonight what an outline Lily has"' (p.138). Although Selden indignantly dismisses such coarse remarks as the judgement of a Caliban on a Miranda, he is clearly aroused by Lily's presence on the stage and the only sexual contact between them in the novel takes place in the garden immediately after the entertainment. There is some pathos in the fact that Selden feels closest to Lily during this public performance, and claims to see the 'real' Lily when, in fact, she is disguised as Mrs Lloyd; the Lily he desires is not Lily Bart but a fantasy who emerges from 'the boundary world between fact and imagination' (p.133) which the *tableaux vivants* provide.

Lily's choice of portrait is highly significant. She chooses to represent Joshua Reynold's painting of Mrs Joanna Lloyd, daughter of John Leigh, of North Court, Isle of Wight, who married R. B. Lloyd, of Maryland, in 1775. The portrait, which is reproduced on the cover of this book, appeared in an exhibition in 1776 and was reviewed in the *Morning Post* in the following manner:

> The whole lengths of the two ladies are fine pictures . . . The designs are pleasing, particularly that of Mrs Lloyd on the left side, a beautiful figure in a loose, fancy vest, inscribing her husband's name on the bark of a tree. The idea is taken from *As You Like It.*[11]

Under a man's direction, Lily thus mimics a portrait of a woman who poses as a Shakespearean heroine who disguises herself as a man who pretends during the course of the play to be a woman. Although, no doubt, Wharton intended the reader to be aware of the complexity of Lily's situation, she allows her heroine to remain ignorant of the web of signification in which she is situated and appropriately, Lily's enactment of the portrait effaces, rather than releases, any 'real self'. There is, then, deep irony in the claim made by both Selden and Gerty Farish that the *tableau vivant* represents 'the real Lily Bart, divested of the trivialities of her little world' (p.135). We are also meant to read as ironic the narrator's description of the *tableau* as 'simply and undisguisedly the portrait of Miss Bart' (p.134). For the characters present during the entertainment, however, Lily seems to come most to life whilst frozen as an object of art:

> It was though she had stepped, not out of, but into, Reynolds's canvas, banishing the phantom of his dead beauty by the beams of her living grace . . . Her pale draperies, and the background of foliage against which she stood, served only to relieve the long dryad-like curves that swept upward from her poised foot to her lifted arm. The noble buoyancy of her attitude, its suggestion of soaring grace, revealed the touch of poetry in her beauty that Selden always felt in her presence, yet lost the sense of when he was not with her. (p.134)

For the reader who knows *As You Like It*, this episode of *The House of Mirth* evokes several ironic contrasts. For example, Rosalind's resourcefulness and initiative are sharply counter-pointed by Lily's vulnerability and passivity; Lily's careful staging of her own physical beauty is very different from Rosalind's deliberate screening of her sexuality within male attire. Moreover, in Reynolds's portrait, Mrs Lloyd is carving her husband's name on the bark of a tree, whereas in Shakespeare's play it is the hero, Orlando, who carves 'on every tree/The fair, the chaste, and unexpressive she' (Act III, sc.ii, 9–10). The writing woman of the portrait obliquely suggests the artistic potential that Lily has chosen to ignore; she also, however, inscribes within the novel Wharton's perception of herself as writing woman.

Reynolds's portrait of Mrs Lloyd is a rather strange work to modern eyes. It is a large scale, somewhat glamorous painting in which the subject has been perceived not directly, but through a fiction of the past. Mary Webster suggests that Reynolds deliberately set about restoring large-scale portraiture to the English tradition and that he designed a specific 'pose and setting for each sitter, whom he endowed with real or imaginary characteristics of a learned nature'. She notes, too, 'his ability to compose his pictures. His sitters, however improbable some may seem to us – and no doubt did when they were painted – are engaged with imposing manner in playing the role in which Reynolds chose to cast them.'[12] Thus not only is Lily playing a role under Paul Morpeth's direction, but the subject of the painting which she imitates is also playing a role, under Sir Joshua Reynolds's direction; Lily's representation of the fiction enacted by Mrs Lloyd is, then, paradigmatic of the way women are constrained and framed by images of women created by men. Reynolds's appropriation of Shakespeare's *As You Like It* involves, as we have seen, a misreading of the play in so far as it is Orlando, not Rosalind, who desecrates the trees of the forest; the portrait is also inaccurate in that Rosalind wears her woman's clothes in the forest only in the last scene when she is to be married to Orlando. In presenting Mrs Lloyd as Rosalind doing something that Rosalind never did – carving her husband's name on a tree – Reynolds tames a play that subversively questions the fixity of gender roles and enfolds it safely within the sphere of sensuous femininity, marital devotion and conjugal loyalty. The positioning and dress of Mrs Lloyd in the portrait also draw attention to what Van Alstyne would call her 'outline': the contours of her body can be clearly seen; the use of *décolletage* erotically leads the eye up from the shape of the breast to a face held in exquisite profile.

There is, then, something of a conflict between this representation of Mrs Lloyd as a beautiful woman and loyal wife and Shakespeare's representation of Rosalind as a woman who screens her female sexuality and who becomes an almost androgynous figure in *As You Like It.* No doubt Reynolds chose the Shakespearean context in order to flatter his subject – to suggest the wit and learning of Mrs Lloyd – but a sceptical reading of the painting also reveals a great deal about his own attitudes to female sexuality and creativity. However, the feminist critique of Reynolds's painting need not be entirely negative. Despite the highly stylised setting, with its conflicting classical and Romantic elements, the subject is, after all, a woman who writes and a woman who has retained some vestiges of Rosalind's androgynous nature. Her feet are free in sandals, her legs are solid and crossed in a carelessly assertive manner; indeed the setting and the pose of the subject, from the waist down, are remarkably reminiscent of Nicholas Hilliard's *Young Man amongst roses* (*c.*1588), traditionally taken to be a portrait of the young man of Shakespeare's sonnet sequence.[13] Her eyes seek not to engage the observer's but to concentrate on what she is writing. She is thus inscribing herself and her own desires in the landscape and recuperating androgyny in a subversive attempt to dissolve the boundaries effected by gender and culture. For the woman who reads *The House of Mirth*, the complex and conflicting messages of this portrait throw Lily's inability to 'read' her own situation into sharp and ironic relief. Allowing herself to be staged and posed by Paul Morpeth, Lily merely colludes with male fantasies of desire and becomes passive subject matter rather than active reader. Wharton, as a woman writer, inscribes Lily's collusion with patriarchy in a complex web of representations of women by men. Griselda Pollock, in her recent book *Vision and Difference*, draws attention to an article by Mary Kelly entitled 'Desiring images/imaging desire'. This article she sees as addressing the dilemma

> wherein the woman who is an artist sees her experience in terms of the feminine position, that is as object of the look, while she must also account for the feeling she experiences as an artist occupying the masculine position as subject of the look.

Pollock believes that one of the ways in which this dilemma can be resolved is by 'the rearticulation of traditional space so that it ceases to function primarily as the space of sight for a mastering gaze, but becomes the locus of relationships'.[14] This, we would suggest, is precisely what Wharton achieves in this episode of *The House of Mirth*. Whilst gazing upon Lily in her moment of triumph, we are asked to read critically the 'fictions' of Rosalind, Mrs Lloyd (who was once Joanna

Leigh) and Lily Bart and to relate them to Shakespeare's plot, the representation of the feminine by Sir Joshua Reynolds and the manipulation of woman as beautiful object by Paul Morpeth. This complex perspective destabilises any notion of femininity as natural or given. We are thus led to glimpse an alternative fiction: the woman who writes and reconstructs herself anew within a space of her own.

Blind to its ideological significance, Lily, however, revels in this triumphant moment since it brings her a temporary power which she draws out to full effect by further timing and staging:

> Not caring to diminish the impression she had produced, she held herself aloof from the audience till the movement of dispersal before supper, and thus had a second opportunity of showing herself to advantage, as the throng poured slowly into the empty drawing-room where she was standing. (p.136)

She has the talent of an actress and an artist, but these gifts find expression only in the pastimes of a frivolous society. Lily's reflections on her appearance during the entertainment range between those of mere vanity and a vague notion that her physical beauty is somehow a beneficent moral force, 'an element shaping all emotions to fresh forms of grace' (p.131). Such belief in the spiritual element of her beauty is, however, somewhat naïve in a New York society which views beautiful women as objects, artefacts and spectacles to be enjoyed visually and physically. Van Alstyne, for all his coarseness, is closer to a truthful assessment of women's role in such a society than Selden who, though he talks of spirituality and the 'real self', closes his eyes to the powerlessness and economic plight of women in the House of Mirth.

The final scenes of Wharton's novel give us Lily's slide into dependency on chloral and gradual oblivion. It is not at all clear whether she means to take her life. Her death-bed scene stands in ironic relation both to the *tableau vivant* episode and, as Cynthia Griffin Wolff has pointed out, to an American literary tradition in which 'the death of a beautiful woman as seen through the eyes of her lover' had become a set piece.[15] Lily has been destroyed by the House of Mirth and turns her own boarding-house room into a House of Mourning; having colluded with an artistic creation of herself as passive and unmoving in the *tableau vivant*, she quite literally creates herself as immobile spectacle in this final scene. The 'living picture' has become a picture of real death. It is not Selden, however, whose heart will become wise as a result of Lily's tragedy; he refuses to accept that the scene is real, seeing only 'the semblance of Lily Bart' before him. He weaves fictions around her, seeing in her corpse only what he wishes to see; her living body was an object of delight for his eye and now her dead body is merely an object of consolation for his mind: 'Yes, he could now read into that farewell all his heart craved to find there; he could even draw from it courage not to accuse himself for having failed to reach the height of his opportunity' (p.329).

It is the woman reader, presumably, who is asked to grow wise through Lily's story; Lily's deep sleep of death is an awakening for her, not Selden. But does Lily herself ever really waken to the nature of the limitations and boundaries which have constrained her development? In an oblique way, it would seem that she does. There is, for example, perhaps a perverse desire to undo the artifice of the *tableau vivant* by staging a scene in which the misery of her situation is evident: Lily's 'estranged and tranquil face' (p.325) in the unglamorous setting of a boarding-house speaks of a dispossession that is both material and emotional. Her drug-induced dream, with its strange image of Nettie Struther's baby lying in her arms, suggests an unconscious exploration of how that dispossessed state could have been avoided. In the course of the novel, Wharton has moved from plain simile to complex image. There is little ambiguity, for example, in the simile which occurs within the first few pages of the novel and which likens the links of Lily's bracelet to 'manacles chaining her to her fate' (p.7). Nettie's baby can, on the other hand, stand for several things. First, it suggests an escape from the misery of isolation Lily feels before her death; it evokes 'the solidarity of life' (p.319) Lily might have experienced if she had been content to live as a working-class girl, like Nettie Struther. Second, it reminds the reader of Lily's own arrested emotional development, an inner state of immaturity which is, in part, the product of social attitudes to women. Third, it refers to Lily's own artistic potential, a potential which has never been allowed to grow and express itself. Fourth, it stands for that work of art which, like a human child, is never born to Lily despite her creative potential. The fact that she breaks through the boundaries of conformity in dream alone is, however, the final note of pathos in her tragedy. In making her heroine experience these insights in such a way, Wharton temporarily abandons realist narrative and allows the reader access to Lily's world of memory, vision and fantasy. The boundaries of realism are stretched to include the irrational, subjective world; the meaning of this inner world is not explained by the narrator but its relation to the House of Mirth is clearly of significance for the reader. There is a sense here of repressed desires speaking through metaphor. Nor is Lily's death allowed to function as an instrument of unproblematic closure in this text: Selden's understanding of her death is alarmingly inadequate and is meant to provoke a more complex response from the woman reader. The end of the novel thereby echoes Wharton's narration of the *tableau vivant* scene which demands a more complex response than Lily is able to give. Like the final unspoken message between Lily and Selden – 'some word that should make life clear between them' (p.323), 'the word which made all clear' (p.329) – the 'moral' of Lily's fate is a blank space for the reader to fill; Wharton was no doubt aware that men and women would fill it differently. We are invited to inscribe meaning within the boundaries of Wharton's novel, whilst recognising that the story itself is about boundaries and enclosures – boundaries and enclosures which 'frame' Lily in more ways than one.

Charlotte Perkins Gilman's *The Yellow Wallpaper*

Charlotte Perkins Gilman's *The Yellow Wallpaper* and Kate

Chopin's *The Awakening* also concern themselves with the boundaries that constrain woman's sense of self. Both works subtly articulate the part played by notions of the 'feminine' in a social structure which limits and contains women's creative potential; both works implicitly condemn the bourgeois family and its role in upholding patriarchy in the late nineteenth century. Looking back on this period from the vantage point of 1939, Virginia Woolf recorded the nature of these constraints quite dispassionately: 'Society in those days was a very competent machine. It was convinced that girls must be changed into married women. It had no doubts, no mercy; no understanding of any other wish; of any other gift. Nothing was taken seriously.'[16] *The Yellow Wallpaper*, published in 1892, gives us a tale of mental breakdown writ large in gothic characters; *The Awakening*, published in 1899, presents us with a heroine who chooses death rather than submission to a marriage (and therefore a society) which oppresses her creative and sexual desires. Marriage, for the creative women of *The Yellow Wallpaper* and *The Awakening*, is an enclosure which becomes gradually suffocating. Rooms, houses, railings and boundaries are important within the plots of these works but they function more importantly as metaphors for the way in which society refuses to let women wander beyond the cultural 'room' of marriage and motherhood.

The Yellow Wallpaper gives us subversive insights in a form which constantly upsets our expectations. Shifting between the conventions of different genres, Gilman deliberately lays trails that lead the reader up various garden paths of fiction. Elements of the country-house novel, the gothic tale, and the horror story all usurp any sense that this is a straightforward account of postnatal depression. The novelist adapts these genres for her own ends; *The Yellow Wallpaper* therefore becomes a verbal landscape which is both strange and familiar. Mary Jacobus suggests that Gilman's skilful adaptation of the gothic tale has itself metaphorical implications:

> It is as if Gilman's story has had to repress its own ancestry in nineteenth-century female gothic, along with the entire history of

> feminine protest. The house in 'The Yellow Wallpaper' is strange because empty. An image of dispossession, it points to what Gilman can't say about the subjection of women, not only in literary terms, but politically – imaging the disinherited state of women in general, and also, perhaps, the symptomatic dispossession which had made Gilman herself feel that she had to take her stand against marriage alone . . . As readers versed in female gothic we know that Bertha Mason haunts this text; as readers of the feminist tradition from Wollstonecraft on, we know that the rights of women have long been denied by treating them as children. The uncanny makes itself felt as the return of a repressed past, a history at once literary and political – here, the history of women's reading.[17]

The narrator in *The Yellow Wallpaper* is contrasted with two women who are paradigms of maternal competence and happy domesticity. There is Mary, presumably the nanny, who 'is so good with the baby' in contrast with the narrator's incompetence with her own child: 'And yet I *cannot* be with him, it makes me so nervous' (p.14).[18] There is her sister-in-law, Jennie, whose domestic competence points to the folly of trying to be an artist and a woman: 'She is a perfect and enthusiastic housekeeper, and hopes for no better profession. I verily believe she thinks it is the writing which made me sick!' (p.18). The sinister implication is that the desire to write is, in a woman, abnormal and might well destroy her 'natural' tendencies towards domesticity and motherhood: the woman artist is, therefore, something to be abhorred. The very thing which would sustain the mental health of the narrator, artistic creativity, is deemed to be the root cause of her malaise, although the narrator herself knows intuitively that this is not so: 'I think sometimes that if I were only well enough to write a little it would relieve the press of ideas and rest me' (p.16). However, the narrator's desire is overruled by her condescending and paternalistic husband who warns her that the combination of 'story-making' and 'nervous weakness . . . is sure to lead to all manner of excited fancies' (pp.15–16). She is also denied access to people whose minds work in the same creative manner as her own; a visit from 'those stimulating people' (p.16), Cousin Henry and Julia, is indefinitely postponed. The 'imaginative power' (p.15) which John suppresses (supposedly for her own good) is also, of course – whether he consciously recognises it or not – a threat to his position of authority and power as a man. If used subversively, it might well result in a 'story-making' which would challenge current ideology, a fact Virginia Woolf was to recognise a few decades later:

> It is probable . . . that both in life and in art the values of a woman are not the values of a man. Thus, when a woman comes to write a novel, she will find that she is perpetually wishing to alter the established values – to make serious what appears insignificant to a man, and trivial what is to him important.[19]

The narrator's 'imaginative power' must, therefore, be inhibited: and it is, through a handling of the woman as if she were mad and infantile. She is denied knowledge of herself both as adult woman (having a child has resulted in a 'temporary nervous depression' according to her husband's diagnosis and suggests her inability to cope with her own female sexuality) and as creative artist – 'he hates to have me write a word' (p.13) the narrator confesses as she hides her writing away. Her husband is also her doctor and his status ensures that her desires are perceived as pathological. We are not allowed the comforting thought that John's attitude might spring from an idiosyncratic marital jealousy or possessiveness: 'My brother is also a physician, and also of high standing, and he says the same thing' (p.10). Thus the discourse of medicine is used to sustain patriarchy. 'Treatment' consists of enforced rest and incarceration in the nursery at the top of the house,

> a big, airy room, the whole floor nearly, with windows that look all ways, and air and sunshine galore. It was nursery first and then playroom and gymnasium, I should judge; for the windows are barred for little children, and there are rings and things in the walls. (p.12)

There is much ambiguity inherent in this description: the room is a place of confinement yet it also gives a vantage point not available to those living in the main rooms of the house; the changed perspective is mental as well as physical. We might remember here the 'wan lucidity of mind' (*House of Mirth*, p.320) which comes to Lily in the isolation of her boarding-house room shortly before her death. However, the windows are 'barred', both to protect small children from falling and to confine them (and adults like the woman) within a prescribed area. This double function neatly suggests the double-speak of patriarchy: women, like children, are confined and protected supposedly for their own good. Her husband addresses the woman as 'a blessed little goose' (p.15) and 'little girl' (p.23), makes her 'take cod liver oil and lots of tonics and things' (p.21) and reads to her in bed (p.21). He insists that his treatment is working and when she demurs, overrules her with '"I am a doctor, dear, and I know"' (p.23). The 'treatment', not surprisingly, results in the narrator's mental decline – 'I'm getting dreadfully fretful and querulous' (p.19) – just as it did for Charlotte Perkins Gilman who was herself prescribed the 'rest cure' treatment by Weir Mitchell.[20] Told in 1887 to give up writing and lead a quiet, domestic life, Gilman – unlike her heroine – rebelled. In an essay entitled 'Why I wrote *The Yellow Wallpaper*', Gilman recorded that she finally

> cast the noted specialist's advice to the winds and went to work again . . . ultimately recovering some measure of power.
>
> Being naturally moved to rejoicing by this narrow escape, I wrote 'The Yellow Wallpaper' . . . and sent a copy to the physician who so nearly drove me mad. He never acknowledged it . . . (But) many years later I was told that the great specialist had admitted to friends of his that he had altered his treatment of neurasthenia since reading 'The Yellow Wallpaper'.[21]

The narrator of *The Yellow Wallpaper* also writes, of course; what we read is her narration but it is one that leads not to a successful writing career and re-integration into society (albeit on her own terms) as it did for Charlotte Perkins Gilman, but one that charts a descent into a state that society defines as insane.

By confining her to a nursery which is papered with a ghastly yellow wallpaper, John forces his wife to concentrate on her immediate surroundings; those immediate surroundings become a metaphor for her position as a woman artist within late nineteenth-century society; his 'diagnosis' and the narrator's 'vision' thus provide the reader with a radical critique of that society. Gilman's critique expresses itself through the narrator's state of alienation, the symptoms of which conflate with those of madness – feelings of persecution, poor self-image, repressed anger, experiences of vision and hallucination. However, this narrative strategy constrained contemporary readings: as Annette Kolodny has pointed out, 'her story located itself not as any deviation from a previous tradition of women's fiction but, instead, as a continuation of a genre popularized by Poe'.[22] It was not until the 1980s that women readers could see beyond the horror story and begin to speculate on the irony and metaphoric meaning of *The Yellow Wallpaper*. It is, for example, no accident that the brief description of the Fourth of July celebrations are followed by John's comment that he will send for Weir Mitchell in the fall if the narrator does not 'pick up faster' (p.18). A sharp irony results from this juxtaposition of the social celebration of America's independence as a nation with the absence of independence for American women. This is a society celebrating its democracy; a society founded on the 'Declaration of Independence' for *man*. It is a society which excludes women from that concept of democracy and one in which they have no vote and little power. The mad woman of *The Yellow Wallpaper* is the narrator created by Gilman; the mad woman *in* the yellow wallpaper is the narrator's vision; our understanding of the relationship between sexual politics, power and the concept of madness depends on our ability to relate these 'mad' women to society's attitude to female creativity and independence. As such, the text is positive even though the ending bodes badly for the narrator; for Gilman it was an instrument of both therapy and insight.

For Gilman's narrator, however, life closes in and her horizons become more and more limited. Initially, there is a sense of space. Like the Lady of Shalott, she is an isolated figure looking out upon an idealised landscape. The house is 'a most beautiful place!' and the garden is '*delicious* . . . large and shady, full of box-bordered paths, and lined with long grape-covered arbors with seats under them' (p.11). She can see this garden from one window, and out of another 'I get a lovely view of the bay and a little private wharf belonging to the estate' (p.15). Another window 'commands the road, a lovely shaded winding road, and one that just looks off over the country. A lovely country, too, full of great elms and velvet meadows' (p.18). She fancies she can see 'people walking' in the 'numerous paths and arbors' around the house; the landscape surrounding the house is both a source of consolation and frustration, as it is to Jane Eyre when she views the surrounding countryside from the attic window at Thornfield:

> I longed for a power of vision which might overpass that limit; which might reach the busy world, towns, regions full of life I had heard of but never seen; that then I desired more of practical experience than I possessed; more of intercourse with my kind, of acquaintance with a variety of character, than was here within my reach.[23]

For both narrators, this glimpsed community of people in a landscape viewed from a room at the top of a house suggests a frustration at being made marginal and peripheral to human affairs; the elevated perspective also, however, metaphorically suggests an intellectual awakening to that process of marginalisation. Not allowed to venture beyond the nursery, unable to leave the house as Jane Eyre left Thornfield, the narrator gradually turns the focus of her attention to her room and its repellent wallpaper. The significance of the landscape outside the house slowly slips away as her chances of freedom and self-expression crumble. Unable to write, she becomes a reader and what she reads is the pattern in the wallpaper:

> I lie here on this great immovable bed – it is nailed down, I believe – and follow that pattern about by the hour. It is as good as gymnastics, I assure you. I start, we'll say, at the bottom, down in the corner over there where it has not been touched, and I determine for the thousandth time that I *will* follow that pointless pattern to some sort of conclusion. (p.19)

Her desire to decipher the meaning of 'the bloated curves and flourishes (p.20) of the pattern becomes, as many feminist critics have noted, paradigmatic of woman's struggle to read and write herself within a man's culture. In Mary Jacobus's interpretation, one which draws heavily on post-Freudian psychoanalysis, the wallpaper itself becomes a symbolic site of repression in which the uncanny and the irrational 'creeps in as both woman's estate and woman's body'[24] despite John's attempts to exclude them from his life. Noting that feminist readings ignore the importance of yellow in the story, Jacobus nevertheless dismisses the historical dimension of yellow as the colour of decadence in the 1890s since 'the *Yellow Book* was not to appear until 1894.'[25] This frees her to argue that the 'smooch' on the wallpaper, and its 'yellow' smell suggest the smell of female genitalia and 'the repression imposed by the 1890s on the representation of female sexuality and, in particular, the repression imposed on women's writing'.[26] For Jacobus, the text speaks, through metaphor, of male hysteria: 'that is, fear of femininity as the body of the mother ("old, foul, bad yellow things") which simultaneously threatens the boy with a return to the powerlessness of infancy and with anxiety about the castration she embodies'.[27] This is an intriguing reading but, deriving from psychoanalytic discourse, it ignores the quite precise associations that yellow carried in England and American during the 1890s – associations of which Gilman would surely have been aware. Connected with the avant-garde and the death of Victorianism, the colour yellow came to suggest the daring subversion of past values.

The Yellow Book, edited by Henry Harland and Aubrey Beardsley, and published in London between 1894 and 1897 was noted for its subversive *fin de siècle* morality; its producers deliberately took the colour of the yellow-backed French novels, according to R. K. R. Thornton, in an attempt to shock English sensibilities.[28] In her book, *A Study in Yellow: The 'Yellow Book' and its contributors*, Katherine Lyon Mix echoes the words of Holbrook Jackson in describing yellow as *the* colour of the 1890s, 'the colour of the hour, the symbol of the time-spirit'. Significantly for our reading of *The Yellow*

Wallpaper, she also argues that its metaphoric importance predated *The Yellow Book* itself:

> *Yellow had assumed significance before the dawn of 1890* [our italics]. It gathered importance during the decade, becoming quite meaningless with the arrival of the new century. A favorite color with the Pre-Raphaelites, with Rossetti and Burne-Jones, it was also affected by Whistler, whose yellow breakfasts with orange nasturtiums or darting goldfish in a flat bowl inspired Lily Langtry to use the same idea, substituting a yellow water lily in antique blue glass – beautiful Lily Langtry, whom he painted so gorgeously in the yellow robe . . .
>
> Yellow sunflowers, painted on the walls of the Oxford Union by William Morris, became the symbol of aestheticism in the hand of Oscar Wilde, who praised the leonine, gaudy beauty of the flower so fervently that American undergraduates at Harvard and Yale marched to his lectures bearing stalks of the yellow blossoms – probably artificial, since it was winter.
>
> . . . the word 'yellow' popped up in book titles – *The Yellow Aster* by Iota and *Le Cahier Jaune* by A.C. Benson, poems privately printed, for which Henry James wrote to 'thank you for your yellow sheaf'.
>
> The editor of *Harper's* wrote on Yellow Literature, declaring, 'The Yellow literature is not new. There have always been diseased people seeking notoriety by reason of their maladies', but Richard Le Gallienne glorified the 'Boom in Yellow'. 'Let us', he invited, 'dream of this: a maid with yellow hair, clad in a yellow gown, seated in a yellow room, at the window a yellow sunset, in the grate a yellow fire, at her side a yellow lamplight, on her knee a Yellow Book.'[29]

Richard Le Gallienne's romantic vision of a woman 'in a yellow room' is, however, a far cry from Gilman's increasingly deranged narrator, for whom the colour yellow seems to carry negative associations: 'It is the strangest yellow, that wallpaper! It makes me think of all the yellow things I ever saw – not beautiful ones like buttercups, but old foul, bad yellow things' (p.28). In giving us a perfectly sane heroine who is driven mad by those around her and who sinks into anonymity, Gilman ironically subverts the idea of 'yellow literature' as a genre in which 'diseased people (seek) notoriety by reason of their maladies'. Further, she makes the yellow wallpaper fearful because it is an instrument of unsettling revelation; through it the narrator learns her own story, the story of a woman who has been imprisoned:

> At night in any kind of light, in twilight, candle light, lamplight, and worst of all by moonlight, it becomes bars! The outside pattern I mean, and the woman behind it as plain as can be.
>
> I didn't realize for a long time what the thing was that showed behind, that dim sub-pattern, but now I am quite sure it is a woman. (p.26)

Yellow in this novella, then, does not simply denote the joyous embrace of hedonism and the 'art for art's sake' philosophy of the 1890s; instead, it anticipates *The Yellow Book*'s concentration on woman's identity and sexuality, an issue which, according to Fraser Harrison, 'dominated . . . an enormous number of *Yellow Book* stories'.[30] Most of these stories were 'fraught with sexual tension' and expressed

> the terror that the possibility of female liberation, in the modern sense of heightened consciousness, must have struck in the hearts of husbands and wives alike during this decade. The middle-class wife who found her repressed situation irksome must have also feared the consequences of her liberty, regardless of whether or not her husband was sympathetic. She not only had to bear and combat the prejudice, hostility and ridicule of society at large, she not only had to put into perspective the propaganda of a century, but she also had to come to terms with the prospect of disastrously upsetting the balance of her domestic life . . . By challenging the concept of male supremacy [women] automatically questioned their husbands' virility.[31]

Thus the awakening of Gilman's narrator derives from a quite specific historical context which was observing the emergence of a new breed of woman who, in her demands for political, artistic and sexual fulfilment, seemed to threaten her male partner with a metaphoric castration. Gilman uses the delirious ramblings of her narrator to inscribe one crucial meaning within the wallpaper pattern: this is the basic insight that the social construction of gender can be a prison house for the growing woman. This perception leads the narrator to feel increasingly alienated from and persecuted by those close to her: 'The fact is I am getting a little afraid of John. He seem very queer sometimes, and even Jennie has an inexplicable look' (p.26). As she struggles to 'find out' what the patterns mean, the smell of the wallpaper continually haunts her:

> It creeps all over the house.
>
> I find it hovering in the dining-room, skulking in the parlor, hiding in the hall, lying in wait for me on the stairs.
>
> It gets into my hair.
>
> Even when I go to ride, if I turn my head suddenly and surprise it – there is that smell!
>
> Such a peculiar odor, too! I have spent hours in trying to analyze it, to find what it smelled like.
>
> It is not bad – at first, and very gentle, but quite the subtlest, most enduring odor I ever met. (pp.28–9)

The ubiquitous nature of this smell is rather like fog in that it can creep round any boundary, escape any enclosure. As such, the smell is elusive, undefinable, uncontainable and leads the woman beyond the confining sense of self with which society has endowed her. To reach it becomes a queer sort of quest: she even thinks of burning the house 'to reach the smell' (p.29). This smell might, then, stand for the narrator's identity which – to her cost – refuses to be confined by the discourse within which nineteenth-century society has defined woman. Like Bernard in *The Waves* (1931), she is perhaps haunted by intimations of a 'real self': 'Yet behold, it returns. One cannot extinguish that persistent smell. It steals in through some crack in the structure – one's identity . . .'[32]

Thus, as the presence of the smell becomes stronger, the figure of the woman behind bars in the wallpaper becomes clearer and her struggle more obvious: 'she is all the time trying to climb through' (p.30). Sometimes she appears to be more than one woman, which suggests that her fate is that of all women during this decade, as does the anonymity of the narrator. Towards the end of the story the narrator sees her outside the house, 'creeping along, and when a carriage comes she hides under the blackberry vines' (p.31). Anticipating the heroine of Margaret Atwood's *Surfacing*, the figure in the wallpaper, who emerges as the narrator's ghostly and ghastly double, takes refuge in nature because it is free from cultural constructions of gender: it knows no such boundaries. This is the landscape that faces the narrator if she wishes to be 'free' and, understandably, she views it with some ambivalence since such 'freedom' inevitably involves the terror of the unknown – or what Fraser Harrison describes as 'the terror' deriving from 'the possibility of female liberation, in the modern sense of heightened consciousness'. At one moment, she wishes to 'jump out of the window' (p.34) and escape, just like the figure in the wallpaper; it is a wish that presages both Septimus Warren Smith's suicidal leap from the window in *Mrs Dalloway* (1928) and Antoinette Cosway's imagined jump to her death in *Wide Sargasso Sea* (1966). All three acts are, metaphorically, a leap into autonomy and an escape from convention and conformity. The next moment, however, she wishes to imprison the figure: 'I've got a rope up here that even Jennie did not find. If that woman does get out, and tries to get away, I can tie her!' (p.34). That act of imprisonment then becomes directed against herself: 'But I am securely fastened now by my well-hidden rope – you don't get *me* out in the road there!' (p.35). She begins to 'creep', in an animal-like fashion, as does the figure in the wallpaper. She develops a fear of the outdoors: 'I don't want to go outside. I won't, even if Jennie asks me to' (p.35). She is, quite literally, torn between cultural constructions of what it means to be a woman – embodied in the house, its boundaries and the role-playing which goes on within it – and the wild space of nature which offers no boundaries but no subjecthood either: she thus stands on the threshold between the two.

This is her awakening; it dawns as she deciphers the meaning of the subtext within the house and the home, contained in the patterns of the yellow wallpaper. There are no easy solutions to the questions it provokes: the narrator is left creeping round the room, maniacally following the yellow 'long smooch around the wall' (p.35). Her continual circling represents the impasse which faces the woman reader: it is left to her to establish a better liaison between women's desires and the cultural construction of gender. The husband, lying in a dead faint 'right across my path by the wall' (p.36) is another obstacle to be negotiated in the struggle; he represents the threshold of Victorian marriage which must be stepped over if woman is ever to attain a more satisfactory sense of 'self'. Lying in a faint on the floor, he not only inverts cultural notions concerning frailty and gender, but becomes, quite literally, a boundary. It is a boundary that the narrator, however, refuses to recognise any longer; she simply crawls over his body. Having come to this awakening in her fiction, Gilman resolved the impasse in her own life by jettisoning the constraints of marriage and by living unconventionally.

The narrator of *The Yellow Wallpaper* is allowed no such solution, however, and the end of the novella is disturbing and ambiguous. Does the narrator's bestial 'creeping' suggest a tragic drop into insanity – or does her final confrontation with her husband suggest an assertion of the self that constitutes a moment of triumph? From whose words do we take our cue? The husband's: '"What is the matter?" he cried, "For God's sake, what are you doing!"' (p.36)? Or the wife's: '"I've got out at last," said I, "in spite of you and Jane. And I've pulled off most of the paper, so you can't put me back!"' (p.36)? And what does she mean by these words when we know that she has deliberately locked herself in the room and thrown the key out of the window? We can only resolve these contradictions by exploring the ironic tension which exists between the narrator as victim and the author as victor. The narrator's awakening is also Gilman's, but for the writer, who can handle fictional madness with cool control, the wild space of nature translates itself more safely into the landscape of the text. The narrator's gradual divorce from her sense of self as conventional American society of the 1890s would define it allows us to perceive her simultaneously as mad and sane, free and imprisoned. This 'doubleness' speaks metaphorically of the author's discovery that femininity is a social construct and that 'story-making' is evaluated by society from the position of the male reader. As Judith Fetterley points out, although 'in going mad [the narrator] fulfils [John's] script and becomes a character in his text', Gilman herself, in exposing his strategy accepts neither conformity nor madness but the autonomy which authorship can give. This escape, however, Gilman 'implicitly recognizes [as] . . . the exception, not the rule'.[33] Through this exception, however, other women can learn to read 'woman' as a social construct: thus the yellow wallpaper itself becomes a metaphor for the process of reading metaphor. Constrained by boundaries not of their own making, women have had to become skilful readers of the patterns on the walls in order to deconstruct them. In Virginia Woolf's words:

> women have sat indoors all these millions of years, so that by this time the very walls are permeated by their creative force, which has, indeed, so overcharged the capacity of bricks and mortar that it must needs harness itself to pens and brushes and business and politics.[34]

Woolf's words help to explain the puzzle of how it is that the narrator of *The Yellow Wallpaper* can claim that she has 'got out at last' whilst she is still locked in her room.

Kate Chopin's *The Awakening*

Edna Pontellier, in Kate Chopin's *The Awakening*, is contrasted with two other women in the text who take on paradigmatic value: Mme Ratignolle comes to represent the concept of motherhood idealised and sentimentalised by late nineteenth-century American society; Mlle Reisz is tolerated and marginalised as the eccentric woman artist. Edna finds neither of these role models satisfactory as her desire for artistic and sexual freedom grows to maturity. The constraints placed upon her development are not legal or monetary, but none the less powerful for being social and intangible. As in *The Yellow Wallpaper*, medical diagnosis is seen to help effect those 'mystic boundaries' (see pages 66–7) which contain women within modes of conventional behaviour appropriate to patriarchy. At the end of the novella, Edna partially confides in Dr Mandelet, a fairly enlightened man and a sympathetic character, and thinks to herself that he might, in time, have understood the nature of her desires. In conversation with her husband, however, the doctor falls back on the stock bourgeois response to her challenge to marriage and motherhood, a response which sees the domestic sphere as woman's 'natural' one. Any deviation from this is perversely unnatural and must stem from external forces of corruption: '"Has she," asked the Doctor, with a smile, "has she been associating of late with a circle of pseudo-intellectual women – super-spiritual beings? My wife has been telling me about them"' (p.118).

Thus, at a stroke, the New Woman is rendered both ludicrous and pretentious. His attempt to reassure Pontellier takes the form of taking refuge in the old myth of woman as unknowable and irrational. This myth, which also implies that man is a rational and intelligent creature, both shrouds woman in mystique and safely marginalises her: '"Woman, my dear friend, is a very peculiar and delicate organism – a sensitive and highly organized woman, such as I know Mrs Pontellier to be, is especially peculiar. It would require an inspired psychologist to deal successfully with them"' (p.119). He dismisses Edna's restlessness as 'some passing whim' (p.119) and thus reduces the need for political and social change to a minor problem of one woman's neurosis. In fact, of course, the changes which come over Edna Pontellier, far from being 'some passing whim', constitute an awakening to the nature of her desires and to the fact that society, as it exists, cannot accommodate them.

She is 29, married to a successful businessmen, and the mother of two small children when she begins to realise that 'She had all her life long been accustomed to harbor thoughts and emotions which never voiced themselves' (p.96). Her struggle in *The Awakening*, like that of Rachel Vinrace in *The Voyage Out*, is to do with finding a way of expressing sexual and creative desires for which late nineteenth-century discourse provides no language. The young and handsome, if somewhat vacuous, Robert Lebrun arouses her sexual desire during a long summer holiday in the Gulf of Mexico; at the same time she begins to feel an 'indescribable oppression' (p.49) at her husband's accusations that she is not properly caring for their children. 'Properly caring' seems to involve fussing at their bedsides if they should become over-warm and – on the example of Mme Ratignolle – spending hours making elaborate winter garments for them during the long, warm days of summer. Edna gradually becomes aware of the subtle manner in which marriage is oppressing her need for growth and, one night after a prolonged battle of wills with Léonce, her husband, she begins 'to feel like one who awakens gradually out of a dream, a delicious, grotesque, impossible dream, to feel again the realities pressing into her soul' (p.78). Robert engineers an abrupt departure to work in Mexico, in order to avoid facing the implications of his relationship with Edna, a married woman. During his absence, Edna decides that her infatuation for Robert has grown into love and, on his return, tells him so. Her love for him does not, however, prevent her from being sexually aroused by other men. After her separation from her husband, and during the time when Robert is absent, she conducts an affair with a notorious womaniser, Alcée Arobin, who is a handsome, fashionable and shallow young man. His physical presence alerts 'all her awakening sensuousness' (p.131) and although he means 'absolutely nothing to her' (p.132) she finds him sexually exciting; his kiss is described as 'a flaming torch that kindled desire' (p.139).

Edna has abandoned the construct of romantic love which can accommodate, albeit with disapproval, the transference of love from one man to another; she desires and wishes to enjoy both men. By conventional moral standards of the 1890s she is 'fallen', 'loose' and 'bad'. These standards have, however, become irrelevant in her independent process of self-exploration:

> 'One of these days,' she said, 'I'm going to pull myself together for a while and think – try to determine what character of a

> woman I am; for, candidly, I don't know. By all the codes which I am acquainted with, I am a devilishly wicked specimen of the sex. But some way I can't convince myself that I am. I must think about it.' (p.138)

Her central blasphemy, of course, is to challenge both monogamy and the notion that chastity and fidelity in woman are necessarily equated with moral good. The hysteria which greeted publications on contraception in nineteenth-century England and America – and the public brouhaha which still surrounds the issue of abortion today – suggest that control of women's sexuality is vital to the maintenance of patriarchy. This control is most effective when internalised through religion so that woman sees deviance from marriage, motherhood and monogamy as a sin. In Western society, this internalised control is percolated through Christianity and is present metaphorically in *The Awakening* as the old woman in black with Bible and beads who chaperones 'the lovers', a nameless couple who continually haunt the text, clasped in each other's arms. Their presence in the story is inexplicable in terms of plot; they exist, however, as a reminder of the way sexual desire is guided by ideology to serve the interests of a particular social system. So although her 'symptoms' – and by implication, her changing consciousness – are marginalised by Dr Mandelet as the result of 'a passing whim', Robert Lebrun comes to recognise that her desire for autonomy is incompatible with his own conventional values and is irreconcilable with the society of which he is part. It threatens, in fact, everything he knows and believes in; it threatens patriarchy itself. Hence his appalled question – which goes unanswered – when Edna laughs at his wish to marry her and points out that she is no longer one of Mr Pontellier's possessions to be disposed of as he thinks fit:

> 'I give myself where I choose. If he were to say, "Here, Robert, take her and be happy; she is yours," I should laugh at you both.'
>
> His face grew a little white. 'What do you mean?' he asked. (p.167)

It is immediately after this conversation that she visits Adèle

Ratignolle, who is in labour. No longer prepared to accept society's sentimental presentation of childbirth and motherhood as woman's true fulfilment, she sees Adèle's suffering as a 'scene of torture' (p.170). Eager for the comfort of Robert's physical presence, she returns from the Ratignolle household only to find his elliptical note: 'I love you, Good-bye – because I love you' (p.172). Edna Pontellier, in breaking through boundaries of conformity and convention, follows the call of her own desire which, 'like the everlasting voice of the sea' (p.49), becomes more insistent as the story of her awakening proceeds. Memories of a summer spent in Robert's company are expressed in language which conflates the movement of the sea itself with her desires:

> She could hear again the ripple of the water, the flapping sail. She could see the glint of the moon upon the bay, and could feel the soft, gusty beating of the hot south wind. A subtle current of desire passed through her body, weakening her hold upon the brushes and making her eyes burn. (p.109)

The expression of these desires is, however, a subversive act in late nineteenth-century American society; even her lover cannot reconcile the radical nature of her ideas with his image of womanhood. The implication is that men, however sympathetic to an individual woman, are unable to face rationally such challenges to patriarchy; its ideology guarantees that such a challenge is seen as deviant and ensures the continuation of a system which works to their advantage.

As Edna's sexual desire begins to express itself, so her desire for artistic self-expression awakens; indeed music and painting seem to offer a way of exploring repression and oppression. Art and music become increasingly important and she eventually places them at the centre of her life, rather than at the periphery: '"I am becoming an artist. Think of it!"' (p.115) she confesses to Mlle Reisz. The process is one of *becoming* rather than *being*; she has to find her proper subject matter and her proper milieu in order to practise effectively as an artist. She has yet to discover her potential which has been cloaked beneath a socially acceptable mere enjoyment of art.

'Edna was what she herself called very fond of music. Musical strains, well rendered, had a way of evoking pictures in her mind' (p.71) the narrator informs us. That same narrator gives us, one paragraph later, Edna's awakening into the 'abiding truth' of art as she listens to Mlle Reisz's piano playing, an awakening which is intensely moving: 'the very passions themselves were aroused within her soul, swaying it, lashing it, as the waves daily beat upon her splendid body. She trembled, she was choking, and the tears blinded her' (p.72). The usual pictures which appear in her mind as she listens to music are conventional compositions: 'a man standing beside a desolate rock on the seashore . . . a dainty young woman in an Empire gown . . . children at play . . . a demure lady stroking a cat' (p.71). Suddenly, these are no longer adequate as images of reality. Similarly, her sketch of Mme Adèle Ratignolle, the friend who is a living incarnation of idealised Victorian motherhood, displeases her: 'After surveying the sketch critically she drew a broad smudge of paint across its surface, and crumpled the paper between her hands' (p.55). She is rejecting Adèle's embrace of the Madonna stereotype and refusing to give it credibility in her art. Michael T. Gilmore is quite right to point out that, as Edna begins to reject 'the constraining model of marriage admired by late Victorian society' so she begins to reject 'realist or representational aesthetics'.[35]

The image of the naked man standing on the seashore is one evoked by a piece played by Mlle Reisz which Edna has entitled 'Solitude', though that is not its correct title. This image, which suggests the lonely spiritual anguish of man in his metaphysical quest for self-knowledge is contrasted with the sociable nature of women and children in her other 'pictures'. These mental pictures are the insidious creations of ideology: they present man as the solitary thinker, woman as social cement. Their refusal to 'appear' in her mind indicates an awakening to the way in which she has allowed herself to become something she does not wish to be. Interestingly, her behaviour before her final swim enacts the 'picture' of the naked man by the sea:

> for the first time in her life she stood naked in the open air, at the mercy of the sun, the breeze that beat upon her, and the waves that invited her.
>
> How strange and awful seemed to stand naked under the sky! how delicious! She felt like some new-born creature, opening its eyes in a familiar world that it had never known. (p.175)

She has appropriated the role of the philosopher and, in so doing, has rejected society's prescribed roles for women. The scene is the antithesis of Lily Bart's moment of triumph: Edna Pontellier divests herself of clothes and roles and needs no audience to affirm her sense of self. *The Awakening* was originally entitled 'A Solitary Soul'; the change of title suggests a shift from the Romantic legacy of man as the solitary thinker in a natural landscape towards an affirmation of one woman's attempt to deconstruct the social meanings in which she finds herself trapped. The metaphoric implications of Edna's naked stance on the beach are presaged by the narrator's comments on her husband's anxiety:

> It sometimes entered Mr Pontellier's mind to wonder if his wife were not growing a little unbalanced mentally. He could see plainly that she was not herself. That is, he could not see that she was becoming herself and daily casting aside that fictitious self which we assume like a garment with which to appear before the world. (p.108)

Edna's highly emotional reaction to Mlle Reisz's playing is part and parcel of this affirmation of 'herself'; through it she realises that good art pushes at the boundaries of representation, struggling against culturally endorsed values and images. Art, if it merely entertains, no longer fulfils this function but is reduced to a trite mimesis; like the parrot whose shrieking words open Edna's story, it mimics, rather than challenges, the world around it. This is something that neither Mme Ratignolle nor Léonce Pontellier understand. The former is talented but subordinates her gift to her domestic persona; she considers her ability merely 'a means of brightening the home and making it attractive' (p.69). This is a strategy of which Edna's husband entirely approves: 'It seems to me the utmost folly for a woman at the head of a household, and the mother of children, to spend in an atelier days which would be better employed contriving for the comfort of her family' (p.108).

Edna's growing desire to paint is not just a desire to escape from the 'appalling and hopeless ennui' (p.107) represented by the domestic harmony of the Ratignolle household; it is a desire to express an alternative sense of self in a medium free from the verbal inscriptions of ideology. Although she accomplishes nothing that really satisfies her, painting becomes positively associated with dreaming and solitude: 'she found it good to dream and to be alone and unmolested' (p.109). She begins to realise that painting can be an instrument of vision and subversion, that it can awaken new voices in her, as does Mlle Reisz's music. Mlle Reisz is, however, Edna's only model for the woman who has devoted herself to art and Chopin presents her with some ambivalence. Perceived as gifted and strange by the society around her, Mlle Reisz is able to enchant people with her musical gift and they tolerate her eccentricity and spleen in exchange for her performances. Indeed, there are echoes of the traditional witch figure in Chopin's first presentation of Mlle Reisz as 'a disagreeable little woman, no longer young' who 'had absolutely no taste in dress, and wore a batch of rusty black lace with a bunch of artificial violets pinned to the side of her hair' (pp. 70, 71). As Cristina Giorcelli has pointed out, she has even the traditional witch's terror of water:[36] 'Mademoiselle Reisz's avoidance of the water had furnished a theme for much pleasantry' (p.97). It is a trait which links her obliquely to Edna, who fears the sea: 'A certain ungovernable dread hung about her when in the water' (p.73). Further, Andrew Delbanco has noticed that Mlle Reisz has 'apartments up under the roof' (p.113):[37] 'There were plenty of windows . . . From her windows could be seen the crescent of the river, the masts of ships and the big chimneys of the Mississippi steamers' (p.113).

Mlle Reisz is thus an ironic inversion of the wicked fairy at the top of the castle in the fairy tale *Sleeping Beauty* in that she awakens the heroine, rather than casting a spell upon her which makes her sleep for a hundred years. She is also, however, linked to the many women in fiction who look obliquely at the world from a room high in the house. Like Jane Eyre in the attic-room at Thornfield and the narrator of *The Yellow Wallpaper* in her nursery room on the top floor, Mlle Reisz has a perspective on the world which is rich and strange. Metaphorically, it is a perspective born out of difference, withdrawal and nonconformity. However, although she encourages Edna in her struggle for independence, telling her that 'to succeed, the artist must possess the courageous soul' (p.115), Mlle Reisz has, in fact, colluded with society's strategy of marginalising the woman of vision. This strategy allows such a woman her freedom provided she lives alone, without lovers and without children – provided, in fact, she denies her sexual desires. The cost of such autonomy is therefore high. It is a strategy Woolf was to recognise some years later in her portrayal of Lily Briscoe and it is one that Chopin exposes in her ambivalent presentation of Mlle Reisz. However, Edna comes to realise that, whilst rejecting the older woman as a role model, she can learn much from her art:

> There was nothing which so quieted the turmoil of Edna's senses as a visit to Mademoiselle Reisz. It was then, in the presence of that personality which was offensive to her, that the woman, by her divine art, seemed to reach Edna's spirit and set it free. (p.133)

What does Edna learn, apart from these vague sensations connected with calm and freedom? The answer is implicit in the musical configurations of Chopin's text. Music as a non-representational form of art confirms Edna's earlier intuition that representational art can never be an adequate mode of expression for challenging the assumptions of current ideology. This is a lesson that Chopin also learnt; consequently *The Awakening* itself moves away from the representational conventions embraced by the nineteenth-century novel or short story and begins to model itself upon the discourse of music. It structures itself, as Elaine Showalter points out, on 'an impressionistic rhythm of epiphany and mood'[38] in a manner which anticipates the prose of Virginia Woolf. Incremental repetition and circularity gradually replace the forward dynamism of the plot; the result, as Michael T. Gilmore suggests, is that 'The novel becomes highly self-referential as it repeats phrases, incidents, and motifs in the manner of a musical composition'.[39] Moreover, the self-referential element of music is used at one point to raise interesting questions about Chopin and her own art of writing, and about women and art generally. 'It is', Elaine Showalter suggests,

> no accident, for example, that it is Chopin's music that Mademoiselle Reisz performs . . . 'Chopin' becomes the code word for a world of repressed passion between Edna and Robert that Mademoiselle Reisz controls . . . These references to 'Chopin' in the text are on one level allusions to an intimate, romantic, and poignant musical *oeuvre* that reinforces the novel's sensual atmosphere. But on another level, they function as what Nancy K. Miller has called the 'internal female signature' in women's writing, here a literary punning signature that alludes to Kate Chopin's ambitions as an artist and to the emotions she wished her book to arouse in its readers.[40]

This constitutes the nature of both Edna's and Chopin's 'becoming' an artist: it is the desire to use art as a medium which deconstructs socially acceptable images of womanhood and inscribes the 'self'. Music and water in *The Awakening* are, therefore, to be understood metaphorically: they are, to use Mary Jacobus's words on the works of George Eliot and Luce Irigaray, 'an imaginative reaching beyond analytic and realist modes to the metaphors of unbounded female desire in which each finds herself as a woman writing'.[41] All this, it is implied, Edna learns from the music of Mlle Reisz; Kate Chopin shows that she has already learnt these lessons by the form and metaphors she chooses for *The Awakening*. Edna's quest, however, is for a self which is wiser and emotionally richer than that of Mlle Reisz; she is not prepared to suppress certain desires in order that others may express themselves. In the spirit of Maggie Tulliver in George Eliot's *The Mill on the Floss* (1860) who protests against the trial of witches by water,

Edna is not prepared to accept society's definition of the deviant, creative woman as witch-like; nor is she prepared to accept Christianity's creed of desire's renunciation.

Edna's quest, as several critics have noticed, appropriates Christian mythology and subsumes it to a paganism which allows a less inhibited expression of desire. The journey across the bay to the *Chênière Caminada* becomes, for Edna, a voyage of spiritual dimensions: 'Edna felt as if she were being borne away from some anchorage which had held her fast, whose chains had been loosening' (p.81). During the service at the 'quaint little Gothic church of Our Lady of Lourdes' on the island, she suddenly feels ill and Robert takes her to rest at Mme Antoine's. The fact that 'Our Lady of Lourdes' brings about no miraculous cure, but an illness, results in an ironic inversion of religious revelation; her giddiness literally forces her to withdraw from the hallowed ground of Christianity. The dark night of the soul is replaced by her sleep at Mme Antoine's which suggests an inner rite of passage resulting in a sense of herself as dislocated from the society in which she is forced to live: '"How many years have I slept?" she inquired. "The whole island seems changed."' Her simple meal of brown bread and wine when she wakes suggests the act of Communion and again appropriates Christian ritual to communicate a sense of deep inner change taking place. The narrator fully understands the nature of this change but does not permit Edna the same insight: 'That she was seeing with different eyes and making the acquaintance of new conditions in herself that colored and changed her environment, she did not yet suspect' (p.88).

Edna's return to New Orleans and its futile round of social calls deepens her sense of frustration. The elegant houses of the city, like the house in *The Yellow Wallpaper*, are cages for intelligent women; the significance of the caged 'green and yellow parrot', whose curses open Edna's story, suddenly becomes clear. The parrot, an exotic bird carrying mystical meaning for the Indians of New Mexico,[42] represents all peoples confined and colonised by a dominant race or sex. (Cf. Jean Rhys's similar metaphoric use of a parrot in *Wide*

Sargasso Sea.) The bird, trapped in the cage of the dominant culture, is forced to echo the language of that culture but has not lost its own tongue: the parrot 'could speak a little Spanish, and also a language which nobody understood' (p.43). Its own unintelligible language represents a 'wild zone' beyond the boundaries of the culture by which it is constrained. Like the parrot's cage, the elegant Lebrun household too has its bars and 'from the outside looked like a prison, with iron bars before the door and lower windows' (p.110). Feeling increasingly alienated from the society in which she lives, Edna resolves 'to do as she liked and to feel as she liked' (p.107).

Her meetings with Mlle Reisz and her desire to return to painting and become independent lead Edna to rent a tiny house in which she will be able to live her life as she chooses. Like Virginia Woolf, she has some financial independence, and is able to acquire a room of her own. Her departure from her husband's home is marked by a farewell dinner which, as Sandra M. Gilbert has pointed out, is something of a 'Swinburnian Last Supper'.[43] Here, too, the colour yellow is important in that it suggests, metaphorically, a *fin de siècle* rejection of nineteenth-century convention and respectability:

> There was something extremely gorgeous about the appearance of the table, an effect of splendor conveyed by a cover of pale yellow satin under strips of lace-work. There were wax candles in massive brass candelabra, burning softly under yellow silk shades; full, fragrant roses, yellow and red, abounded. There were silver and gold, as she had said there would be, and crystal which glittered like the gems which the women wore. (p.143)

Edna herself is dressed in gold satin and her attitude suggests 'the regal woman, the one who rules, who looks on, who stands alone' (p.145). The evening ends with the enactment of a strange *tableau.* Mrs Highcamp places a garland of yellow and red roses on Victor Lebrun's black curls. The handsome young man, who is drunk with the wine, is suddenly metamorphosed: 'As if a magician's wand had touched him, the garland of roses transformed him into a vision of oriental beauty. His cheeks were the color of crushed grapes, and his dusky eyes glowed with a languishing fire' (p.146). Mrs Highcamp then swathes Victor in her white evening scarf, so that his black suit is hidden from view, turning him momentarily into a figure of classical mythology. His beauty thus transformed, Victor Lebrun evokes Adonis and Bacchus; he becomes a physical manifestation of earthly desire. Another male guest finds himself whispering lines from Swinburne's sonnet, 'A Cameo':

> '"There was a graven image of Desire
> Painted with red blood on a ground of gold"'
> (p.146)

The choice of these lines is significant. During the *fin de siècle* period, Swinburne's work was seen as a poetic rejection of all that the nineteenth century stood for. Leonard Woolf, in his book *Sowing: An autobiography of the years 1880–1904* (1960) recalls how, during his own undergraduate career, Swinburne, Shaw, Butler, Hardy and Wells were regarded as 'champions of freedom of speech and freedom of thought, of commonsense and reason. We felt that, with them as our leaders, we were struggling against a religious and moral code of cant and hypocrisy.'[44] Chopin's use of Swinburne's lines in this episode represents, therefore, Edna Pontellier's embrace of that tide of anti-Victorianism. Moreover, the combination of Edna as a prototype New Woman and Victor as the decadent dandy encapsulates exactly that alliance of the New Woman and the decadent which Linda Dowling suggests the late Victorians found so alarming, 'perceiving in the ambitions of both a profound threat to established culture'.[45] During this decade the figure of the New Woman strode through the pages of *Punch* and *The Yellow Book*, trailing in her wake male nightmares of impotence; holding her hand was the decadent young man who found fulfilment in homosexual relationships. These two unlikely companions were bracketed together in the Victorian mind as presenting a joint threat to the nation's eugenic health. Edna's dinner party is, then, the final heresy in a book of heresies: woman as the erotic object of desire has become the observer, the painter, the writer, the New Woman; man as observer, voyeur, artist has become translated into an aesthetic object of erotic longing. The scene in *The House of Mirth*, in which Lily poses at the centre of a *tableau vivant*, reinforces the role of woman as passive model; here, however, she is the creator of spectacles.

The implications of the shift in power are fascinating for the reader but merely embarrassing for the fictional characters: 'Miss Mayblunt and Mr Gourvernail suddenly conceived the notion that it was time to say good night. And Mr and Mrs Merriman wondered how it could be so late' (p.147). Beneath their shock at such impropriety is a fear of what overstepping such boundaries might mean. In the midst of Edna's moment of triumph, however, a 'hopelessness' and 'a chill breath' sweep through her: 'There came over her the acute longing which always summoned into her spiritual vision the presence of the beloved one, overpowering her at once with a sense of the unattainable' (p.145). It is as if she suddenly realises, as does Virginia Woolf at the end of her essay 'Professions for women', that a room of one's own is not enough; taking that room involves asking questions about how such a life will be lived. The 'unattainable' 'presence of the beloved one' which causes Edna such momentary despair is not simply a romantic yearning for Robert Lebrun; it expresses the frustration of desire in the widest sense. She may well have a room of her own, but that is only the first hurdle to be crossed in achieving complete autonomy; the struggle to find a language in which to express a particular vision is yet to come. Edna's new home, 'Le Pigeonnier' is an important step on the road to freedom; Shirley Foster claims that its name 'suggests a cage'[46] but the word also carries the meaning of attic or garret-room as well as pigeon-loft. The name of Edna's new home therefore suggests changed perspective, drawing her closer to the artistic vision of Mlle Reisz.

The central metaphor used to express the struggle for freedom in *The Awakening* is swimming. Edna learns to swim during her summer stay in the Gulf and gradually overcomes her 'ungovernable dread' (p.73) of the sea. During the night swim early on in the tale, her newly found confidence results in fresh feelings of strength and power:

> A feeling of exultation overtook her, as if some power of significant import had been given her to control the working of her body and her soul. She grew daring and reckless, overestimating her strength. She wanted to swim far out, where no woman had swum before . . . As she swam she seemed to be reaching out for the unlimited in which to lose herself. (pp.73,74)

However, she is suddenly almost overcome by a 'quick vision of death' (p.74) and struggles to regain the shore. She comments to her husband, '"I thought I should have perished out there alone"' (p.74) – words which strikingly anticipate Woolf's use of William Cowper's line, 'We perished, each alone' from his poem 'The Castaway', as a dominant motif of *To the Lighthouse*. Her sudden fear here is like that of the narrator of *The Yellow Wallpaper* as she realises that in jettisoning the cultural construction of gender she runs the risk of jettisoning the boundaries of her own being in what Chopin calls 'the unlimited'. Her final swim in the sea, which invites 'the soul to wander in abysses of solitude' (p.175), is therefore highly ambiguous: most readers assume that Edna commits suicide but as Sandra Gilbert and Susan Gubar point out, '*how, after all, do we know that she ever dies*? What critics have called her "suicide" is simply our interpretation of her motion, our "realistic" idea about the direction in which she is swimming.'[47]

The ambiguous nature of Chopin's conclusion, in which Edna's final swim can be construed either as an act of despair or a moment of triumph, owes much to the fact that the meaning of metaphor is to a certain extent culturally relative. 'Readers of the 1890s', as Elaine Showalter points out 'were well accustomed to drowning as the fictional punishment for female transgression against morality, and most contemporary critics of *The Awakening* thus automatically interpreted Edna's suicide as the wages of sin.'[48] Although no recent readings embrace such a censorious morality, there is still no consensus about the metaphorical 'meaning' of Edna's last swim. Suzanne

Wolkenfeld, for example, reads it negatively as 'a defeat and a regression'.[49] Sandra Gilbert and Susan Gubar's reading is much more celebratory:

> Chopin's Aphrodite, like Hesiod's, is born from the sea, and born because the colony where she comes to consciousness is situated, like so many places that are significant for women, outside culture, beyond the limits and limitations of the cities where men make culture, on one of those magical shores that mark the margin where nature and culture intersect.[50]

Reading her death on one level as the crucifixion of a goddess who has no viable role in Victorian culture, they also argue, on another level, that 'Edna's supposed suicide enacts not a refusal to accept the limitations of reality but a subversive questioning of the limitations of both reality and "realism".'[51]

In more metaphysical and interrogative vein, Michael T. Gilmore suggests that *The Awakening* 'remains alive because it attempts to make sense of two enigmas, nature and the self, that continue to challenge and frustrate modern understanding . . . Does nature have objective meaning or is it always a social construct?'[52] For Cristina Giorcelli, however, Chopin's conclusion presents no such problems: Edna simply 'enters a love relationship with the sun and the sea, the primal elemental factors' and attains 'fulfillment with Nature, with the Emersonian Not-Me, with the universe'.[53]

Undoubtedly, many readers are drawn into a positive reading of Edna's last swim because the final words of Chopin's work return her heroine to scenes of childhood which seem, on the surface, comforting. The sea becomes conflated with 'the blue-grass meadow that she had traversed when a little child, believing that it had no beginning and no end' (p.176); the final lines are a flashback to her early days:

> Edna heard her father's voice and her sister Margaret's. She heard the barking of an old dog that was chained to the sycamore tree. The spurs of the cavalry officer clanged as he walked across the porch. There was the hum of bees, and the musky odor of pinks filled the air. (p.176)

These memories suggest a pre-pubertal self that is free from cultural definitions of the feminine; the infinite space of the blue-grass meadow which 'had no beginning and no end', like the moors in *Wuthering Heights*, is a landscape which is free from such boundaries. To go back to that former pre-sexual self is both release and regression, both death and *jouissance*. In psychoanalytic terms, Edna's return voyage is a metaphoric journey to the stage before the Symbolic Order of the Father, and an embrace of the Imaginary pre-Oedipal stage where the opposition between masculine and feminine does not exist. It represents a rejection of the cultural order, and the psychic impossibility of such rejection.

It can also be argued that the language of *The Awakening* anticipates the work of both Hélène Cixous and Julia Kristeva in its articulation of the nature of gender and writing. Chopin's description of the sea as an embrace of the mother appears *verbatim*, twice, in *The Awakening*: 'The touch of the sea is sensuous, enfolding the body in its soft, close embrace' (pp. 57,176). Chopin's equation of the return to the mother with the sea – which, like the meadow, has 'no beginning and no end' – could be seen as presaging Cixous's mythological use of water. For Cixous, as Toril Moi has pointed out, water is 'the feminine element *par excellence* . . . It is within this space that Cixous's speaking subject is free to move from one subject position to another, or to merge oceanically with the world.'[54] It is only in *writing*, however, that this freedom is available and the sea is a metaphor for that writing. Reflecting the constraints and tensions of a certain historical moment, writing also provides the opportunity for their disruption. Cixous's own work celebrates such artistic freedom with vatic lyricism:

> Write! and your self-seeking text will know itself better than flesh and blood, rising, insurrectionary dough kneading itself, with sonorous, perfumed ingredients, a lively combination of flying colors, leaves, and rivers plunging into the sea we feed . . . our seas are what we make of them, full of fish or not, opaque or transparent, red or black, high or smooth, narrow or bankless; and we are ourselves sea, sand, coral, sea-weed, beaches, tides, swimmers, children, waves . . . Heterogeneous, yes. For her

> joyous benefits she is erogenous; she is the erotogeneity of the heterogeneous: airborne swimmer, in flight, she does not cling to herself; she is dispersible, prodigious, stunning, desirous and capable of others, of the other woman that she will be, of the other woman she isn't, of him, of you.[55]

Thus, reading *The Awakening* with reference to Cixous suggests that Edna's swim is metaphorically a swim into the realm of women's writing. To this end, Chopin's narrative severs itself from nineteenth-century realism and moves towards the subjective and the musical; the carefully observed world is replaced by one of memory, vision and dream: Chopin thus begins to anticipate modernist writing and feminist theory. In Catherine Clément's words, 'Somewhere every culture has an imaginary zone for what it excludes';[56] metaphorically, the sea in *The Awakening* could be read as that 'imaginary zone' where the social construction of the self can be dissolved. Harder to image, and to conceive of intellectually, is the notion of the 'real self' which, like the ghost of a living self, haunts all three texts examined in this chapter. The philosophical difficulty of conceiving a more 'real self' beyond the boundaries of a socially constructed world is communicated by the vagueness of this 'self' in fiction and by closures embracing elements which cannot be reconciled or resolved. The ambiguous nature of Edna's death recognises the high price to be paid for the freedom of 'the other woman that she will be' who lies beyond language and culture in a discourse yet to be articulated. In her own life Chopin paid a very high price for her heresies: the publication of *The Awakening* brought bad reviews, rejection of future work and social isolation.

It is clear, then, that the metaphoric value of the sea and Edna's last swim in *The Awakening* is inherently unstable. This is not surprising, since as readers we inscribe ourselves and our values within the fluidity of metaphor. As D. Davidson has remarked:

> Metaphor is the dreamwork of language and, like all dreamwork, its interpretation reflects as much on the interpreter as originator . . . So too understanding a metaphor is as much a creative endeavor as making a metaphor, and as little guided by rules.[57]

The various critical readings of metaphor in Kate Chopin's work are all interpretations of linguistic 'dreamwork' and as such they express changing perceptions of woman and society. Refusing fixity of meaning, metaphor is itself essentially accommodating; the woman reader's implicit recognition of this phenomenon allows her to engage actively with the woman writer's text in a continuing dialogue of feminist hermeneutics.

Engaging with *The House of Mirth*, *The Yellow Wallpaper* and *The Awakening* in this way, we have constructed a narrative around the metaphorical configuration of room, house, landscape and sea. Ignoring the actual chronology of these works, we have traced a movement from enclosure to openness and see this as a narrative attempt to map metaphorically a recognition of the constraints of discourse. Lily Bart accepts the confinement of a socially constructed sexual identity and dies appropriately within a small room; Gilman's narrator hovers, in a state of madness, on the threshold of her room, a boundary that separates culture and ideology from nature and wildness; Edna Pontellier embraces that wildness in her last suicidal swim, a swim that perhaps expresses a rejection of the boundaries and boundedness effected by nineteenth-century culture. Indeed, a certain optimism about the future for the writing woman is to be found in Chopin's choice of name for her heroine: Edna means 'rejuvenation' in Hebrew[58] and Pontellier, with its allusion to bridges, suggests a woman who can imaginatively cross from the Victorian social and linguistic construction of woman to a perhaps more liberating narrative of woman to be offered by the twentieth century.

All three works examined in this chapter present women who have artistic and imaginative potential, a potential which is not fulfilled within their fictional worlds since none of these women becomes an artist proper. However, in inscribing their stories, Gilman, Chopin and Wharton themselves become artists and the mismatch between their success and the failure of their heroines suggests the difficulty of traversing the ground between woman as object of desire and woman as desiring subject. The woman writer thus deconstructs the obstacles to her own fulfilment, including femininity itself, and thereby makes the page itself a landscape of desire. As Eleanor Munro has remarked: 'Now, the thing about emptiness is that one can fill it: an empty landscape, an empty paper. One can make one's own mark. And in a wide, flat, empty landscape, one is centred wherever one is.'[59]

2
Virginia Woolf's 'mystic boundaries'

Woolf's fiction, like that of Wharton, Gilman and Chopin, portrays women of artistic sensibility enmeshed in social circumstances, surrounded and influenced by cultural paradigms of 'femininity'. Virginia Woolf lived through the late Victorian period and much of the first half of the twentieth century. Born in 1882, she was little more than a child when Gilman and Chopin were writing their 'awakenings' and she lived to see the outbreak of the Second World War before taking her own life in 1941. In her non-fiction works she articulates the problems faced by the woman writer and foregrounds the issues which the 'awakenings' texts of the previous chapter probe obliquely. The intervening years, it would seem, have not resolved these issues in spite of the political successes of the suffragettes. In Woolf's novels there is a preoccupation with boundary, threshold and fluidity; through the room/house, water/sea configuration of metaphor, her works explore the hidden boundaries which constrain women within the construct 'woman'. They also go further: whereas in *The Voyage Out* there is no resolution of the clash between Rachel's desire for artistic expression and the social roles available to her, in *Mrs Dalloway* we see a woman living within social constraints but having access to a private space – a room – in which her imagination can run free of gender boundaries and into that state which Woolf calls androgyny in *A Room of One's Own*. In *To the Lighthouse*, Lily Briscoe – the woman artist – moves into a central position in the text and the novel ends with her vision.

Woolf's most polemical work, *Three Guineas*, is not overtly concerned with the role of the woman artist at all. However, it serves to emphasise Woolf's understanding that the political disabilities of women overcome by the struggles of the suffragettes were only part of a more complex picture. Published in 1938, *Three Guineas* was written towards the end of Virginia Woolf's life and in the shadow of the impending world war. Taking as its ostensible theme the prevention of war, it offers a searching critique of patriarchal society which argues that authoritarianism in the political sphere is a logical development of patriarchal oppression within the family. Cast in a fictional framework as a letter of reply to a lawyer who has offered her three guineas to spend in the cause of pacificism, it contains this arresting metaphorical articulation of the workings of ideology:

> Inevitably we look upon society, so kind to you, so harsh to us, as an ill-fitting form that distorts the truth; deforms the mind; fetters the will. Inevitably we look upon societies as conspiracies that sink the private brother, whom many of us have reason to respect, and inflate in his stead a monstrous male, loud of voice, hard of fist, childishly intent upon scoring the floor of the earth with chalk marks, within whose *mystic boundaries* human beings are penned, rigidly, separately, artificially; where, daubed red and gold, decorated like a savage with feathers he goes through mystic rites and enjoys the dubious pleasures of power and dominion while we, 'his' women, are locked in the private house without share in the many societies of which his society is composed. (p.121, our italics)[1]

The language is harsh in its repetition of verbs of physical restraint – 'distorts', 'deforms', 'fetters' – while the image of the savage drawing the 'mystic boundaries' shows a symbolic act which is followed by forceful physical description – human beings are 'penned', by implication against nature: 'rigidly, separately, artificially'. This exotic image is domesticated at the end of the passage: the symbolic boundary becomes the private house. In Woolf's fiction the private house is a recurrent and ambiguous metaphor in an exploration of the concept of boundary. The phrase 'mystic boundaries' is of key importance here. These boundaries which constrain and distort are not the social and political disabilities which feminism had challenged, but something more insidious and more powerful, constituted in discourse itself. It is interesting that in *Three Guineas* Woolf advocates abandoning the term 'feminist' – which 'according to the dictionary, means "one who champions the rights of women"' (*TG*, p.117) – as obsolete. Since the right to earn a living has been won, she says, the word no longer has any meaning and being dead, its corpse should be cremated. She goes on, however, to quote Josephine Butler:

> Our claim was no claim of women's rights only . . . it was larger and deeper; it was a claim for the rights of all – all men and women – to the respect in their persons of the great principles of Justice and Equality and Liberty. (*TG*, p.117)

Woolf concludes that the fight against the tyranny of the Fascist state is the same fight as that against the patriarchal state. The term 'feminist' has shades of meaning which are specific and limited; Woolf is concerned with a struggle against all-pervasive ways of thinking which constrain the manner in which women live their lives. The suffragettes battered against a particular wall; it gave way under the onslaught, but the 'mystic boundaries' remain as powerful as ever.

Three Guineas enjoyed a mixed reception. Some contemporary reviewers poured scorn on Woolf's linking of militarism and the patriarchal oppression of women and the book was unfavourably received by other members of the Bloomsbury set. Woolf's diary entry for 22 November 1938 contains the following comment:

> Yes I used to be praised by the young and attacked by the elderly. *Three Guineas* has queered the pitch. For the G. M. Youngs and the Scrutineers both attack that. And my own friends have sent me to Coventry over it. So my position is ambiguous. Undoubtedly Morgan's reputation is much higher than my own. So is Tom's. Well? In a way it is a relief. I'm fundamentally an outsider. I do my best work and feel most braced with my back to the wall.[2]

Woolf's sense of herself as on the edge here is interesting, as if she perceives her own position of marginality as being artistically fruitful. The reception of *Three Guineas* was not wholly condemnatory, however. Some reviewers recognised its significance. Theodora Bosanquet described *Three Guineas* as 'a revolutionary bomb of a book'[3] and *The Times Literary Supplement* called Woolf 'the most brilliant pamphleteer in England'.[4] The strength of *Three Guineas* lies in its sharp analysis of the working of power and ideology. *Three Guineas* appeared towards the end of Virginia Woolf's career and towards the end of her life. It seems to be a more explicit statement of what we would now call her 'feminism' than anything that had gone before.

However, while not denying the force of Woolf's polemical writing, we wish to argue that it is the fiction which presents a far more radical critique of woman within society. This critique is all the more searching for having been developed obliquely through metaphor, through which it probes the limits of the signifying practices of her own culture. Woolf herself bears testimony to the effect of such signifying practices upon the lives of women and more specifically upon the life of the aspiring woman writer. A powerful stereotype had developed by the later years of Victoria's reign. Woolf names it by appropriating the figure of 'The Angel in the House' from Coventry Patmore's famous poem. In the essay 'Professions for women' (1931)[5] she recognises this figure as a phantom. Woolf says she will describe her as briefly as she can:

> She was intensely sympathetic. She was immensely charming. She was utterly unselfish. She excelled in the difficult arts of family life. She sacrificed herself daily. If there was chicken, she took the leg; if there was a draught she sat in it – in short she was so constituted that she never had a mind or a wish of her own, but preferred to sympathize with the minds and wishes of others. Above all – I need not say it – she was pure. Her purity was supposed to be her chief beauty – her blushes, her great grace. In those days – the last of Queen Victoria – every house had its Angel.[6]

Allowing for a rhetorical quality in the language of what was originally a speech, this description is distinguished by its difference from the poetic lyricism of much of Woolf's fiction. The rhythmic fluidity which characterises the style of, for example, *To the Lighthouse* and *The Waves* is here replaced by a deliberate jauntiness which points up the ironic defensiveness in this description of practical self-sacrifice. In Woolf's brief allegory, the phantom of the Angel hovers over the page of the woman writer, keeping her within the bounds of propriety and admonishing her for daring to write honestly about the work of a 'great man'. In the interests of self-preservation, Woolf kills her with a judiciously aimed inkpot but 'she died hard' (*Virginia Woolf*, p.60). Victorian man, depicted in *Three Guineas* as scoring his 'mystic boundaries' on the earth floor has circumscribed the cultural construct of woman and she is 'locked' in the private house, sometimes literally but in an even more insidious way, metaphorically. For this 'phantom' issues another injunction: 'Above all, be pure' (*VW*, p.59). Artistic expression meets a 'mystic boundary' when Woolf attempts 'to tell the truth' about her 'own experiences as a body' (*VW*, p.62). For Woolf the body is a site of conflict between the cultural construct 'woman' and her own experiences. Emphatically, she believes it to be a problem common to all women writers: 'I doubt that any woman has solved it yet' (*VW*, p.62).

Like 'Professions for women', *A Room of One's Own* discusses the problems of the woman writer. Originally to be called *Women and Fiction*, the change of title is significant in foregrounding a central metaphor in Woolf's work. The text, published in 1929, resists easy categorisation. Although it presents a controversial materialist argument which explains the suppression of women's talent and the marginalisation of women as writers, it is not generally regarded as being polemical. Indeed, it is for this very reason that Elaine Showalter criticises it; it is, she claims, 'evasive' in its textual strategies, lacking real awareness of women's experiences and real commitment to feminism. Showalter finds the 'teasing, sly elusive'[7] quality of the text almost offensive and symptomatic of Woolf's unwillingness to commit herself to a firm feminist argument. It is arguable, however, that Woolf's assumption of different personae in *A Room of One's Own* is a positive attempt to remove the ego from the text, to speak for other women, not least those who, through historical circumstances, have been prevented from speaking for themselves. As the title suggests, the text appropriates what has become a recognised metaphor for women's cultural limitation. The image of the room as enclosure in nineteenth-century fiction has been identified and examined by a number of feminist critics (notably Elaine Showalter in *A Literature of Their Own* and Sandra M. Gilbert and Susan Gubar in their important work, *The Madwoman in the Attic: The woman writer and the nineteenth-century literary imagination*). In *A Room of One's Own*, the room comes to signify freedom from interference and – along with the £500 p.a. which Woolf also identifies as essential for the aspiring woman writer – independence. The room, most significantly, is one's own; not the guest rooms and boarding-house rooms through which Lily Bart makes her descent, nor the inflicted prison at the top of the house in *The Yellow Wallpaper*. Yet this is a Utopian vision, set against a series of speculations as to the fate of potential women writers of the past and present. It is particularly interesting that the speaking voice at the beginning of the essay juxtaposes the image of the room of one's own with her own image for the search for inspiration: 'When you asked me to speak about women and fiction I sat down on the banks of a river and began to wonder what the words meant.'[8] She expands this image a little further into the essay:

> Thought – to call it by a prouder name than it deserved – had let its line down into the stream. It swayed, minute after minute, hither and thither among the reflections and the weeds, letting the water lift it and sink it until – you know the little tug – the sudden conglomeration of an idea at the end of one's line: and then the cautious hauling of it in, and the careful laying of it out? (*Room*, p.7)

This is of course a familiar Woolf image for the process of creative thought, and the one which we find in 'Professions for women' when she describes the difficulty of writing about her own experiences as a body. Fluidity, expressed through the trope of water – the sea or the river – may be understood as a rejection of the boundedness of life within existing society. It may be seen as an escape from the 'mystic boundaries' of cultural constructs. The self-defined, new female space of the female writer – the room of one's own – becomes an alternative construct, a newly defined boundedness of a newly defined cultural order. The very act of writing self-consciously through metaphor involves such a process.

The topological nature of metaphor (to follow Patricia Parker's terminology referred to in our Introduction) is emphasised as *A Room of One's Own* follows the river fishing image with another short narrative:

> It was thus I found myself walking with extreme rapidity across a grass plot. Instantly a man's figure rose to intercept me. Nor did I at first understand that the gesticulations of a curious-looking object, in a cut-away coat and evening shirt, were aimed at me. His face expressed horror and indignation. Instinct rather than reason came to my help; he was a Beadle; I was a woman. This was the turf; there was the path. Only the Fellows and Scholars are allowed here; the gravel is the place for me. (*Room*, p.7)

The irony here is unmistakable, especially for a woman reader. Reason would indeed have been of little help. The boundary of the Fellows' lawn has achieved the status of a 'mystic boundary' and all Woolf's contempt for the pomposity of male official dress, which achieves such forthright expression in *Three Guineas*, is apparent here. The ironic humour is, however, grimly underscored by the postscript to this little story which concludes with the reflection, 'What idea it had been that had set me so audaciously trespassing I could not now remember' (*Room*, p.8). Thus we see, in miniature, the inhibition of female creativity at work.

To inscribe this inhibition of female creativity on a grander scale, Woolf tells another story: that of Judith Shakespeare, imaginary sister of the more famous William. Judith stands for all the muted female voices of the past, and her story must of necessity be a fiction, 'since facts are so hard to come by'

(*Room*, p.46). The tale of this 'extraordinarily gifted' (*Room*, p.46) but uneducated girl is short and tragic; her attempt to escape her destiny of marriage and domestic duty is ill-fated. Her artistic talent can find no way of expressing itself in sixteenth-century England and her approach to Nick Greene, the actor-manager, leads not to work in the theatre, but to pregnancy and suicide. The story is alluded to again at the end of *A Room of One's Own* and its point driven home:

> I told you in the course of this paper that Shakespeare had a sister; but do not look for her in Sir Sidney Lee's life of the poet. She died young – alas, she never wrote a word. She lies buried where the omnibuses now stop, opposite the Elephant and Castle. Now my belief is that this poet who never wrote a word and was buried at the cross-roads still lives. She lives in you and in me, and in many other women who are not here tonight, for they are washing up the dishes and putting the children to bed. But she lives; for great poets do not die; they are continuing presences; they need only the opportunity to walk among us in the flesh. (*Room*, p.108)

This tale of thwarted artistic talent may be read as a materialist argument, but it has a metaphorical dimension too. 'The ultimate room of one's own is the grave', says Showalter in her essay 'The flight into androgyny';[9] but it is exactly Judith Shakespeare's failure to find a room of her own within the house of sixteenth-century culture which led to her premature grave. In Woolf's novels, fictional women demonstrate the artist who 'lives in you and in me'. Rachel Vinrace, Clarissa Dalloway and Mrs Ramsay are all examples of women of artistic sensibility and their position within a patriarchal culture is explored in the works in which they appear. After the death of Mrs Ramsay in *To the Lighthouse*, the vision of the woman artist in the figure of Lily Briscoe occupies the foreground of the novel.

The inscription of culture in language is an issue which *A Room of One's Own* touches upon in a tantalising way. In a passage which seems to anticipate the ideas of *écriture féminine*, we find the statement, 'The book has to be adapted to the body' (*Room*, p.74) and, a little earlier, reflections on how literary forms have been shaped by men: 'There is no reason to think that the form of the epic or the poetic play suits a woman more than the sentence suits her' (*Room*, p.74). The notion of specifically female language and writing is one which appears to contradict the most problematical concept in *A Room of One's Own*: that of androgyny. It is here that the concept of boundary becomes central. 'No age can have been as stridently sex-conscious as our own' (*Room*, p.94) Woolf says in an observation that gender divisions are more sharply delineated now than ever before. Such sharp gender division effaces women and this is reflected in the text, as the anecdote about Mr A's new novel suggests:

> But after reading a chapter or two a shadow seemed to lie across the page. It was a straight dark bar, a shadow shaped something like the letter 'I'. One began dodging this way and that to catch a glimpse of the landscape behind it. Whether that was indeed a tree or a woman walking I was not quite sure . . . the worst of it is that in the shadow of a letter 'I' all is shapeless as mist. (*Room*, p.95)

This shadowed landscape behind the monolithic 'I' is the landscape of Woolf's fiction in which, striving to find a language which will evaporate those 'mystic boundaries', she aspires towards 'the androgynous mind' which is 'resonant and porous . . . transmits emotion without impediment' and which is 'naturally creative, incandescent and *undivided*' (*Room*, p.94, our italics). It is only when that sharp gender polarity has been deconstructed, and the phantom of the Angel annihilated, that women can escape the boundaries of the 'feminine' and establish rooms of their own in the house of fiction. To see this process at work, we must turn to the novels.

The Voyage Out

It is Virginia Woolf's remarkable first novel, *The Voyage Out*, published in 1915, which inscribes the initial struggle to establish such a room of her own in the house of fiction. Re-reading it in 1920, Woolf wrote in her diary that she did not know what to make of it and called it a 'harlequinade', 'an assortment of patches – here simple and severe – here frivolous and shallow – here like God's truth – here strong and free flowing as I could wish'.[10] Louise DeSalvo's book, *Virginia Woolf's First Voyage*,[11] has painstakingly charted the struggle which Woolf had in writing the novel with its numerous drafts and alterations. Both she and other commentators, notably Stephen Trombley in *All that Summer she was Mad* and Roger Poole in *The Unknown Virginia Woolf*,[12] have seen the novel as a painful attempt on Woolf's part to work through the traumas of a childhood and youth beset by bereavement and sexual abuse. This very fruitful kind of reading, however, does not emphasise the formal problems that the text presents. As well as being a very personal expression of female experience, Woolf's novel also begins to probe the landscape behind the 'straight dark bar'. In so doing, it begins to undermine the conventional form of realist narrative and to create tensions within the text, tensions which Woolf perceived in the 1920 reading. In the novel we may discern two kinds of landscape. Using the term 'landscape' literally, we can recognise the 'setting' or background which realist conventions of the novel demand: the wide vistas of the Atlantic Ocean and the exotic terrain of the South American country where most of the novel's action takes place. If we use the term 'landscape' metaphorically to refer to the structure of the text, however, there are narrative landscapes superimposed upon each other to create the 'harlequinade effect' to which Woolf herself refers. One of these is the landscape of the realist novel, concerned with the interaction of 'characters' in their social and moral behaviour. Another is the archetypal symbolic landscape of the voyage, carrying with it the structuring principle of quest. A third narrative landscape is the metaphorical configuration of house, room/water, sea which is central to much of Virginia Woolf's work. Reading *The Voyage Out* through the grid of this metaphorical structure enables us to read positively and to reject the view of many early reviewers, and indeed recent critics, that the death of Rachel is a reflection of Woolf's inability both to solve the problems she had set her heroine and the aesthetic problems she had set herself.[13]

Rachel Vinrace, the heroine of *The Voyage Out* is – unlike the heroines of the Gilman, Chopin and Wharton texts – a very young woman, and the story of her voyage to South America may be viewed within the conventions of the *Bildungsroman* as a voyage of self-development. As Susan J. Rosowski suggests in her essay 'The novel of awakening' (see pages 15–16) the distinctively female *Bildungsroman* involves an awakening to limitations rather than to possibilities and the novel illustrates this in the case of Rachel. The plot may be summarised quite simply. A young woman, Rachel Vinrace, the product of a sheltered upbringing and a limited education but with a talent for music, accompanies her father on board his ship on a voyage to South America. Also on board are her aunt and uncle, Helen and Ridley Ambrose, a beautiful and unconventional woman married to a single-minded academic. On the way, the ship picks up a couple, the Dalloways, who are sophisticated and worldly. Richard Dalloway kisses Rachel during a storm and this disturbs her profoundly. When they reach South America, Helen decides that Rachel should stay with them on the coast instead of going up the Amazon with her father. This gives Rachel the opportunity to meet a group of English tourists who are staying at the hotel in the resort of Santa Marina, in particular a young aspiring novelist, Terence Hewet. On an expedition up the river, she becomes engaged to Terence. They return to Santa Marina, where they appear to be settling into the role of an engaged couple, when Rachel is taken ill with fever and after several weeks of sickness, dies. The novel ends with life resuming its humdrum course for the tourists at the hotel.

It is impossible, of course, with such a plot, to overlook the presence of water in the text. In one sense it has a metonymic dimension as an integral part of the setting of the realist novel. Its metaphoric significance, however, can only be understood by looking carefully at its binary opposite within the metaphoric pattern – the room. These two metaphors are poised one against the other in a pattern which seems to fix and then dissolves. It is through the interplay of these opposites that Rachel's progress in the novel is charted. It is also through them that both the constraints and potential freedom of the text, the novel form itself, are acknowledged. Rachel's 'awakening' takes her into several rooms, and also gives her visions through dream and delirium of sinister distortions of the room in the form of vaults and tunnels. In the end, if she is to reconcile the room that is left to her with the desire which she cannot articulate but only image through visions of the sea, she must again take possession of it. In the existing state of culture, the only way she can do this is, like Lily Bart and Edna Pontellier, through death. Woolf's third person narration functions like that of a realist novel in providing the 'staircases'[14] of the plot but, in anticipation of her later work, frequently privileges the subjective over the collective values of the social world.

Rachel Vinrace, as she appears at the beginning of the novel, is not so much a defined 'character' as a deliberate presentation of undeveloped potentiality. The reader sees her largely through the eyes of her aunt, Helen Ambrose, herself by contrast a worldly woman, who views her niece as unformed and naive: '"She really might be six years old"', she says when speaking of 'the smooth unmarked outline of the girl's face'.[15] Such apparent immaturity is also reflected in Rachel's difficulties with language: 'a tendency to use the wrong words, made her seem more than normally incompetent for her years' (p.16). This discomfort with language persists throughout the novel and increasingly enacts Rachel's inability to accommodate herself within the categories imposed by her society. Her immersion in music suggests the possibility of an alternative discourse; her lack of formal education has given her time and opportunity to teach herself and develop her talents on her own. In her room on board ship, she divides her time between 'playing very difficult music', dabbling in a little reading and 'doing . . . absolutely nothing' (p.29). Only the music suggests definite purpose; apart from this she is in a state of stasis. This state is expressed metaphorically through the unlikely person of Richard Dalloway who, in discussing hazards to navigation, tells how he asked a sea captain what perils he dreaded most for his ship: 'expecting him to say icebergs, or derelicts, or fog or something of that sort. Not a bit of it. I've always remembered his answer. "*Sedgius acquatici*", he said, which I take to be a kind of duckweed' (p.38). Read in the context of the pervasive sea imagery in the novel, this anecdote assumes a significance beyond itself, although it is interestingly divested of its sinister mystique by the prosaic Richard in the phrase, 'a kind of duckweed';[16] he is unable to perceive its significance. The full import of such an image in the female *Bildungsroman* was to be explored by Jean Rhys half a century later in *Wide Sargasso Sea*.

The arrival of the sophisticated Dalloways, however, prompts Rachel to an expression of dissatisfaction with herself and her body; she begins to harbour a desire to be something other than she is. Her development into an adult woman involves the awareness of a self, or an image of the self, which other people see. The image of the mirror expresses this: looking in the mirror, she reflects that 'she had come to the depressing conclusion, since the arrival of the Dalloways, that her face was not the face she wanted, and in all probability never would be' (p.37). Richard Dalloway is the agency through which Rachel's sexual naiveté is exposed within the novel. The tumult his kiss causes Rachel is presaged by the storm in which it happens. Significantly, it is in Rachel's own room aboard the ship that the incident takes place; it is thus a metaphorical intrusion upon Rachel's personal space. His words leading up to the kiss are symptomatic of an ideology which hypocritically ascribes power to Rachel simply because she is able to attract sexually: '"A young and beautiful woman", he continued sententiously, "has the whole world at her feet. That's true, Miss Vinrace. You have an inestimable power – for good or evil. What couldn't you do –" he broke off' (p. 73). Thus divesting himself of responsibility for his actions, he kisses Rachel and establishes over her his physical power. In so doing, he exposes the treachery of his own language and the discourse of sexuality which it represents. Her reaction seems out of all proportion to the event and is fraught with ambivalence: 'she became peaceful too, at the same time possessed with a strange exultation' (p.73). Any sense that this is a sexual awakening – 'Life seemed to hold infinite possibilities she had never guessed at' (p.73) – is qualified by the feeling of dislocation she experiences from her own body as she looks out across the sea: 'She leant upon the rail of the ship and gradually ceased to feel, for a chill of mind and body crept over her' (p.73). By contrast, the dream she has that night is all too physical as images of physical constraint condense into a distorted room containing a distorted form of manhood:

> She dreamt that she was walking down a long tunnel, which grew so narrow by degrees that she could touch the damp bricks on either side. At length the tunnel opened and became a vault; she found herself trapped in it, bricks meeting her wherever she turned, alone with a little deformed man who squatted on the floor gibbering, with long nails. His face was pitted and like the face of an animal. The wall behind him oozed with damp, which collected into drops and slid down. Still and cold as death she lay, not daring to move, until she broke the agony by tossing herself across the bed, and woke crying 'Oh!'. (p.74)

Not surprisingly, this passage (and the delirium which echoes it as Rachel lies dying) has attracted a great deal of critical attention, lending itself as it does to a variety of psychoanalytic interpretations. Some critics have chosen to read the passage as illuminating Woolf's own traumas; Poole and Trombley, for example, see the gibbering deformed man as George Duckworth, who subjected his half-sister to sexual interference for a number of years.[17]

Changing the focus, however, we can see the room/sea opposition at work in the metaphorical expression of Rachel's reaction to the experience. Her conscious mind detaches itself from her body and travels over the surface of troubled waters to 'glimpse infinite possibilities'. Her subconscious, however, is repelled by the implications of Dalloway's kiss. The image of enclosure thrust upon her by the dream carries with it suggestions of death in the word 'vault'.[18] Rachel's sexual awakening, therefore, involves an awakening to a sense of threat. Even after waking from the dream, Rachel perceives of herself as prey. In the manner of nightmares, it will not go away on waking, and she locks the door of her cabin, as if to reassert her own space. She is, however, under siege: 'A voice moaned for her; eyes desired her. All night long barbarian men harassed the ship; they came scuffling down the passages, and stopped to snuffle at her door. She could not sleep again' (p.74). The language here suggests animal behaviour and an ugly perception of sexual desire involving herself as prey. This echoes an earlier observation as Helen sees Rachel asleep over the piano: 'she looked somehow like a victim dropped from the claws of a bird of prey' (p.33). Now, not only is Rachel vulnerable; she also sees herself as vulnerable. On confiding in Helen about the episode, her thoughts run on and are related in language uncannily reminiscent of *The Yellow Wallpaper*:

> By this new light she saw her life for the first time as a creeping hedged-in thing, driven cautiously between high walls, here turned aside, there plunged in darkness, made dull and crippled for ever – her life that was the only chance she had – a thousand words and actions became plain to her.
>
> 'Because men are brutes! I hate men!' she exclaimed.
>
> 'I thought you said you liked him?' said Helen.
>
> 'I liked him, and I liked being kissed', she answered, as if that only added more difficulties to her problem. (p.79)

What is it that is such a revelation for Rachel? The problem is that she now recognises her own sexual desire but has also grasped intuitively the basis of the relationships between the sexes and understands its core to be power. Far from ascribing that power to herself, as Dalloway's words suggest she should, she sees herself as the potential victim of any man who might choose to make her one: 'So that's why I can't walk alone!' (p.79) she bursts out. It is because of this revelation that she sees her life now as 'a creeping hedged-in thing'; she experiences her sexual awakening as a closing off of possibilities, a denial of freedom imposed by this particularly forceful form of gender differentiation within her culture.

Arrival at Santa Marina moves Rachel on to a different phase in her 'awakening', an intellectual awakening imaged in a temporary room of her own. It is in an attempt to stimulate Rachel and to broaden her outlook that Helen suggests that she spend the months in South America with her and her husband at the villa they have borrowed. In this villa, Helen gives Rachel a room of her own which is to be 'a fortress as well as a sanctuary' (p.122). Here, Rachel moves further away from that state of stasis in which she first appears aboard the ship. In this room of her own, there is a subordination of her physical self to more cerebral demands:

> Far from looking bored or absent-minded, her eyes were concentrated almost sternly on the page, and from her breathing, which was slow but repressed, it could be seen that her whole body was constrained by the working of her mind. (p.122)

She is described as acting out the parts of female characters in plays by Ibsen and a novel by Meredith, both male writers associated with late nineteenth-century feminism. Nora in *The Doll's House* and Diana of the Crossways, in the novel of the same name, are both female figures who flout convention and assert their independence by leaving their husbands. It is as though Rachel is trying out alternative social roles. Her own choice of fiction is interesting as she selects

> modern books, books in shiny yellow covers, books with a great deal of gilding on the back, which were tokens in her aunts' eyes of harsh wrangling and disputes about facts which had no such importance as the moderns claimed for them. (p.123)

Given the significance of yellow at the turn of the century (discussed in the previous chapter on pages 39–41), Rachel's awakening seems to place her in the same historical context as the heroines of the 'Awakenings' texts. Rachel's provisional autonomy in her room remains intact until her engagement to Terence Hewet when they spend many hours together alone in it. This personal space then becomes eroded and, as a result, Rachel experiences desires which she is unable to articulate.

Rachel's intellectual awakening is paralleled at this point by a new experience of social life. The residents at the villa become acquainted with the English tourists at the hotel and Rachel's involvement with them reaches its culmination at the dance, held in the hotel's public room.[19] Here, Rachel's artistic gift is pressed into service; she plays so that the dance can continue after the professional musicians have left. The episode provides another expression of how women are constrained: Rachel's music in *this* context is quite acceptable, just as is Adèle Ratignolle's music when she plays for her family in *The Awakening*. It is no accident that, on the same occasion, she is badly upset by the patronising views of a young academic, St John Hirst, on women's intellectual inferiority.

The relationship between Rachel and Terence Hewet provides the focus for the remainder of the novel. The single most significant thing about Terence is that he is trying to write novels. Early in their relationship, in a parody of the text's own delineation of the range of characters who cluster around the hotel at Santa Marina, he observes the people at the picnic he has organised. His observations are, for the most part, cynical and reductive whereas Rachel, by contrast, is not judgemental but open in her attitude to the others. When Terence asks her what she is looking at, she simply replies, 'Human beings' (p.134). The chapter ends here as if there is no more to be said. Rachel's phrasing of her answer is significantly ungendered and indicates the distance between herself and Hewet who, as it emerges from the long conversations he subsequently has with Rachel, is acutely aware of the sharp gender divisions in society. The separate spheres imposed by ideology fascinate him and he makes Rachel tell him all about her domestic life in Richmond. At this point in the novel, he seems to become a mouthpiece for indignation at the lot of women and he voices ideas later to be found in *A Room of One's Own* and *Three Guineas*. Such ideas express the social disabilities of women exemplified in the fate of his friend

St John Hirst's sister, who is sent to feed the rabbits while her brother pursues his studies in order to make a success of his academic career. Such is his own indignation that Terence finally blurts out: 'If I were a woman I'd blow someone's brains out' (p.217). This conversation is yet another stage in Rachel's 'awakening', altering as it does her perspective on life in English society. Yet she does not repudiate the female sphere but rather re-evaluates the role played by her father ('She had always taken it for granted that his point of view was just' (p.218)) and asserts that the domestic life carries 'a sort of beauty in it', that it is 'making an atmosphere and building up a solid mass, a background' (p.218). (This affirmation of the value of domestic life is embraced by Lily Briscoe at the end of *To the Lighthouse* and incorporated into her artistic vision.) For Rachel, the distance that her voyage has now given her enables her to tell Terence that she was both happy and miserable, but further attempts to tell him how it is to be a young woman lead her to thoughts of sex and a failure of language: 'Here came in the great space of life into which no one had ever penetrated . . . Did he demand that she should describe that also?' (p.219). Her reflections on this seem to evoke the freedom of a pre-pubertal self for which the closest analogy is the sea. Describing walking alone in Richmond Park and singing to herself, she says, 'I love the freedom of it – it's like being the wind or the sea' (p.219).

Terence tells Rachel that he is trying to write a novel about 'Silence . . . the things people don't say (p.220). At this point, he seems to articulate what Woolf herself was trying to do; in a very important sense *The Voyage Out* is itself a novel about silence. Working within the house of realist fiction with plot, characters and setting, it continually probes the inadequacies of such a structure in its passages of lyrical intensity and surrealism. The shortcomings of the realist novel are particularly apparent at those moments when Rachel herself no longer finds language adequate – points at which the fluidity of water is invoked. Terence, however, is doomed to failure, working as he is within a literary discourse which cannot give form to such a conception. His own comparison of himself with Thackeray is a powerful indicator of this. As for Rachel, at this stage in the novel she becomes aware that the books she is reading are inadequate representations of her own feelings:

> none of the books she read, from *Wuthering Heights* to *Man and Superman*, and the plays of Ibsen, suggested from their analysis of love that what their heroines felt was what she was feeling now. It seemed to her that her sensations had no name. (pp.228–9)

The omniscient narrator, however, echoes Helen in comparing her mind to 'racing water' (p.227), an image which suggests inner tumult. This inability to give language to her feelings and to express her desire is represented very powerfully just before the expedition up the Amazon and it signifies a turning point in her 'awakening'. Rachel is at the hotel, the setting for social life, but she is ill at ease with herself and her place in that social world. She feels alienated from other people, experiencing only the reality of her body:

> For the time, her own body was the source of all the life in the world, which tried to burst forth here – there – and was repressed now by Mr Bax, now by Evelyn, now by the imposition of ponderous stupidity, the weight of the entire world. (p.264)

It is here that the metaphor of the room expresses the inability of Rachel not only to fulfil her desire, but even to name it: 'Physical movement was the only refuge, in and out of rooms, in and out of people's minds, seeking she knew not what' (p.265).

From this point in the novel, the inherent contradictions involved in Rachel's 'awakening' are brought into dramatic conflict. The expedition up the Amazon draws on literary conventions of quest and self discovery but subverts them by creating further ambiguity and conflict. The sense of language as both inadequate and alien is rendered in the dream-like surrealism of the scenes in the interior. Rachel and Terence's love for each other is presented in a dialogue where each seems to be speaking mechanically as if performing a kind of ritual; the silence surrounding their words is emphasised (p.278). The scene suggests that they are both submitting to pre-ordained roles; however, Rachel's inner turmoil is conveyed by her words '"Terrible – terrible"' as she looks at 'the senseless and cruel churning of the water' (p.279). The ambiguities of Helen's relationship with Rachel come into focus at this point. She has performed the role of mentor to Rachel, attempting to educate her in the ways of the world. As an exemplar of 'woman', she herself displays contradictions. Apparently worldly, she has chosen marriage to a scholar whose absorption in the Pindar Odes gives her a measure of personal freedom. She has accommodated her Bohemianism within marriage, but none the less is circumscribed by marital boundaries. Like Mrs Ramsay, she is interested in personal relationships; also like Mrs Ramsay, her artistic sensibility finds expression through traditional female craft (in her case, tapestry). She has accepted marriage as natural and right, both for herself and for others. As far as Helen is concerned, it is the most natural thing for Rachel to marry; Rachel, however, by this time intuitively understands that marriage will inevitably inhibit both her artistic development and her sexual freedom. Helen becomes transformed into an agent of constraint, immediate in her physicality (in a strange way, rather like the deformed man in Rachel's dream) in what is almost a physical assault on Rachel:

> A hand dropped abrupt as iron on Rachel's shoulder; it might have been a bolt from heaven. She fell beneath it, and the grass whipped across her eyes and filled her mouth and ears. Through the waving stems she saw a figure, large and shapeless against the sky. Helen was upon her. Rolled this way and that, now seeing only forests of green, and now the high blue heaven; she was speechless and almost without sense. (p.290)

Accounts of earlier drafts suggest that the violence of this scene became moderated as Woolf revised it over and over again. It presents Helen as a threatening figure, defamiliarised in the surroundings of the forest. Significantly, then, in this strange scene in the forest Rachel actually seems to see Terence with Helen rather than herself in the role of lover, a delusion which suggests her alienation from her own situation:

> Over her loomed two great heads, the heads of a man and woman, of Terence and Helen.
>
> Both were flushed, both laughing, and the lips were moving; they came together and kissed in the air above her. Broken fragments of speech came down to her on the ground. She thought she heard them speak of love and then of marriage. Raising herself and sitting up, she too realized Helen's soft body, the strong and hospitable arms, and happiness swelling and breaking in one vast wave. (pp.290–1)

Here, the sea imagery suggests fulfilment but this is associated with the female body rather than the male. When Rachel gains control of her own body, it is in an identification with Helen's which is a far more sensual experience for her than her relationship with Terence. Thus Rachel's state is one of ambivalence; outwardly conforming to the ritual of engagement and marriage, she experiences Helen's physical nearness as both erotic presence and social constraint.

After their return to the coast, the room again becomes foregrounded. The engagement becomes official and Rachel has great difficulty in adjusting to the behaviour expected of her by 'society'; the writing of acknowledgements to notes of congratulation, for example, is irksome to her. Conventional behaviour, by contrast, is provided by Susan Warrington and Arthur Venning, whose relationship is presented in some detail. For Susan, the offer of marriage holds out the promise of salvation from a life dogged by the petty demands placed upon spinsters by their families. Susan's situation is a vivid example of the oppressive constraints placed upon women of her class and, superficially, her situation parallels Rachel's. For Rachel, however, there is a growing sense of unease at the constraints that will be placed upon her through marriage. The room of her own at the villa is no longer that, as she and Terence spend many hours in it together. On one occasion, Rachel is playing the piano and Terence is trying to write. She is absorbed in the difficult music, while he is pondering his book, *Silence*. He displays an ambivalent attitude to Rachel's absorption in her art. On the one hand, he 'liked the impersonality which it produced in her' (p.298). On the other, he persists in interrupting her to ask her for comments on some notes he is writing about 'women'. She, however, cannot accept the interruption of her playing; her half-playful objection meets with an egotism which threatens to destroy her artistry: '"I've no objection to nice simple tunes – indeed, I find them very helpful to my literary composition, but that kind of thing is merely like an unfortunate old dog going on its hind legs in the rain"' (p.299). That he then turns to the engagement congratulations is no accident, but a pointed ironic juxtaposition; at this moment, the engagement appears as a socially sanctioned means of suppressing her musical talent. In an ensuing mock fight, which is described in very physical terms, 'they fought for mastery, imagining a rock, and the sea heaving beneath them' (p.305). Here the physical intimacy is combative and contrasts with the soft enfolding experience which she associates with Helen. Terence is the stronger and overpowers her, but her reply, although playful, expresses a desire for escape through its sea imagery: '"I'm a mermaid! I can swim", she cried, "so the game's up"' (p.305). Anticipating an image applied to Mrs Dalloway in the novel of the same name, she thus expresses a desire for a freedom and power beyond the bounds of existing culture; the image is necessarily that of a mythical creature.

It becomes apparent to Rachel that the exclusivity accorded to the romantic relationship within popular mythology does not satisfy, although what it is she does want she cannot express: 'She turned again and looked at the distant blue, which was so smooth and serene where the sky met the sea' (p.309). In an echo of Rachel's looking at herself in the mirror on board ship, the looking glass is used here to express a confrontation with desire which is not accommodated by this romantic mythology: 'But it chilled them to see themselves in the glass, for instead of being vast and indivisible they were really very small and separate, the size of the glass leaving a large space for the reflection of other things' (p.310).

Rachel's final illness is presaged by a psychic withdrawal from the ebb and flow of social life; she sits in the hall at the hotel where the dance was held and can hardly believe it is the same room. This withdrawal is paralleled by a repudiation of the myth of romantic sexual love: 'Although they sat close together, they had ceased . . . to struggle and desire one another. There seemed to be peace between them. It might be love, but it was not the love of man for woman' (p.322). Further, in contrast with these semi-mystical feelings of peace and understanding there are, just before this, destructive images within the text which herald the onset of Rachel's fatal illness: she and Terence 'were seen pulling flowers to pieces in the garden' (p.312) and news is received in a letter to St John of the death of a parlourmaid by poison: 'Why had she done it? He shrugged his shoulders. Why do people kill themselves? Why do the lower orders do any of the things they do? Nobody knows. They sat in silence' (p.313). A subject for Terence's novel perhaps? Certainly a story never to be told of one who was victim by virtue of both her sex and her class.

When Rachel first begins to feel ill, Terence is reading Milton to her[20] and this time, in a different way, language breaks down:

> The words, in spite of what Terence had said, seemed to be laden with meaning, and perhaps it was for this reason that it was painful to listen to them; they sounded strange; they meant different things from what they usually meant. Rachel at any rate could not keep her attention fixed upon them, but went off upon curious trains of thought suggested by words such as 'curb' and 'Locrine' and 'Brute', which brought unpleasant sights before her eyes, independently of their meaning. (pp.333–4)

Thus the discourse of English literary culture becomes alien to her; the signifiers of Milton's verse float free, but the freedom is menacing. Rachel's illness involves her final retreat into that room of her own where all intruders are seen in her delirium as vicious and threatening. The room itself takes on a different aspect for her and this is emphasised in the narrative. At the boundary of the room at the window, there is threat:

> Turning her eyes to the window, she was not reassured by what she saw there. The movement of the blind as it filled with air and blew slowly out, drawing the cord with a little trailing sound along the floor, seemed to her terrifying, as if it were the movement of an animal in the room. (p.335)

This is very evocative of the fears that she experiences after her nightmare on board ship, and suggests a violation of boundary, a threat to autonomy. Indeed, the horrific dream is echoed in Rachel's delirium but the gibbering little man has been transformed into 'little deformed women' playing cards who become Helen and Nurse McInnis '*standing in the window* together whispering, whispering incessantly' (p.338, our italics). This threat therefore is now more than male sexual desire; the conspiratorial aspect of the two women suggests a collusion with male dominance which, for Rachel, is destructive. Terence himself becomes 'an old woman slicing a man's head off with a knife' (p.346). Left alone with her own body, Rachel becomes detached even from that; mind and body separate, and her delirium is described in terms of a retreat into the medium of water:

> At last the faces went further away; she fell into a deep pool of sticky water, which eventually closed over her head. She saw nothing and heard nothing but a faint booming sound, which was the sound of the sea rolling over her head. While all her tormentors thought that she was dead, she was not dead, but curled up at the bottom of the sea. There she lay, sometimes seeing darkness, sometimes light, while every now and then someone turned her over at the bottom of the sea. (p.348)

Stephen Trombley sees the water image as an image of fluidity, softness, comfort, 'the antidote for the hardness of male abstraction'.[21] However, as Rachel sees her 'tormentors' as women, this reading is difficult to sustain; this total retreat is rather an escape from the enclosures of civil society perceived in a delirious or nightmare state as being menacing and violent. Such enclosures include the cultural construct of femininity and the complicity of women in sustaining it.

It is at this point in the novel that Rachel enacts a

withdrawal from the role of 'character' in a novel which conveys 'meaning' through plot. In her delirium, she sees a series of sights 'all concerned in some plot, some adventure, some escape' but is unable to 'grasp their meaning' (pp.348 and 347). The vision expresses Rachel's situation both within society and within the novel. She is onlooker in a 'plot' which will not give up its meaning. Through her delirium here the text creates an enactment of the failure of the plot's internal logic; the retreat into the deep pool is also a metaphorical retreat from the realist novel's assertion that it is capable of conveying 'truth'. Her death, which the reader experiences through Terence's consciousness, is closely associated with the parameters of the room and what lies beyond its boundaries. In his mind the mystic consummation of their union which her death represents involves an outward movement from the room: 'The windows were uncurtained, and showed the moon, and a long silver pathway upon the surface of the waves' (p.361). Through the threshold of the window the long silver pathway on the surface of the waves suggests a different voyage into the beyond, one which would exclude the demands of the body – in life not possible, of course. Rachel's supremacy in the room after death is emphasised by Terence's having to leave it and return to the mundane world outside: 'As he saw the passage outside the room, and the table with the cups and plates, it suddenly came over him that here was a world in which he would never see Rachel again' (p.361).

Thus Rachel's death is presented as ambiguously as that of Edna Pontellier, as loss and negation but also as gain and assertion. To achieve such autonomy, Rachel must go beyond the confines of society and beyond, in textual terms, the confines of plot. Her death is not the final chapter; the novel returns to the hotel where life resumes in a round of knitting and novel reading. The woman as artist within the text is destroyed. The novel ends, therefore, by re-establishing the values of the social world and keeping the realist framework intact. However, the power of such a framework to express the central concerns of the novel is constantly under strain and this is metaphorically expressed in an extraordinary scene when Helen and Rachel, after several months of seclusion in their villa, pay an evening visit to the hotel. Instead of going in, they move around the building, looking in at the lighted windows and seeing a series of scenes from the outside. The effect of this scenario is to place them in a marginal position *vis-à-vis* the other English characters. They see their social interaction and are able to interpret it without being a part of it. They are on a threshold between one world and another, just as Catherine and Heathcliff are when they look in at the windows of Thrushcross Grange in *Wuthering Heights*. What they see, however, is not alien and unfamiliar but a replication of the drawing-room society of their own class at home. The anomalousness of their position is emphasised when they are sighted and run away, as if having performed some delinquent action: 'They did not stop running until they felt certain that no eye could penetrate the darkness and the hotel was only a square shadow in the distance, with red holes regularly cut in it' (p.101). For the reader, too, the hotel – as this description suggests – is defamiliarised as are the people, the 'characters' within it. They are, as it were, 'framed' in a series of rooms as they are viewed through the windows. They are contained in the same way that the realist novel 'contains' its characters.

In his review of *The Voyage Out* in 1915, Woolf's friend, E. M. Forster, claimed that 'her chief characters are not vivid', but that nevertheless he considered the novel to be a success because 'she believes in adventure . . . and knows that it can only be taken alone'. This comment brings together two of the landscapes in the novel – that of the realist fiction and that of the inward quest for self-discovery. His subsequent assertion that 'It is for a voyage into solitude that man was created',[22] however, does not acknowledge that both Woolf herself and Rachel are women, not the allegedly ungendered 'man' and that their desire for self-discovery strains at the very bounds of language and fictional form itself. A comparison with Forster's *A Room with a View* (1908) illustrates the point well. Here again we find the metaphor of the room, the journey to a foreign country and at their centre a young and naive heroine. Lucy Honeychurch is also an accomplished pianist, a fact which leads the clergyman, Mr Beebe, to say, 'If Miss

Honeychurch ever takes to live as she plays it will be very exciting – both for us and for her.'[23] What Lucy's 'awakening' consists of, however, is a growing realisation that the manners and attitudes of her own upper middle-class society are artificial and that what she really wants is George, a young man of lower social status, who is somehow associated with natural impulses and true feelings. In contrast, Woolf's work suggests that such a version of the fairy tale happy ending is one more cultural construct which does not adequately explore the shadowy landscape behind the monolithic 'I'.

Mrs Dalloway

In *Mrs Dalloway* and *To the Lighthouse* we see two women who, unlike Edna Pontellier, Lily Bart, the anonymous heroine of *The Yellow Wallpaper* – and indeed unlike Woolf's own Rachel Vinrace – are well into middle age. Clarissa Dalloway and Mrs Ramsay occupy the centre of the two novels in which they appear, a centre which becomes displaced in *To the Lighthouse*. Both novels situate their heroines very precisely in a society which defines the two women by their marital status. Unlike the other heroines, neither of these two women does anything which challenges her established social role. The texts, however, interrogate that role in a complex and problematical way; the pervasive metaphors of room and sea are not merely devices which give aesthetic unity, but constitute the parameters by which we as readers may construct the meaning of both works. In *To the Lighthouse*, the sea is an ever present force and, as in *The Awakening* and *The Voyage Out*, it is an integral part of the plot. However, *Mrs Dalloway* is different in that the novel appears, on a superficial reading, to present us with a very urban world. In terms of plot, the sea does not figure, yet images of water and the sea appear at a number of points in the text, setting up a metaphorical structure which contrasts images of fluidity with those of constraint. The shifting pattern between these two abstractions suggests that the view of Hafley – that the sea represents 'unity'[24] – is perhaps too simple. The metaphor of the room manifests itself ambiguously in both novels, enclosure and confinement giving way to a more positive appropriation of space.

Mrs Dalloway and *To the Lighthouse* also place their heroines against a background of historical change in a more precise way than the other novels discussed in this book. Both are novels of the 1920s – written considerably later than *The Voyage Out* – and in both texts the First World War is a dominating event, not actually present but acknowledged as influencing in a profound way how the characters think and behave. *Mrs Dalloway* is a novel about a post-war world; it is set in 1923. (A recent essay by Jeremy Tambling has examined in some detail the historical preciseness of the novel and the bearing of this on its central thematic concerns.)[25] As Clarissa Dalloway wanders through the streets of London at the opening of the novel, she reflects on how people have endured personal sacrifice and comforts herself with the thought that the war is over. Five years later, she believes, London is back to normal and people have returned to the business of daily life. One of the major themes of the novel, however, illustrates how the damaging effects of war have reached far beyond the armistice. The long opening section of *To the Lighthouse* evokes the sense of a long Edwardian summer in which traditional values hold – just – and the middle section, spanning ten years, covers the war period. We return to the Hebrides in the final section to a world irrevocably changed.

Mrs Ramsay and Mrs Dalloway, therefore, are situated very precisely, both historically and socially. The society lady of the 1920s and the all-beneficent mother-figure of the Edwardian era are, we will argue, presented in Woolf's fiction as social constructs. Neither novel carries the theme of quest for a 'real self' within the plot and it is difficult to see how either work could be characterised as a *Bildungsroman*, even of the specifically female kind which involves an awakening to limitations (see pages 15–16). The search for meaning, however, permeates both novels and preoccupies both characters although it is never resolved. What we are left with, rather, is an awareness of the provisional nature of meaning itself and a conviction that a self which is constructed in discourse is one which is open to disruption and reconstitution. It is the achievement of *Mrs Dalloway* to link militarism, patriarchy and sexual ideology in a way that anticipates the polemic of *Three Guineas*; it is the achievement of *To the Lighthouse* to both celebrate and displace 'woman' as domestic angel, a figure which Woolf was to identify in 'Professions for women' as such an obstacle to her development as a writer. Mrs Ramsay dies and the closure of the novel focuses on the woman artist, Lily Briscoe, who achieves the artistic fulfilment which has evaded her throughout the novel. Taken together, the two novels present a critique of early twentieth-century society from a feminist perspective. The critical view that water imagery in Woolf's work represents 'life, time and reality'[26] takes us only so far; we would suggest that a richer understanding of the novel results from reading the water imagery as expressing a potentially infinite realm of meaning outside the illusory fixities of social 'truths'. Those social 'truths' may be metaphorically likened to the rooms and houses which we inhabit; for women they have often been oppressive, even imprisoning, but they are not absolute – their boundaries may be redrawn and the woman artist must have a room of her own.

Kate Millett's statement in 1969 that Virginia Woolf 'glorified two housewives'[27] set the tone for certain subsequent feminist critiques of Woolf's work, characterising her as betraying the cause of feminism in her fiction. Certainly both Mrs Dalloway and Mrs Ramsay have received a staggering range of critical interpretation and this is probably especially true of Mrs Dalloway, who has been variously described as a pagan goddess figure, a spiritual recluse, a frigid repressed neurotic and an expression of alienation within contemporary society.[28] None of these characterisations is wholly true; all represent a partial truth. Woolf herself expressed anxiety and misgivings about the presentation of Mrs Dalloway as the novel was in progress, writing in her diary: 'The doubtful point is, I think, the character of Mrs Dalloway. It may be too stiff, too glittering and too tinselly.'[29]

The choice of a fashionable society lady as the central figure is crucial. In a recent work on Woolf, Rachel Bowlby makes the following points:

> Clarissa is both perfectly conventional in her role as lady and hostess and, at the same time, a misfit: *Mrs Dalloway* is all about the fact that she is still unresolved in a choice apparently completed a generation before . . . Like Mrs Ramsay, to all appearances a model of maternal equilibrium, she is in reality anything but 'composed', except in the sense of being put together from disparate parts.[30]

Critics like Jeremy Hawthorn see Clarissa's social status as the ultimate weakness of the novel: Clarissa experiences alienation, desires to connect, but – like her creator – is too far removed from the ordinary concerns of life as it is lived by most people. He advances the view of William Troy, claiming that Woolf came from a class whose experience was largely vicarious, one whose 'contacts with actuality were incomplete, unsatisfactory or inhibited'.[31] There is a surprisingly naive confidence here that 'actuality' is a given objective condition. We shall argue that, on the contrary, in a novel which explores and exposes how the social self is moulded by ideology, Clarissa may be seen as the perfect focus precisely *because* her way of life is all too obviously artificial. Just as Rachel Vinrace is presented as undeveloped and immature in order to illustrate the encroaching constraints of ideology, Clarissa Dalloway's 'artificiality' shows a woman living within those constraints. The novel also presents women characters who are exemplary figures for the heroine. The alliterative trio of Ladies Bruton, Bexborough and Bradshaw illustrates certain aspects of 'woman' which constitute the 'lady' and the three women therefore provide points of reference in Clarissa's negotiation of her social identity. Further, the party which is the culmination of the novel, far from being simply the 'offering' (p.109)[32] Clarissa wishes it to be, represents the superficial role play of 'civilised' society.

Clarissa's acceptance of her society's values is illustrated by her reaction on returning from a trip to Bond Street to find that her husband, Richard, has been invited to lunch by Lady Bruton without her. This apparently trivial occurrence provokes an extreme reaction from Clarissa, seemingly out of all proportion to the event and carrying for her alarming intimations of mortality. Lady Bruton is one of the women she most admires, a woman who embraces the most masculine values of militarism and political dealing and who exercises powerful influence on the establishment world of London. Even her name, Millicent Bruton, suggests a militant patriotism, Millicent being an ancient German name meaning 'strong worker' or 'energetic' and Bruton evoking the mythical ancestor of the British. The language in which Clarissa's misgivings are expressed, presented as her own consciousness, deserves close attention:

> Millicent Bruton, whose lunch parties were said to be extraordinarily amusing, had not asked her. No vulgar jealousy could separate her from Richard. But she feared time itself and read on Lady Bruton's face, as if it had been a dial cut in impassive stone, the dwindling of life. (pp.28–9)

The simile of the dial which describes Lady Bruton's face is intimately linked with the metaphorical structure of the novel. It encapsulates the solidity of linear time, is associated with the periodic chiming of Big Ben ('The leaden circles dissolved in the air' (pp.6 and 165)) and resonates with the line from *Cymbeline* which runs through the novel, 'Fear no more the heat of the sun'. Its solidity connects, too, with the language used to describe Peter Walsh's interruption of the intimate moment between Sally Seton and Clarissa at Bourton which Clarissa is about to relive in her attic room: 'It was like running one's face against a granite wall in the darkness' (p.33). It suggests Clarissa's sense of constraint at the frailty of her own body – she has a weak heart – and her all too acute awareness of the inevitability of her own death; it also represents the constraints of life lived in society from childhood to old age. Clarissa has chosen to espouse the role of politician's wife and society hostess: she identifies with a vision of England in which 'The King and Queen were at the Palace. And everywhere . . . there was a beating, a stirring of galloping ponies, tapping of cricket bats; Lords, Ascot, Ranelagh and all the rest of it' (p.6). She sees herself as part of a tradition: 'since her people were courtiers once in the time of the Georges' (p.7). There is a sense here of an idealised vision of stability and entrenched privilege. It is one critical view that Clarissa loves life, is a 'good liver',[33] yet implicated in Clarissa's sense of herself as a social being is this acute sense of her own vulnerability and susceptibility to the erosions of time. Clarissa would most like to be like Lady Bexborough, the second of the trio of Lady Bs who provide role models for women in this patriarchal society: 'Lady Bexborough who opened a bazaar, they said, with the telegram in her hand, John, her favourite, killed' (p.6). This woman demonstrates the British 'stiff upper lip' attitude and faithfully allows her son to be sacrificed in the cause of patriotism: the image she represents – the woman exhorting her son to fight for his country – had entered the public imagination through the recruiting posters of the Great War. Clarissa's acceptance that Lady Bexborough's behaviour is exemplary reveals the true cost of Clarissa's social role: she is constrained not by social disabilities but by her own assumptions of what is normal and what is right.

Acutely aware of the frailty of her own body and its sterility – 'feeling herself suddenly shrivelled, aged, breastless' (p.29), she retreats from a perception of herself as living flesh and blood into her own room. Clarissa's attic at the top of the fashionable marital home in Westminster (with all the connotations of politics and government that such an address involves) is the most striking example of the room image in the novel and one which has occasioned considerable critical debate. As women readers, we are now familiar with the image of the woman in the third storey and, following Gilbert and Gubar, we associate such a trope with both repression and vision. In contrast with Bertha Mason and the heroine of *The Yellow Wallpaper*, however, Clarissa's habitation of the room is by choice. Although Richard's concern that 'after her illness she must sleep undisturbed' (p.29) provides an overt rationale for the separation, there is a tacit agreement between them that this arrangement is to her liking: 'And really she preferred to read of the retreat from Moscow. He knew it' (p.29).

Her withdrawal to her room on this occasion is coloured by two different notions of herself, one as a 'nun withdrawing' and one 'as a child exploring a tower' (p.29) – both of which place her outside the role of sexual woman. This personal space, therefore, is achieved at a cost: 'There was an emptiness about the heart of life; an attic room' (p.29). Psychoanalytic critics tend to see this retreat into the self as a regression to the state of virginity. Makiko Minow-Pinkney, for example, in a recent application of Kristevan theory to Woolf's fiction, sees the attic as the space where Clarissa 'rejects all men',[34] and likens the sheets of the attic bed which are 'clean, tight stretched in a broad white band' to her intact hymen. Clarissa withdraws from sexual commitment – hence her rejection of Peter Walsh – in favour of a more amicable and less demanding relationship with her husband, Richard. Although Minow-Pinkney sees the sexual implications of Clarissa's withdrawal to the attic as complex, she chooses to read the reference to Clarissa laughing at Richard's dropping of the hot water bottle as a demonstration of Clarissa's antagonism towards him. For Minow-Pinkney, Richard has become a threatening figure who relegates Clarissa to the attic in the process of adopting the 'Bradshaw approach, invoking the "disinterested" authority of medical science to impose constraints on female desire'.[35] She believes that this is how Clarissa sees Richard. However, it is significant that Richard, like Clarissa, has an instinctive dislike of Bradshaw and does not share his passion for 'conversion' (p.89). Further, it is Richard's willingness to give Clarissa personal space, rather than absorb her in heterosexual passion, which led to her choice of him over Peter Walsh. Marriage to Richard gives Clarissa the freedom to step outside her allotted gender role, literally in the sexual sense, but also metaphorically if the room is interpreted as an imaginative space. Peter Walsh would not have allowed her a room of her own. When she is in the room, a mental process takes place during which we see her sense of sexual failure transformed into something more positive. At first, she seems to judge herself by the male-oriented standards of her society. She is hard on herself:

> Lovely in girlhood, suddenly there came a moment – for example on the river beneath the woods at Clieveden – when, through some contraction of this cold spirit, she had failed him. And then at Constantinople, and then again and again. (pp.29–30)

Is this Clarissa's acknowledgement of her own frigidity, judged from the male point of reference? Beverly Ann Schlack, in a stimulating study of literary allusion in *Mrs Dalloway*, points to Clarissa's reading of Baron Marbot's memoirs in her room and perceptively suggests that, because they deal with war and the masculine life, they subtly relate Clarissa to 'her male double, Septimus Smith'.[36] Schlack further argues that Clarissa's frigidity is echoed in the scenes of frozen desolation, and that 'Napoleon's failure at Moscow is the analogue of Clarissa's failure of Richard.'[37] It is difficult to accept, however, that Woolf would choose to parallel Clarissa with a figure so symbolic of imperialism and militarism as Napoleon. Certainly, Clarissa's choice of 'this tale of agony, suffering, death and defeat'[38] as bedtime reading is significant. Marbot's experience involves the most extreme horror and privation:

> Marbot's descriptions of the Russian campaign, particularly of Napoleon's ignominious retreat, are harrowing. The battlefield was covered with 'thirty thousand corpses half devoured by wolves'; soldiers died of exposure to the freezing cold or of starvation, despite eating their horses. When one of the bridges over the Beresina River broke under the combined weight of men, horses and wagons, those who were not crushed or drowned were killed by Russian guns firing 'upon the wretches who were struggling to cross the river'. Nearly 25,000 men were lost.[39]

In a sympathetic identification with Marbot, Clarissa does not establish herself as an analogue of Napoleon and his failure to capture Moscow. Quite the reverse; she identifies with the victims of such attempts at imperial aggrandisement as she is to identify later with Septimus Warren Smith's gruesome death. In imagination she is already experiencing those same horrors and privations which forced 'manliness' (p.79) on Septimus. In her room, Clarissa takes herself outside the constraints of her gender, even though the reminder of the inevitability of mortal life is there in the form of the half-burnt candle which is mentioned several times. Memoirs by definition attempt to make sense of a life; the writer tries to give permanence to the experience of living. In this respect, Baron Marbot's work resonates with Clarissa's memories as they appear throughout the novel, surfacing in her consciousness as she attempts to confer meaning on her own life.

It is significant that in her thoughts in the attic room, Clarissa gradually moves away from the language of failure in which desire is associated with her failure in the eyes of another. She reflects on how sometimes, when a woman confesses to her some sexual scrape, she achieves a moment of 'illumination; a match burning in a crocus; an inner meaning almost expressed' (p.30):

> It was a sudden revelation, a tinge like a blush which one tried to check and then, as it spread, one yielded to its expansion, and rushed to the farthest verge and there quivered and felt the world come closer, swollen with some astonishing significance, some pressure of rapture, which split its thin skin and gushed and poured with an extraordinary alleviation over the cracks and sores. (p.30)

Some critics have observed that the language describing this process is essentially phallic.[40] However, we would argue that the image of the match in the crocus unites both male (the hard, elongated match) and female (the crocus, petalled and folded like the vulva) in a mystic burning. The imagery here is therefore appropriate to both male and female orgasm. Clarissa reflects at this point that 'she did undoubtedly then feel what men felt' (p.30). It would be a mistake, however, to interpret this as expressing a deep-seated desire on Clarissa's part to be a man, or even to limit its interpretation to a suggestion of her latent lesbianism. The attic room and Clarissa's thoughts when she is there offer a movement towards that principle of androgyny which, Woolf states in *A Room of One's Own*, is the principle upon which the minds of all artists must be based. What we see in Clarissa Dalloway is the artistic process at work, an imaginative and creative sensibility which cannot translate itself into artefact in the world outside because of the choices she has made in her life. It is in this light that we ought to interpret Clarissa's reading of Baron Marbot's memoirs. What her choice of reading suggests is not a desire for vicarious experience, but a potential for artistic thought: the withering of that potential into the social façade of creating flower arrangements and groups of people at parties is the price she pays for her social conformity. In that, she and Septimus have something else in common apart from their contingency in time and space: sexual and social conformity cost Clarissa her creative powers; sexual and social conformity cost Septimus his sanity. The price of social acceptability for both is high indeed.

The attic room is a special place poised outside the normal spaces of everyday life; it is a place where, for Clarissa, the negative effects of such withdrawal are offset by the freedom to reflect alone. Possibilities not pursued are part of this reflective picture. The most significant of these is the exploration through memory of Clarissa's girlhood relationship with the exotic Sally Seton. For Clarissa, Sally offered a view into a life more liberated than her own both sexually and intellectually. Sally felt at ease with her body in a way that Clarissa did not – 'she forgot her sponge and then ran along the passage naked' (p.32). She was intellectually stimulating too and the young Clarissa found this infectious: 'but very soon she was just as excited – read Plato in bed before breakfast; read Morris; read Shelley by the hour' (p.31). Clarissa remembers this relationship as love: 'this falling in love with women . . . Had not that, after all been love?' (p.30). It is with Sally at Bourton that Clarissa has experienced 'the most exquisite moment of her whole life passing a stone urn with flowers in it. Sally stopped; picked a flower; kissed her on the lips. The whole world might have turned upside down!' (p.33). Clarissa's response to the kiss is expressed through an arresting image:

> And she felt that she had been given a present, wrapped up and told just to keep it, not to look at it – a diamond, something infinitely precious, wrapped up, which as they walked (up and down, up and down), she uncovered, or the radiance burnt through, the revelation, the religious feeling! (p.33)

What does this jewel, the diamond, stand for? Hard and glittering, it contrasts with the living flower that Sally has just given her. A sense of secrecy is carried by the phrases 'wrapped up', 'not to look at it yet'. The image is repeated a few pages later in the novel when Clarissa prepares to come down from her room and looks in the mirror:

> That was her self – pointed; dart-like; definite. That was her self when some effort, some call on her to be her self, drew the parts together, she alone knew how different, how incompatible and composed so for the world only into one centre, one diamond, one woman who sat in her drawing-room and made a meeting-point, a radiancy no doubt in some dull lives, a refuge for the lonely to come to, perhaps; she had helped young people, who were grateful to her; had tried to be the same always, never showing a sign of all the other sides of her – faults, jealousies, vanities, suspicions, like this of Lady Bruton not asking her to lunch; which, she thought (combing her hair finally), is utterly base! Now, where was her dress? (pp.34–5)

The nature of the image seems to have changed here. In the first extract, if the diamond is to be seen as representing for Clarissa a 'real self', that 'real self' has become transformed in the older Clarissa into a social being effected through a willed composition of parts. The earlier perception of the 'real self' can only be experienced through withdrawal into the room and then only imaged through metaphor. In the second passage the language enacts Clarissa's emergence from the room and the mental state which it represents; as she returns to the outside world she becomes more concerned with the superficial matters of everyday life, thinks again of Lady

Bruton and asks herself a quite practical question about her dress. Her initial retreat to the room had been accompanied by thoughts of undressing expressed in strangely impersonal language: 'Women must put off their rich apparel. At midday they must disrobe' (p.29), and the shedding of clothes here perhaps suggests the laying aside of social roles. The reference to the diamond is repeated as she goes along the landing: 'pausing on the landing, and assembling that diamond shape, that single person' (p.35). The diamond here is, however, a shape rather than the real thing suggesting representation rather than actuality. The diamond image, therefore, is closely associated with the concept of selfhood. In Clarissa's consciousness it metaphorically expresses for her a sense of her 'real' self, deeply hidden; the willed composition of parts which form the diamond shape presents to the world a social self which may be seen as the construct 'woman'. The use of granite, another hard, crystalline substance – neither lustrous nor prismatic – to express the boundaries and repressions of male-dominated society conveys a much more negative sense of limitation. The retreat into the attic room allows Clarissa to remember the hidden diamond which she cherishes as an image of self-fulfilment. The attic room therefore restores her to another sense of self and, returning to the drawing room, she is at peace with her desire.

The sea metaphor structures the text in a different way from that of the room. It is present in the consciousness of the characters and in the narrative voice rather than in the setting. Clarissa, 'on the threshold of her drawing-room' (p.28) just before retreating to the attic, feels

> an exquisite suspense, such as might stay a diver before plunging while the sea darkens and brightens beneath him, and the waves which threaten to break, but only gently split their surface, roll and conceal and encrust as they just turn over the weeds with pearl. (pp.28–9)

In this passage the image of the room and that of the sea are counterpointed and the sense of boundary and threshold foregrounded. The doorway is that of the drawing-room, the most public room in the house and what is to be the scene of Clarissa's party. The 'one moment', the 'exquisite suspense', suggest a crystallisation of the awareness of desire, both a reluctance and an anticipation before entering the room; the language then moves into sea imagery which expresses both fear and delight ('the sea darkens and brightens beneath him, and the waves which *threaten* (our italics) to break'). Diving into the depths, the immersion in fluidity is imagined; 'plunging' evokes the opening page of the novel when Clarissa, going out into the June morning in London, likens the feeling to standing on another threshold, many years before – that of the French windows at Bourton:

> And then, thought Clarissa Dalloway, what a morning – fresh as if issued to children on a beach.
>
> What a lark! What a plunge! For so it had always seemed to her when, with a little squeak of the hinges, which she could hear now she had burst open the French windows and plunged at Bourton into the open air. How fresh, how calm, stiller than this of course, the air was in the early morning; like the flap of a wave; the kiss of a wave. (p.5)

Septimus's later actual plunge out of the window of Mrs Filmer's boarding house darkly undermines, of course, the positive connotations that these earlier uses of the verb seem to carry. Clarissa's mood of contentment, as she returns to the drawing-room, is expressed through the language of the sea:

> Quiet descended on her, calm, content, as her needle, drawing the silk smoothly to its gentle pause, collected the green folds together and attached them, very lightly to the belt. So on a summer's day waves collect, overbalance; collect and fall; and the whole world seems to be saying 'that is all' more and more ponderously, until even the heart in the body which lies in the sun on the beach says too, that is all. Fear no more says the heart. Fear no more, says the heart, committing its burden to some sea, which sighs collectively for all sorrows, and renews, begins, collects, lets fall. And the body alone listens to the passing bee; the wave breaking, the dog barking, far away barking and barking. (pp.36–7)

Peter Walsh's interruption of this trance-like state as he comes into the drawing-room parallels his earlier intrusion at Bourton when the flower and the kiss gave intimations of the fulfilment of desire. For Clarissa, his hand on the door to the room betokens this violation, expressed metaphorically through the language of sexuality: 'She made to hide her dress, like a virgin protecting chastity, respecting privacy' (p.37).

The essential thing about Peter is that he represents in the text all that would conspire to rob Clarissa of her own room and, as such, contrasts sharply with the benign conformist that Richard Dalloway has become since his appearance in *The Voyage Out*. Like Clarissa and Richard, Peter identifies with a set of social values and this is illustrated by his sentimental attitude to King and Country which he demonstrates in his admiration for the 'Boys in uniform carrying guns' who are marching through the London streets (p.46). This sentimentality is ironically undermined by his choosing to see an ambulance as emblematic of 'civilisation'; this is the very ambulance which is carrying Septimus's mutilated body to the hospital. His emotional commitment to these beliefs is mirrored by his personal relationships. Peter is emotionally demanding. A volatile personality, he bursts into tears during his reunion with Clarissa; his passion for women demands total commitment from them. This is illustrated in his latest relationship with Daisy who is leaving her husband and possibly her children for him – and it is something that the young Clarissa was able to intuit. Wisely, then, she has chosen Richard Dalloway instead, although when she first met him, she mistakenly thought his name was Wickham, thus subconsciously evoking the sexually flamboyant character from Jane Austen's *Pride and Prejudice*. This indeed is how he appears in *The Voyage Out*, but the Richard of *Mrs Dalloway* is much closer to Jane Austen's Mr Knightley and it is Peter Walsh who has become a middle-aged Wickham. His insistent fingering of his pocket knife suggests an insecure masculinity which must be constantly asserted. For the woman reader, the episode where he follows a girl home, weaving as he goes a fantasy of being 'an adventurer . . . a romantic buccaneer, careless of all these damned proprieties' (p.49) is sinister. For Clarissa, then, marriage to Peter would have meant 'forcing your soul' (p.163), a submission of self which is enforced in society at large by Holmes and Bradshaw.

Clarissa is halfway to knowing this through intuition and thus she has an instinctive distrust and dislike of Sir William Bradshaw: 'But she did not know what it was about Sir William; what exactly she disliked' (p.162). Sir William Bradshaw's treatment of his wife in comparison with Richard's treatment of his is highly significant. Lady Bradshaw, the third Lady B., is a personification of the 'Angel in the House'. In a passage in which a narrative voice remote from any one character speaks with bitter irony, the link between this treatment and his other activities is established beyond question:

> Worshipping proportion, Sir William not only prospered himself but made England prosper, secluded her lunatics, forbade childbirth, penalized despair, made it impossible for the unfit to propagate their views until they, too, shared his sense of proportion – his, if they were men, Lady Bradshaw's if they were women (she embroidered, knitted, spent four nights out of seven at home with her son). (p.89)

The scepticism of this passage should warn us against an interpretation which celebrates knitting and embroidery as womanly pursuits. Woolf's ironic presentation of Lady Bradshaw far from glorifies the 'feminine' and negates sewing and knitting as metaphors for an admirable feminine principle of connection and synthesis.[41] It is surely such gender stereotyping that Woolf is undermining here where the 'feminine' imprisons women. The description of Lady Bradshaw's submission to her husband's perception of her: 'she felt wedged on a calm ocean' (p.85) echoes the state of stasis metaphorically expressed in *The Voyage Out* through the reference to duckweed and anticipates the use of the word 'marooned' in *Wide Sargasso Sea*.

Lady Bradshaw, 'like a sea-lion at the edge of its tank, barking for invitations' (p.161), is presented in a parodic way which evokes Clarissa's own disappointment at being excluded from Lady Bruton's lunch party and it is in the light of this that we must consider Clarissa's party. Many critics have accepted Clarissa's own feeling that her party is an 'offering' to be its true meaning within the context of the novel. Her desire that it should 'kindle and illuminate' (p.7) must be considered in the light of how the party is actually presented in the text. What we see there, in fact, is a gathering of people who are wrapped up in their own concerns. The more selfish side of Clarissa's nature is shown in her desire to exclude Ellie Henderson, a poor cousin of the Dalloways. It is difficult to resist the notion that Ellie, like other poor relation figures in literature, is being presented as a touchstone for Clarissa's moral integrity. Her reaction to Richard's suggestion that she invite Ellie is indicative of more than mere irritation – 'But Richard has no notion of the look of a room' (p.106) – and suggests the withering of aesthetic sensibility into the social discernment of mere snobbery. Lord Gayton and Nancy Blow are depicted as being absorbed only in each other and anxious to leave; Lord Lexham is concerned for his wife's health. Peter Walsh and the gatecrashing Sally Seton speak of their youth, but the keynote in their reminiscences is that of loss and failure. 'Not a word!', is Peter Walsh's reply to Sally's question, 'Have you written?' (p.166). As for Sally, the bohemian non-conformist, she has married a self-made man and lives in great affluence, the mother of 'five enormous boys' (p.152). She has become the ultimate in convention, channelling her sexuality into an acceptable social role, and raising exotic flowers in suburban beds near Manchester – a metaphor for her own life. The Prime Minister, who is the guest of honour at Clarissa's party, is presented satirically as a figure in gold lace – a costume not meant to inspire admiration in the reader. The deflating observation, 'One couldn't laugh at him. He looked so ordinary. You might have stood him behind a counter and bought biscuits' (p.152), is not clearly attributed to any one character in the text. Clarissa's daughter, Elizabeth, is thoroughly bored: 'Oh how much nicer to be in the country and do what one liked!' (p.167). In her own way she is quite resistant to the romanticised image that men have of her and this remark is juxtaposed with the musings of Willie Titcomb (hardly to be taken seriously with such a name): 'She was like a poplar, she was like a river, she was like a hyacinth' (p.167). Only Richard, true to his Mr Knightley role, bothers to speak to Ellie Henderson. The party is, in fact, quite pedestrian and the buried metaphor of that particular word is subtly foregrounded when the curtains bearing their design of birds of paradise blow into the room and are pushed back – twice. Sir William Bradshaw's late arrival at Clarissa's party effects the tangential connection between Clarissa and Septimus in terms of plot; in order to assimilate the experience of Septimus's death, Clarissa withdraws from the social hubbub of the drawing-room into a smaller room where she can be alone.

It is to escape Sir William Bradshaw and his twin goddesses of 'Proportion' and 'Conversion' that Septimus makes his final leap from the window in a Bloomsbury lodging house. If we see the room as metaphor, it is significant that this is a rented room in a society which metaphorically allows Septimus no room of his own. The establishment of Sir William Bradshaw in the novel as a bastion of patriarchal values places Septimus as the victim of a society which is based on those values. The link between patriarchy in its domestic manifestations and the conduct of society in its political and military undertakings, so explicitly argued fifteen years later in *Three Guineas*, is made through metaphor in *Mrs Dalloway*. It is obvious that he is a parallel to Clarissa – one critic sees him as scapegoat who dies so that Clarissa might live[42] – and although they never meet, his tragic destiny constitutes a meaning which has significance for her own life. Woolf herself said of the novel: 'I adumbrate here a study of insanity and suicide; the world seen by the sane and the insane side by side.'[43]

Much critical work has been done on the nature of Septimus's madness[44] and on how the boundary between himself and the outer world is dissolved so that he no longer has a sense of himself. If we see madness as a metaphor in the text, however, it represents all that cannot be contained in discourse, a total vision of which Clarissa can apprehend only through intimation if she is to keep her sanity but which the woman writer or artist must represent if she is to retain any artistic integrity. Beverly Anne Schlack puts forward a powerful argument which links Septimus and Clarissa in their repressed homosexuality through the web of allusion to Dante.[45] This gives meaning to Septimus's unusual forename by identifying the seventh circle of hell in *The Inferno* as the one reserved for 'sodomites': Schlack sees his intense friendship with Evans as repressed homosexual love. Septimus's madness is for him both illuminating and terrifying: he thinks he has been shown the meaning of life but is tortured by visions of eternal damnation. Neither can be contained in language and Septimus's writings amount to little more than banalities. The flower image which pervades the novel is defamiliarised horrifically in his imagination: 'The red flowers grew through his flesh; their stiff leaves rustled by his head' (p.62). Recurrently he sees the figure of his dead friend Evans, killed before the armistice. The spectre of Evans represents, through Septimus's distorted or enhanced consciousness, a constant reminder in the text of the cost of the war. Septimus's condition is induced by the horror of war itself which has disabused him of the idealised concept of 'England': 'Septimus was one of the first to volunteer. He went to France to save an England which consisted almost entirely of Shakespeare's plays and Miss Isabel Pole in a green dress walking in a square' (p.77).[46] The 'manliness' imposed on this sensitive young man from Stroud (another link with Clarissa through the Cotswold name of her family home?) – taken to its logical conclusion – leads him into a terrible numbness: he had become engaged to Rezia 'one evening when panic was on him – that he could not feel' (p.78). Only Clarissa in the novel, reading Baron Marbot's *Memoirs* in her own attic room, is able to relate imaginatively to the horrors of war which Septimus has actually experienced.

Significantly, for most of the novel, Septimus and Rezia are shown out of doors and it is only just before his death that the domestic life of the Warren Smiths is portrayed. This rented room is seen as a temporary resting place which is violated by the intrusion of Holmes, the Smiths' doctor who has referred Septimus to Bradshaw. Holmes's intrusion into the room echoes Peter Walsh's intrusion into Clarissa's drawing room earlier in the novel. There is an evocation of the earlier scene through the use of very similar language to express a state of peace:

> Every power poured its treasures on his head, and his hand lay there on the back of the sofa, as he had seen his hand lie when he was bathing, floating, on the top of the waves, while far away on shore he heard dogs barking and barking far away. Fear no more, says the heart in the body; fear no more. (p.124)

There is one very significant difference between these two passages, so similar yet separated by about ninety pages in the novel: Clarissa conceives of herself as a body on the beach, lulled by the sea, but still there on solid land. Septimus, however, is out to sea, and in that state he watches the gold spot on the wall of the room. Both here and earlier in the novel there are uncanny echoes of *The Yellow Wallpaper*:

> He had grown stranger and stranger. He said people were talking behind the bedroom walls. Mrs Filmer thought it odd. He saw things too . . . He lay on the sofa and made her hold his hand to prevent him from falling down, down, he cried into the flames! and saw faces laughing at him, calling him horrible disgusting names, from the walls and hands pointing round the screen. (p.60)

> Going and coming, beckoning, signalling, so the light and shadow, which now made the wall grey, now the bananas bright yellow, now made the Strand grey, now made the omnibuses bright yellow, seemed to Septimus Warren Smith lying on the sofa in the sitting-room; watching the watery gold glow and fade with the astonishing sensibility of some live creature on the roses, on the wall-paper. (p.124)

The image of the live creature in the wallpaper is acutely reminiscent of the Gilman story and the colour yellow is here too, but transmuted from the foul yellow in the earlier text to a 'watery gold' which is associated with the shifting pattern of yellow and grey. This contrast of yellow and grey is subtly present at other points in the text. Grey is associated with conformity; the colour of granite, it becomes identified with establishment values: the interior of the car carrying the distinguished person in Bond Street is 'dove grey' (p.14); a 'grey tide of service . . . washed round Lady Bruton' (p.96); the churches of the Strand are like 'shapes of grey paper' (p.121). Yellow, however, seems to have a less precise connotation: it is the colour of the curtains bearing the bird of paradise design in Mrs Dalloway's drawing-room and it is the colour of the hat which Clarissa removes so ritualistically in her attic room. Seemingly inconsequential details offer the contrast between yellow and grey as a binary opposition which perhaps metaphorically represents non-conformity versus the crushing weight of convention and respectability.[47] In choosing a pair of gloves, for example, Clarissa has to decide '. . . should they be to the elbow or above it, lemon or pale grey?' (p.17). This apparently trivial detail is given significance by the information a few pages before that Clarissa 'had a passion for gloves' (p.12) and, when seen as part of the binary metaphorical pattern in the novel, perhaps represents the choices that Clarissa makes in her life. The contrast between the grey of the Strand and the yellow of the omnibuses in the passage quoted above is evocative of Elizabeth's sense of release after leaving Miss Kilman when she boards an omnibus and goes up the Strand – this occurs in the text just before the narrative moves to Septimus in the room. Clarissa's hat represents a 'femininity' and the removal of it signals the onset of the more androgynous reflections that take place within the room; the fact that it is yellow is perhaps a hint of her repressed desire for a less orthodox way of life. Septimus comes nearest to sanity in the novel when he helps to trim Mrs Peters's hat, an occupation conventionally classified as feminine. In moving away from the extreme form of gender identification which has resulted in his 'manliness', he unconsciously acknowledges the repressed part of his nature and release from his madness begins to seem a possibility. It is into this precarious space, metaphorically expressed by the rented room, that Holmes – the envoy of Bradshaw – thrusts his way, penetrating Septimus's sanctuary. Septimus's thoughts as he hears Holmes's approach are rendered in the text with utmost clarity: they seem to be the product of a supremely rational consciousness. The window is seen as the last practical resort, the only escape from all that Holmes and Bradshaw represent; his suicide becomes, paradoxically, not a rejection but an embrace of life: 'Life was good. The sun hot. Only human beings?' (p.132). Like Hardy's heroine, Sue Bridehead, he releases himself from the constraint that a room dominated by others involves, but in his case the leap from the window proves fatal. At the very end, we are no longer privileged to share Septimus's thoughts; the externalised dispassionate description of his action shocks by its lack of emotion: 'Holmes was at the door. "I'll give it to you!" he cried, and flung himself vigorously, violently down on to Mrs Filmer's area railings' (p.132).

It is left to Clarissa to recreate imaginatively Septimus's experience in the midst of her party. The news of Septimus's death comes with the arrival of Sir William and Lady Bradshaw and Clarissa withdraws from the party itself into a smaller room. There are echoes here of her earlier withdrawal into the attic room in the metaphor which evokes her rather ritualistic disrobing on that occasion: 'the party's splendour fell to the floor' (p.163). Again, there is the sense that this is a provisional space created within a culture which holds different values: 'The chairs still kept the impress of the Prime Minister and Lady Bruton, she turned deferentially, he sitting four-square, authoritatively' (p.163). Clarissa's imaginative identification with Septimus in his fatal plunge enacts in the text the horror of Baron Marbot's memoirs which is present only through allusion earlier in the novel. The language of the description conflates an image of bayonets of war with the aggressive boundary markers of private property, thus implicitly linking the two: 'Up had flashed the ground; through him, blundering, bruising, went the rusty spikes. There he lay with a thud, thud, thud in his brain, and then a suffocation of blackness' (p.163). The violent imagery of sexual penetration in the language Clarissa finds for her perception of Septimus's fate, in intimating her own sexual fears, completes the textual identification of Clarissa with Septimus as victim of an aggressively 'masculine' society. Clarissa's physical identification is an immediate imaginative re-enactment: 'Always her body went through it, when she was told, first, suddenly, of an accident; her dress flamed, her body burnt' (p.163). Yet she moves forward to greater insight concerning the significance of the act itself. However, it is an insight to which she finds difficulty in giving language. She perceives something which she cannot name:

> But he had flung *it* away. They went on living (she would have to go back; the rooms were still crowded; people kept on coming). They (all day she had been thinking of Bourton, of Peter, of Sally), they would grow old. A *thing* there was that mattered; a *thing*, wreathed about with chatter, defaced, obscured in her own life, let drop every day in corruption, lies, chatter. This he had preserved. (p.163, our italics)

The repetition of the word 'chatter' twice draws attention to the emptiness of much everyday language. What is 'it'? Clarissa has a vision of 'it', but there is no language available to express this vision. The closest she is able to come is when she asks herself 'had he plunged holding his treasure?' (p.163). The word 'treasure' here evokes the earlier image of the diamond as 'something infinitely precious, wrapped up' (p.33) which – treasured since youth – Clarissa has associated with a 'real' self. Having understood at an intuitive level the perniciousness of Bradshaw and all that he stands for, Clarissa indeed understands, as no one else does, how he is responsible for Septimus's death. She knows him to be 'capable of some indescribable outrage – forcing your soul, that was it' (p.163).

Clarissa's power of vision is for her a source of both extreme distress and delight. It brings with it an acute sense of her own complicity with her society's values: 'She had schemed, she had pilfered. She was never wholly admirable. She had wanted success, Lady Bexborough and the rest of it. And once she had walked on the terrace at Bourton' (p.164). This sense of loss of the potential self that Bourton represents gives way, however, to a perception of happiness, expressed in a sentence which is ambiguous and syntactically elusive: 'No pleasure could equal, she thought, straightening the chairs, pushing in one book on the shelf, this having done with the triumphs of youth, lost herself in the process of living, to find it as the sun rose, as the day sank' (p.164). The strange syntax of this sentence itself suggests the difficulty of finding language to express the elusive 'it'.

This vision, however, is essentially private and surfaces in the text only when Clarissa is in this state of withdrawal metaphorically represented by the attic room and the small room at the party. Even then it is expressed in the text elusively and metaphorically; Clarissa has no language for it and no medium in which to communicate it to others. This intense inner life remains an inner life. Clarissa has an artist's power of vision but it cannot be translated into art; her social role has closed off this possibility. While young men like Septimus suffer and die, the implication of the novel must be that society is the worse without it. As Clarissa returns to the party, Big Ben sounds again and 'the leaden circles dissolved in the air' (p.165).

Before Clarissa returns, however, she watches the old lady opposite going to bed. Totally extraneous to the plot, this old lady has earlier appeared in the text: Clarissa has watched her before and seen her, framed in the window of her room, as representing the 'privacy of the soul' which is prey to the destructive power of 'love and religion' (p.113). On this occasion, however, Clarissa consciously projects no such thoughts but watches, fascinated, the old lady 'crossing the room, coming to the window' (p.165). There is a curious sense here of Clarissa watching herself, and the pulling of the blind echoes Clarissa's retreat to her own room and the containment it offers. This oblique image of Clarissa's own withdrawal into a space in which she can contemplate a 'real self' leads her suddenly to a moment of illumination: 'She felt somehow very like him – the young man who had killed himself. She felt glad he had done it; thrown it away while they went on living' (p.165). She now understands the significance of his act in preserving his integrity. Thus she is ready to return to the outer world and the 'leaden circles' of the striking clock mark this transition.

Parallel to this anonymous old lady on the margins of the text is another old woman who is quite unrelated, apparently, to anyone else yet who may be seen as being placed in opposition to the lady in the room. This is the old woman opposite Regents Park Tube Station who sings in 'a voice bubbling up without direction, vigour, beginning or end, running weakly and shrilly and with an absence of all human meaning into

> ee um fah um so
> foo swee too eem oo –'
> (p.73)

We are here made aware of a space beyond culture and beyond the novel itself by the eruption into the text of a voice without 'human meaning'. Through the old woman, who sings of 'her lover, who had been dead these centuries' (p.73), we are given an historical perspective which reaches back far before human society and promises a future which will last until 'the pageant of the universe would be over' (p.73). As she sings of how 'she had walked in May, where the sea flows now' (p.74), the constructs of contemporary society – contained within its 'mystic boundaries' – are seen for the ephemera that they are.

To the Lighthouse

Problems of language and meaning are associated in other works by Woolf with the image of the lighthouse. The lighthouse in *To the Lighthouse* has caused much critical debate as commentators have attempted to identify 'what it stands for', as if this were necessarily some metaphysical truth. The image appears elsewhere in Woolf's fiction. In *Mrs Dalloway*, for example, Peter Walsh on his way to Clarissa's party thinks of her Aunt Helena whom he presumes to be dead and sees her as 'like a lighthouse marking some past stage on this adventurous long, long voyage . . . this interminable life' (p.144). In a much earlier novel, *Night and Day*, the main male character, Ralph Denham, finds himself on the Embankment sitting next to an elderly man, who is the worse for drink. They attempt to talk to each other, but communication is impossible; the man is absorbed in his own woes and talks on into the wind. What Ralph hears is fragmented: 'disconnected syllables flying past Ralph's ears' (p.417). Angered and frustrated by this, he expresses his feelings through the image of the lighthouse:

> And when the elderly man refused to listen and mumbled on, an odd image came to his mind of a lighthouse besieged by the flying bodies of lost birds, who were dashed senseless by the gale against the glass. He had a strange sensation that he was both lighthouse and bird; he was steadfast and brilliant; and at the same time he was whirled, with all other things, senseless against the glass.[48]

Both these instances seem to offer the lighthouse as an image which signifies order and meaning but this is not posited as absolute and immutable. Peter Walsh's view is not only subjective and ideologically conditioned, it is also mellowed by nostalgia. Ralph Denham's disorientation is replaced by a more positive image of the lighthouse as he approaches the house of the woman he loves and the restoration of order and meaning joins the lighthouse image to that of the room:

> The space of the room behind became, in Ralph's vision, the centre of the dark, flying wilderness of the world; the justification for the welter of confusion surrounding it; the steady light which cast its beams, like those of a lighthouse, with searching composure over the trackless waste. (p.418)

This seems to illustrate very well the way in which the metaphor of the room in Woolf's work suggests the construction of meaning from a potentially limitless range of signifiers. Here, the room and the lighthouse become conflated in the eyes of the character. In *To the Lighthouse*, however, the room and the lighthouse are separated by the stretch of the sea which lies between. The presence of the sea in this novel therefore involves both a literal voyage from room to lighthouse and a metaphorical one in the form of the completion of Lily's painting. In the process, the book's most dominating character, Mrs Ramsay, who is closely associated with the room and the house, dies. Woolf herself cautions the reader to beware of assuming that the lighthouse has an immutable symbolic meaning in her reply to Roger Fry's enquiry concerning the significance of the characters' arrival at the lighthouse:

> I meant *nothing* by *The Lighthouse*. One has to have a central line down the middle of the book to hold the design together. I saw that all sorts of feelings would accrue to this, but I refused to think them out & trusted that people would make it the deposit for their own emotions – which they have done, one thinking that it means one thing and another another. I can't manage Symbolism except in this vague, generalised way. Whether its [*sic*] right or wrong I don't know; but directly I'm told what a thing means, it becomes hateful to me.[49]

Mrs Ramsay, whom Woolf claimed to have modelled on her own mother,[50] is her creation in fiction of that artistically inhibiting stereotype which, in 'Professions for women', she called 'The Angel in the House'. Interestingly, the house here is presented as a temporary dwelling, a rented holiday house on the Hebrides. Admittedly the Ramsays have been tenants for a long time and return year after year, but the sense of impermanence is important – as is the state of repair of the house, which deteriorates year by year. (One of Mrs Ramsay's preoccupations is the fifty pounds needed to mend the greenhouse roof.) It is already subject to the ravages of time and these are exacerbated in the central section of the novel which spans ten years and during which the house deteriorates almost, but not quite, beyond salvation.

Mrs Ramsay is associated very closely with the house in a positive way as its sustaining and controlling hand. It is an intrinsic part of Mrs Ramsay's relationship with her husband that she should see herself in the context of the house – and he demands this. He wants 'all the rooms of the house made full of life – the drawing-room; behind the drawing-room the kitchen; above the kitchen the bedrooms; and beyond them the nurseries; they must be furnished, they must be filled with life' (p.39).[51] However, there is a sense of tension for Mrs Ramsay in this as the effort to maintain the house in a satisfactory state is constantly undermined by the activities of weather and children. At times, Mrs Ramsay seems to be shoring up the house and its power to contain:

> The drawing-room door was open; the hall door was open; it sounded as if the bedroom doors were open; and certainly the window on the landing was open, for that she had opened herself. That windows should be open, and doors shut – simple as it was, could none of them remember it? (p.30)

Not all her daughters, however, are happy to model themselves on their mother. This is particularly so in the case of Nancy, where the desire for something different is expressed metaphorically (as with Clarissa Dalloway) by withdrawal to an attic room. From this vantage point, she is able to give shape to what are possibly incipient lesbian tendencies, as she reflects on how, when Minta Doyle took her hand, she 'saw the whole world spread out beneath her as if it were Constantinople seen through a mist' (p.70). Mrs Ramsay's role in the family as nurturer reaches a symbolic culmination in the novel in the famous scene of the dinner party with its mouth-watering 'boeuf en daube'. The almost mystic sense of communion effected by this celebratory meal is expressed again through images of the room and the sea, the room being perceived by the participants as a benign haven of fixity amid threatening chaos:

> for the night was now shut off by panes of glass, which far from giving any accurate view of the outside world, rippled it so strangely that here, inside the room, seemed to be order and dry land; there, outside, a reflection in which things wavered and vanished, waterily.
>
> Some change at once went through them all, as if this had really happened, and they were all conscious of making a party together in a hollow, on an island; had their common cause against the fluidity out there. (p.91)

Thus, even at the height of her power, Mrs Ramsay's domain is presented as being in a state of siege. For Mrs Ramsay herself, carrying out her allotted role involves the suppression of other possibilities, books which she has never had time to read (and which merely proliferate in the house and make a mess (p.29)) and a desire to become 'an investigator elucidating the social problem' instead of 'a private woman whose charity was half a sop to her own indignation' (p.14). None the less, her belief in marriage as the proper destiny for all human beings and the only possible fulfilment for women remains unshaken and she is shown in the role of matchmaker to Minta Doyle and Paul Rayley (whose marriage is revealed in the last section of the novel as having 'turned out rather badly' (p.161)) and, unsuccessfuly, to Lily Briscoe and William Bankes.

Mrs Ramsay's attitude to men exemplifies some of the commonplaces of nineteenth-century ideology and illustrates well the assertion that Woolf makes in *A Room of One's Own* that 'women have served all these centuries as looking-glasses possessing the magic and delicious power of reflecting the figure of man at twice its natural size' (*Room*, p.35). She sees her role as that of assuring Mr Ramsay of his genius and filling the rooms of his house with life; she thus displays an acceptance of male and female endeavour as separate spheres which are circumscribed by invisiblc 'mystic boundaries'. She has, therefore, internalised a set of values which place her precisely in historical terms:

> Indeed she had the whole of the other sex under her protection; her reasons she could not explain, for their chivalry and valour, for the fact that they negotiated treaties, ruled India, controlled finance; finally for an attitude towards herself which no woman could fail to feel or to find agreeable, something trustful, childlike, reverential; which an old woman could take from a young man without loss of dignity, and woe betide the girl – pray Heaven it was none of her daughters! – who did not feel the worth of it, and all that it implied to the marrow of her bones. (p.11)

That these beliefs are already under threat is illustrated by the fact that she has to assert them to her daughters who are entertaining

> infidel ideas which they had brewed for themselves of a life different from hers; in Paris, perhaps; a wilder life; not always taking care of some man or other; for there was in all their minds a mute questioning of deference and chivalry, of the Bank of England and the Indian Empire, of ringed fingers and lace. (p.12)

Any reading of this passage must be influenced by the way that such a male world is presented in *Mrs Dalloway* and the contempt expressed by Woolf for 'ringed fingers and lace' and the whole panoply of state pomp in *Three Guineas*.

Yet Mrs Ramsay also has an intense inner life, intimately bound up with a refined aesthetic sensibility and a creative imagination which often expresses itself through images of sea and landscape. Looking at the display of fruit that Rose has made for the dinner party

> made her think of a trophy fetched from the bottom of the sea, of Neptune's banquet, of the bunch that hangs with vine leaves over the shoulder of Bacchus (in some picture), among the leopard skins and the torches lolloping red and gold . . . Thus brought up suddenly into the light it seemed possessed of great size and depth, was like a world in which one could take one's staff and climb up hills, she thought, and go down into valleys. (p.90)

This power of imagination, this way of seeing, is closely associated for Mrs Ramsay with the lighthouse and is a way of knowing what she believes to be her 'real self'. Sitting in the window, collecting James's pictures, she thinks about when the children go to bed and she is able to 'be herself, by herself' (p.60). She can express her knowledge of this 'real self' only through metaphor: she has a sense of a 'wedge-shaped core of darkness, something invisible to others' which 'having shed its attachments was free for the strangest adventures' (p.60). The realm of this 'self' is imaged through the language of the sea: 'Beneath it is all dark, it is all spreading, it is unfathomably deep; but now and again we rise to the surface and that is what you see us by' (p.60). As she muses, she imagines this 'real self' being able to go anywhere ('The

Indian plains', 'a church in Rome' (p.61)) in a freedom to travel the world which Mrs Ramsay herself does not actually possess. As she moves out into the landscape she reflects that 'there was freedom, there was peace, there was, most welcome of all, a summoning together, a resting on a platform of stability' (p.61). Such freedom and such rest are only to be found as 'a wedge of darkness'. This sense of being able to go out of oneself only as one's 'real self' is summed up in the image of the lighthouse:

> she looked out to meet that stroke of the Lighthouse, the long steady stroke, the last of the three, which was her stroke, for watching them in this mood always at this hour one could not help attaching oneself to one thing especially of the things one saw; and this thing, the long steady stroke, was her stroke. (p.61)

Thus the lighthouse becomes, for Mrs Ramsay, an outward correlative for this inner sense of self. The connection, however, is quite subjective; it is Mrs Ramsay who confers meaning on the stroke and she knows this. Yet as she looks at the light, her social self asserts itself again in the form of the constraints imposed by the state of motherhood which she is so glad to escape when the children have gone to bed:

> it would lift up on it some little phrase or other which had been lying in her mind like that – 'Children don't forget, children don't forget' – which she would repeat and begin adding to it, It will end, It will end, she said. It will come, it will come, when suddenly she added, We are in the hands of the Lord. (p.61)

This last statement she can recognise as a religious platitude, something she does not mean ('instantly she was annoyed with herself for saying that' (p.61)), but she has been lulled almost hypnotically by the strokes of the lighthouse into saying it. The lighthouse, therefore, has become in the course of the paragraph, an oblique correlative for social identity. The identification between Mrs Ramsay and the lighthouse is about her way of seeing things; it involves the way in which she looks into herself, the way in which she views the outer world and the way in which she sees the relationship between the two. Poised as she is in the window, at the boundary of the house looking out across the sea to the lighthouse, this way of seeing is shown to be in a state of flux, to be radically unstable. That sense of the social self gives way again to an inward vision, a quest for the 'true self'. This movement is conveyed by a metaphor which links her own 'seeing' power with that of the lighthouse:

> She looked up over her knitting and met the third stroke and it seemed to her like her own eyes meeting her own eyes, searching as she alone could search into her mind and her heart, purifying out of existence that lie, any lie. (p.61)

The assertion that she is one with the light gives way again to an acknowledgement of the arbitrariness of this identification, so confidently stated in the sentence that goes before:

> She praised herself in praising the light, without vanity, for she was stern, she was searching, she was beautiful like that light. It was odd, she thought, how if one was alone, one leant to things, inanimate things; trees, streams, flowers; felt they expressed one; felt they became one; felt they knew one, in a sense were one; felt an irrational tenderness thus (she looked at that long steady light) as for oneself. (p.61)

Mrs Ramsay's awareness of the tensions and conflicts which her relationship with the light involves, is expressed a little later in the words: 'she looked at the steady light, the pitiless, the remorseless, which was so much her, yet so little her, which had her at its beck and call' (p.62). It is after this that Mrs Ramsay's reflections reach a state of lyrical climax, a state which finds expression through the metaphor of the sea:

> but for all that she thought, watching it with fascination, hypnotised, as if it were stroking with its silver fingers some sealed vessel in her brain whose bursting would flood her with delight, she had known happiness, exquisite happiness, intense happiness, and it silvered the rough waves a little more brightly, as daylight faded, and the blue went out of the sea and it rolled in waves of pure lemon which curved and swelled and broke upon the beach and the ecstasy burst in her eyes and waves of pure delight raced over the floor of her mind and she felt, It is enough! It is enough! (pp.62–3)

Such moments of intensely heightened sensibility, orgasmic in their climactic quality, are for Mrs Ramsay private and incommunicable. Mr Ramsay, turning and looking at her as she remembers these moments, interprets her expression as one of sadness: 'and he passed her without a word though it hurt him that she should look so distant, and he could not reach her' (p.63). These moments set her apart from her family in a private interior world. Her return to the role she plays out in marriage is voluntary. She now gives Mr Ramsay her full attention 'of her own free will' (p.63). Her acquiescence in a system of belief which requires women to give themselves completely in marriage is voluntary but involves a struggle. Woolf said of the 'Angel in the House', 'she was so constituted that she never had a mind or wish of her own, but preferred to sympathize always with the minds and wishes of others'.[52] This is not true of Mrs Ramsay; she does have a mind and wishes of her own but she subordinates them to the minds and wishes of her family.

In various ways, Mr and Mrs Ramsay have been seen as embodying opposing principles. James Hafley calls it two different kinds of truth;[53] more recent critics tend to see the polarisation as one based on extreme gender stereotyping, an argument which is neatly summed up by Toril Moi:

> *To the Lighthouse* illustrates the destructive nature of a metaphysical belief in strong, immutably fixed gender identities – as represented by Mr and Mrs Ramsay – whereas Lily Briscoe (an artist) represents the subject who deconstructs this opposition, perceives its pernicious influence and tries as far as is possible in a still rigidly patriarchal order to live as her own woman, without regard for the crippling definitions of sexual identity to which society would have her conform.[54]

It is Lily's struggle for artistic vision which becomes paramount in the novel. She must both embrace Mrs Ramsay's imaginative vision and repudiate the gender stereotyping which prevents women from expressing that vision through art. Her relationship with Mrs Ramsay is, from the outset, complex. Mrs Ramsay 'cared not a fig for her painting' (p.49) and urges Lily to marry: 'an unmarried woman has missed the best of life' (p.54). Yet for Lily, Mrs Ramsay remains special but enigmatic: 'she knew knowledge and wisdom were stored in Mrs Ramsay's heart. How then, she had asked herself, did one know one thing or another about people, sealed as they were?' (p.51). Lily's attempt to paint Mrs Ramsay sitting in the window with James is an attempt to render in art what is special about Mrs Ramsay. It also, however, implicitly suggests Lily's perception of her as there at the threshold of the house with all that this metaphorically conveys about the 'framing' of the self within the 'feminine' role. In painting, Lily is pursuing an activity not only considered unimportant by Mrs Ramsay, but also something considered by the male establishment as being not the preserve of women. Charles Tansley, acolyte and caricature of Mr Ramsay, says as much to her: 'Women can't paint, women can't write' (p.48), a denigration which applies both to Woolf's art as a writer and Lily's as a painter. But Lily has her vision, and in her own mind she knows she must be true to it. Not for her the effete pastels of the fashionable Mr Paunceforte (p.48) nor the representational art admired by the scientist, William Bankes, whose favourite picture is of cherry trees on the banks of the Kennet (p.52). She sees the purple jackmanna against a startling white wall and she sees what Mrs Ramsay, sitting in the window, musing on being 'herself', thinks that no one else can see – that 'wedge-shaped core of darkness'. Painting a picture of Mrs Ramsay and James in the window, Lily has, in her struggle to express her vision, depicted Mrs Ramsay as a 'triangular purple shape' (p.52). Interrogated by William Bankes on the picture, she cannot articulate in language the rationale for her depiction, except in terms of light and dark: 'here . . . she felt the need of darkness' (p.52). Interestingly, William Bankes's objection to this presentation of Mrs Ramsay betrays his perception of woman as idealised and sentimentalised object of the male gaze: 'Mother and child then objects of universal veneration, and in this case the mother was famous for her beauty – might be reduced, he pondered, to a purple shadow without irreverence' (p.52). For Lily the form of the picture is a problem: she is dissatisfied with it. 'It was a question, she remembered, how to connect this mass on the right hand with that on the left' (p.53). The problem is not solved and this picture remains unfinished.

Only in the last section of the novel, 'The lighthouse', is Lily able to paint the picture to her satisfaction and this is after a period of ten years has passed. The changes brought by those ten years are crucial in enabling Lily to have her artistic vision. Interestingly, the middle section of the novel, 'Time passes', focuses on the changes wrought by time and weather on the house itself, changes feared and forestalled by Mrs Ramsay earlier. During this period it is brought close to ruin and saved only late in the day by the exertions of Mrs McNab and Mrs Bast, working women who represent all those women who hold the fabric of domestic life together. It seems during this time that the encroachment of chaos which Mrs Ramsay was perpetually staving off has actually triumphed. If we see the house as a metaphorical expression of society's norms, the enclosure of the 'Angel in the House' has been severely under attack. In historical terms, of course, this does make sense. The period covers the First World War which, as well as killing the Andrew Ramsays, also delivered a death blow to the already wavering stereotype of the 'Angel in the House'. Women came out of the private home in unprecedented numbers and into occupations hitherto only performed by men. Mrs Ramsay, as the Angel figure in the novel, dies; it is this death which eventually enables Lily to have confidence in herself as an artist while absorbing the vision that Mrs Ramsay has bequeathed to her. Much of the last section of the novel, while Mr Ramsay and the children make their journey to the lighthouse and find a literal edifice there, inscribes Lily's ambivalent and anguished struggle both to assimilate and repudiate Mrs Ramsay; it culminates in the completion of her painting, the expression of her vision.

In spite of her admiration for Mrs Ramsay, Lily cannot emulate her. The intervening years have not seen her take Mrs Ramsay's advice on marriage and she and William

Bankes have remained only friends. She is now 44, Woolf's age when she was writing the novel. The return to the Hebrides awakens memories and confronts her with Mr Ramsay, widowed and bereft of the sympathy and support that his wife had always given him. He seeks it now from Lily, but she is unable to give it. His presence inhibits her work: 'Every time he approached – he was walking up and down the terrace – ruin approached, chaos approached' (p.139). Lily now understands that Mrs Ramsay's ready sympathy and infinite tolerance have encouraged Mr Ramsay in his egotistical self-absorption. All this crystallises into anger as she sees herself as implicated in the pattern of man–woman relationships that this suggests:

> That man, she thought, her anger rising in her, never gave; that man took. She, on the other hand, would be forced to give. Mrs Ramsay had given. Giving, giving, giving, she had died – and had left all this. Really, she was angry with Mrs Ramsay. (p.140)

Lily's anger is compounded with grief at the loss of Mrs Ramsay. As she looks at 'the hedge, the step, the wall' (p.140), her frustration as an artist is expressed in images of enclosure. The step by the window is the boundary occupied by Mrs Ramsay but now empty; exactly why Lily is so angry at Mrs Ramsay is not clear, even to herself. Is she angry at her for having been what she was, or for no longer being there – or both? These conflicting feelings have to be resolved before she can fulfil herself as an artist. The first stage in this process is to reach an accommodation with Mr Ramsay; she cannot extend to him the bolstering sympathy that Mrs Ramsay would have given, yet she feels impelled to make a conciliatory gesture and so admires his boots. The positive response that this elicits brings them to a companionable state in which the emotional intensity has been defused; Lily is able to feel a sympathy for him that is no longer threatening to herself: 'There was no helping Mr Ramsay on the journey he was going' (p.145).

Mr Ramsay is about to make a sea crossing. Lily, too, as she embarks on the painting she was unable to finish all those years ago, is about to move metaphorically into the sea. 'Why, thought Mr Ramsay, should she look at the sea when I am here?' (p.142); it is from this kind of male demand that she must free herself. Lily's struggle to paint her picture, expressed through her anguished memories of Mrs Ramsay and through images of the sea, is interleaved in the narrative's account of Mr Ramsay's literal voyage over the sea which reaches a literal, very concrete lighthouse.

For Lily, her own personal voyage to the lighthouse consists of assimilating Mrs Ramsay's power of vision, but asserting her own autonomy as an artist in order to be able to translate it into outward form through her painting. Lily's work as an artist is her 'treasure' (p.80); the denial of other kinds of satisfaction is insignificant by comparison. She had already reached this insight at the dinner party in the first section of the novel. In contrast, Minta Doyle, who has just become engaged, has lost her brooch in an episode which signifies the loss of her 'treasure'. Lily has preserved her treasure whereas Clarissa Dalloway's has been wrapped up and hidden away. Lily must now capture Mrs Ramsay's power to bring together, to synthesise; it was the failure to achieve artistic unity in her painting on the earlier occasion that forced her to abandon it. Lily sees Mrs Ramsay as having been an artist in life:

> she brought together this and that and then this, and so made out of that miserable silliness and spite . . . something . . . which survived, after all these years, complete, so that she dipped into it to re-fashion her memory of him, and it stayed in the mind almost like a work of art. (p.150)

The difficulty of expressing this in the medium of painting, however, entails an exploration that takes her as a woman artist beyond the bounds of a discourse which posits that women 'can't paint, can't write' (p.149). The language of the narrative therefore moves into images of the sea:

> All that in idea seemed simple became in practice immediately complex; as the waves shape themselves symmetrically from the cliff top, but to the swimmer among them are divided by steep gulfs, and foaming crests. Still the risk must be run; the mark made. (p.147)

The sea here metaphorically expresses a notionally infinite choice. To commit brush to canvas involves making a choice, using and paradoxically surrendering the freedom of choice. As Lily does this, her brush strokes are described as enclosing a space and her painting is described in language which is evocative of Mrs Ramsay's reflections on the lighthouse; she attains 'a dancing rhythmical movement, as if the pauses were one part of the rhythm and the strokes another' (p.148). The process that Lily is going through (in the garden, outside the house, looking at the sea) is to do with creating her own space, her own enclosure in the form of art itself. In her painting she is metaphorically creating the room of the woman artist. In doing so, she must reject the domestic room which is part of Mrs Ramsay's legacy at the same time as embracing her vision. This involves an enormous struggle on Lily's part:

> She had felt now she could stand up to Mrs Ramsay – a tribute to the astonishing power that Mrs Ramsay had over one. Do this, she said, and one did it. Even her shadow at the window with James was full of authority. (p.163)

Yet her grief for Mrs Ramsay's death evokes in her a feeling of desire which is beyond language and is physical in its manifestation, sending: 'all up her body a hardness, a hollowness, a strain. And then to want and not to have – to want and want – how that wrung the heart, and wrung it again and again! Oh Mrs Ramsay!' (p.165).

Painting is likened to walking a plank: 'out and out one went, further and further, until at last one seemed to be on a narrow plank, perfectly alone, over the sea' (p.160). Overcome with emotion for Mrs Ramsay, Lily feels herself to have stepped 'off her strip of board into the waters of annihilation' (p.167). As she does so, the narrative cuts back to the boat: '[Macalister's boy took one of the fish and cut a square out of its side to bait his hook with. The mutilated body (it was alive still) was thrown back into the sea]' (p.167). This eruption of violence and pain into the text is a correlative of Lily's anguish and invokes in the reader an almost physical identification with her pain. The regularity of the 'square' cut out of the fish recalls the 'angular essences' (p.26) through which Lily was able to visualise Mr Ramsay's philosophical speculations; the thoughtless cruelty which mutilates the living creature implies a parallel with Mr Ramsay's effect on the family; the whole image evokes the psychic pain suffered by Lily and the Ramsays in this last section of the novel.

The narrative then returns again to Lily who, returned to her 'plank', is still 'a skimpy old maid, holding a paint-brush on the lawn' (p.167), an image which defuses the intensity of the preceding lines. She reflects that her picture may be 'hung in the attics . . . rolled up and flung under a sofa' (p.166). Such may be the fate of women's art, marginalised in the existing house of culture. Yet Lily believes that her painting will endure as a work of art; it is an artefact in the way that Mrs Ramsay's artistry in life is not. After her crisis of grief, Lily, metaphorically back on her plank, is able to envisage Mrs Ramsay and attacks 'the problem of the hedge' (p.168). Her vision of Mrs Ramsay pictures her merging with a landscape of flowers: 'It was strange how clearly she saw her, stepping with her usual quickness across fields among whose folds, purplish and soft, among whose flowers, hyacinths or lilies, she vanished' (p.168). This vision of Mrs Ramsay merging with a purple landscape contrasts with the descriptions of her earlier in the novel when she is always described as being dressed in grey, a colour which, as in *Mrs Dalloway*, suggests conformity. However, it is Lily's artistic gift to see through exteriors, as she does at the dinner party, seeing Charles Tansley 'as in an X-ray photograph' (p.85). As Lily thinks about this internal landscape of Mrs Ramsay's, she feels 'some instinctive need of distance' (p.168) and, looking out at the bay, sees 'something incongruous' (p.168). This is the 'brown spot' that is Mr Ramsay's boat in the middle of the bay.

The boat carrying Mr Ramsay and his children, Cam and James, is the scene of another narrative which re-enacts through the next generation the gender stereotyping that Lily is struggling to overcome. Cam, with her reveries and her desire to please her father overcoming her resentment of his tyranny, is an embryonic Mrs Ramsay. For James, there is acknowledgement that the lighthouse, long cherished in memory as a 'silvery, misty-looking tower' (p.172) is also a 'tower, stark and straight . . . barred with black and white' (p.172). Thus the world of 'facts' that his father represents, the 'male world', is borne in on him. However, the conflict of identification that James suffers is not resolved. Just as the stereotype of the 'Angel in the House' has disintegrated over the period covered by the novel, so the Victorian stereotype of masculinity is also under threat. James's unease with the image of masculinity represented by his father is symptomatic of this and is metaphorically expressed by his refusal to reject the earlier image of the lighthouse together with his reflection that 'the other was also the Lighthouse. For nothing was simply one thing' (p.172).

Lily, too, has this insight; hence her need of 'distance'. While she is absorbed in her own feelings about Mrs Ramsay, she cannot achieve the artistic distance needed to paint her picture. Casting her memory back to the earlier days on the island with the Ramsays, Lily remembers a 'feeling of completeness' (p.178) which she yearns to recapture. Looking out to sea, she sees a scene which 'a moment before had seemed miraculously fixed, was now unsatisfactory'; to her artist's eye 'there was something displeasing about the placing of the ships' (p.178). This becomes for Lily a metaphorical expression of instability: 'The disproportion there seemed to upset some harmony in her own mind' (p.178) and she intuitively understands that her art must somehow encompass Mr Ramsay and all that he represents for her and therefore achieve some kind of ideal balance: 'For whatever reason she could not achieve that razor edge of balance between two opposite forces; Mr Ramsay and the picture; which was necessary' (p.178).

Lily sees the problem as manifesting itself in the form of the picture itself: 'There was perhaps something wrong with the design? Was it, she wondered, that the line of the wall wanted breaking, was it that the mass of the trees was too heavy?' (p.178). The need to encompass both Mrs and Mr Ramsay in her artistic vision entails the exercise of the androgynous quality that Woolf felt that all artists must possess. This involves, for Lily, capturing something elusive: 'She must try to get hold of something that evaded her. It evaded her when she thought of Mrs Ramsay; it evaded her now when she thought of her picture' (p.178). At the moment when her commitment to her painting wavers most and she has to reassert her determination to find this elusive 'thing itself' (the elusiveness of the language echoes Clarissa Dalloway's 'it'), Mr Carmichael appears.

Augustus Carmichael, a silent enigmatic figure, has hovered on the margins of the novel throughout. A guest of the Ramsays in the earlier days, he is pitied by Mrs Ramsay; here in the last section of the novel, he is a silent presence while Lily paints in the garden. His art is poetry not painting, but through his own form he too captures his vision. For many years, his poetry has been rejected by an unappreciative public – just as Lily's painting may be 'hung in attics' or 'flung behind a sofa' – but now, as times have changed, he has achieved fame. He is a *fin de siècle* figure: his yellow slippers, the yellow stain on his beard, his French novel all associate him with the last years of the nineteenth century. However, it is through the war and its attendant suffering that he has now found a public. Mr Carmichael, Lily reflects, 'did not much like' Mrs Ramsay (p.180); the artist in him perhaps resented the violation of his autonomy that her desire to sympathise and connect represented for him. At the dinner party when Mrs Ramsay weaves a fantasy around the plate of fruit, she recognises that Mr Carmichael's imagination is focusing on the same object:

> she saw that Augustus too feasted his eyes on the plate of fruit, plunged in, broke off a bloom there, a tassel here, and returned, after feasting, to his hive. That was his way of looking, different from hers. But looking together united them. (p.90)

Mrs Ramsay's artistic sensibilities and Mr Carmichael's are quite different. Hers bring things together – his takes apart. His 'way of looking' is expressed in his poetry: 'It was about the desert and the camel. It was about the palm tree and the sunset. It was extremely impersonal; it said something about death; it said very little about love' (p.180). The stark images of these poetic landscapes suggest a way of looking that strips bare. While Mr Carmichael represents commitment to art, his is the vision of a male artist. This is not Lily's artistic landscape; hers is an internal landscape and must say a great deal about love. Her painting must represent the balance of relationships; between the inner and the outer landscape and between people. Hers is not the art of photographic representation, any more than Woolf's is that of the realist novel. However, neither is it the 'impersonal' art which found expression in the imagist movement in modernism.

When Lily's thoughts return to Mrs Ramsay, she begins to think of her again in her social role, visiting the sick for example. The problem of seeing, in all its aspects, preoccupies Lily: 'One wanted fifty pairs of eyes to see with, she reflected. Fifty pairs of eyes were not enough to get round that woman with, she thought' (p.182). Lily must insert herself as a seeing eye/I into a cultural tradition which has treated 'woman' as the object of the male gaze, the 'object of the look' to use Griselda Pollock's phrase (see page 29). Pollock believes that the woman artist's dilemma is resolved by 'the rearticulation of traditional space so that it ceases to function primarily as the space of sight for a mastering gaze, but becomes the locus of relationships.'[55] Whereas Wharton achieves this through writing by destabilising notions of femininity within the text in the *tableau vivant* scene in *The House of Mirth*, Woolf shows us the figure of the woman artist struggling to achieve it. As Lily allows her mind to wander and reflect on the inner Mrs Ramsay, 'her thoughts, her imaginations, her desires' (p.182), she imaginatively evokes the scene when Mrs Ramsay is sitting in the window thinking about the lighthouse. The scene recreated in memory sees Mrs Ramsay from the outside: 'She would stop knitting for a second. She would look intent' (p.182). But this is not enough for Lily; she needs to synthesise the outer vision with an inner knowledge: 'What did the hedge mean to her, what did the garden mean to her, what did it mean to her when a wave broke?' (p.182). It is only when someone by chance goes into the drawing-room and 'by some stroke of luck as to throw an odd-shaped triangular shadow over the step' (p.185), that she is able to recapture her vision of the inner Mrs Ramsay as 'the wedge-shaped core of darkness' (p.186); however this evokes in her a feeling of painful ecstasy as 'some wave of white went over the window pane' (p.186) unsettling the vision. The window here becomes a threshold of artistic vision, itself a seeing eye in the house of the woman artist. Lily feels for a moment the old horror of unfulfilled desire and then she is able to distance it; only then does she have her complete vision of Mrs Ramsay: 'Mrs Ramsay – it was part of her perfect goodness to Lily – sat there quite simply, in the chair, flicked her needles to and fro, knitted her reddish-brown stocking, cast her shadow on the step. There she sat' (p.186). Only then can she turn her mind to Mr Ramsay: 'Where was that boat now? Mr Ramsay? She wanted him' (p.186).

The narrative moves to the landing at the lighthouse, the culmination of that other literal voyage. As Lily says 'He must have reached it' (p.191), she feels relief: 'Whatever she had wanted to give him, when he left her that morning, she had given him at last' (p.191). This is not the mournful sympathy which Mr Ramsay had demanded, but an immortalisation of Mrs Ramsay through art. Conventional images are rejected in favour of a different perspective. Even so, the picture is not complete and it is the sight of Mr Carmichael resembling a pagan god which prompts her to turn to it again. The picture, enclosing a space 'with its lines running up and across' (p.191) and its colours of the sea 'with all its blues and greens' (p.191), she sees as 'an attempt at something' (p.191). The final line which she draws 'With a sudden intensity . . . in the centre' (p.192) is not a boundary line of constraint but marks the satisfying completion of her vision. The novel thus ends by affirming the vision of the woman artist, as she rejects cultural constructs of woman and their representation in visual art. The completion of Lily's painting is an analogue of the way in which the text itself constitutes a space for the woman writer.

3
'...marooned...': Jean Rhys's desolate women

Good Morning, Midnight

Sasha Jansen, heroine of Jean Rhys's *Good Morning, Midnight* published in 1939, is a woman very much in the mould of Wharton's Lily Bart. Both collude with a society which likes its women pretty and 'feminine' in the traditional sense, with all the dependency upon men that that entails. The two heroines have much else in common: they inhabit a very urban world in which natural scenery plays little part; neither woman has a room of her own, and each moves in a downward social spiral through a number of rented rooms; both subscribe to cultural rituals of femininity and thus spend much time choosing hats, dresses and looking in mirrors; both, in their subsequent despair, relieve inner pain by recourse to drugs – veronal in Lily Bart's case, luminal and alcohol in the case of Sasha Jansen. This despair is not articulated in any overt critique of patriarchal society within the text; indeed throughout her life, Jean Rhys emphatically denied any sympathy with feminism; according to Carole Angier, 'whenever she read a review that was even mildly feminist, she laughed and tore it up'.[1] There is, however, a covert critique of patriarchy in the metaphorical structure of *Good Morning, Midnight* as there is in *The House of Mirth*, particularly in the emphasis on rooms. Further, symptoms of 'hysteria' in the heroines of the early novels suggest repressed feelings of alienation which emerge as signs of physical dis-ease. These signs of muted resistance are later translated into the image of the wide Sargasso Sea, the involuntary passivity of being marooned being linked to woman's ambivalent acceptance of what Catherine Belsey describes as 'the specifically feminine discourse offered by society of submission, relative inadequacy and irrational intuition'.[2] Thus, although Rhys was clearly consciously antagonistic to feminism, her figurative writing presents an anguished picture of woman as constrained and oppressed by patriarchy.

Staying in Paris alone in 1937, approaching middle age, Sasha moves in a twilight world of seedy rented rooms and *demi-monde* companions. Separated from her husband, Enno, with the painful memory of her infant son's death still haunting her, she turns to luminal, drink and sleep to deaden the misery. The fortnight's trip to Paris, where she lived with Enno for eight years or so after the First World War, has been financed by a friend as a holiday away from her lonely and near alcoholic existence in London. In fact, however, it comes to replicate the miseries of her bed-sit life at home in a room 'just off the Gray's Inn Road' (p.30)[3] and the two cities become blurred together as places where streets and rooms form a warren in which one tries to survive. Sasha is an intelligent woman who regards her brain as a liability rather than an asset and in this she is typical of Rhys's heroines: a character in *Tigers are Better Looking*, for example, prays to herself 'Oh God, I'm going to think, don't let me think' (p.176). The novel presents a France of the late 1930s contaminated by an ugly streak of anti-Semitism and incipient Fascism. In this context, a clever woman is seen as anomalous and unnatural, as Sasha's conversation with René, the young gigolo illustrates:

> 'I'm no use to anybody,' I say, 'I'm a cérébrale, can't you see that?' . . .
>
> 'A cérébrale,' he says seriously, 'is a woman who doesn't like men or need them.'
>
> 'Oh, is that it? I've often wondered. Well, there are quite a lot of those, and the ranks are daily increasing.'
>
> 'Ah, but a cérébrale doesn't like women either. Oh, no. The true cérébrale is a woman who likes nothing and nobody except

herself and her own damned brain or what she thinks is her brain.'

So pleased with herself, like a little black boy in a top-hat . . .

'In fact, a monster.'

'Yes, a monster.' (pp.135–6)

This conversation springs from a France in which women were clearly disadvantaged: in 1937 French women were unable to open bank accounts without the permission of their husbands; they had no automatic legal control over their own property and were not to gain the right to vote until 1945.[4] In the Paris of *Good Morning, Midnight*, therefore, all women are legally and socially inferior to men; in this world the intelligent woman, or 'cérébrale', is an uncomfortable threat to that status quo. 'Mystic boundaries' are evoked to constrain her: associated with the monstrous and the abnormal, like the Jew or the 'little black boy', she is safely marginalised and her threat to the dominant discourse is contained.

Sasha has long lived by the rules of the game: we learn that as a young woman in the 1920s she took jobs which complied with the social expectation that women are charming, beautiful creatures obsessed with appearance: in the past she has been both 'mannequin' and 'vendeuse', but successful at neither. The lesson she learnt from the world of work was that men had power and she had none:

> Well, let's argue this out, Mr Blank. You, who represent Society, have the right to pay me four hundred francs a month . . . to lodge me in a small, dark room, to clothe me shabbily, to harass me with worry and monotony and unsatisfied longings till you get me to the point when I blush at a look, cry at a word. (pp.25–6)

Such frustrating and tedious work failed to give her any sense of identity or satisfaction and the novel charts, in a series of flashbacks, how she drifted into relationships with men who exploited her financially and sexually. The pattern is repeated when she visits Paris in 1937. Alone and wearing an old fur coat, she becomes the prey of various men who think they might be able to make something out of her: two men claiming to be Russians (but more probably refugee Jews) pick her up in the street and one of them, Nicholas Delmar, eventually persuades her to buy a painting from a friend of his at an extravagant price; she is also picked up by the young gigolo, René, who claims rather unconvincingly that he is a French Canadian who has just arrived in Paris, having deserted the Foreign Legion.

The Paris of *Good Morning, Midnight* is full of victims struggling to survive as best they can. Rhys was not sentimental about her sex and in her fiction the bond between victims is often stronger than the bond of gender; the narrator of the short story, 'Vienne', for example, thinks to herself: 'I could have shaken his hand and said, "Hail, brother Doormat, in a world of Boots"' (*Tigers Are Better Looking*, p.199). Here, the terrible scar on René's neck and Sasha's inner wounds strangely unite them even as they spar in the game of sexual exploitation. As a man in the Paris of 1937, however, René is better placed than Sasha to survive in such circumstances. Having become economically and emotionally dependent on men, as her culture has encouraged her to, Sasha realises that she has no resources and that she desperately needs 'money, for the night is coming' (p.120). Growing older, she knows that her only asset in Parisian society – her beauty – is rapidly fading and that she is being edged towards the night and the abyss of destitution. The macaronic text, a novel written in English but shot through with French phrases, songs and slang, captures the voice of someone at home in both languages but who has no real sense of worth or 'home' in either country: 'I have no pride – no pride, no name, no face, no country. I don't belong anywhere. Too sad, too sad' (p.38).

Increasingly Sasha sees herself, through the eyes of the French, as absurd: 'A strange client, l'étrangère' (p.59); 'Qu'est-ce qu'elle fout ici, la vieille? What the devil (translating it politely) is she doing here, that old woman? What is she doing here, the stranger, the alien, the old one?' (p.46). She is filled with horror and compassion early in the novel by the sight of an old Englishwoman – 'perfectly bald on top – a white, bald skull with a fringe of grey hair' (p.19) – taking a great deal of time to choose something pretty to wear in her hair. By the end of the novel, however, she sees herself as old and has become involved with a gigolo. Her absurdity, as an ageing woman in a society which values only young, beautiful or rich women, is emphasised by her dislocation from both French and English cultures; she drifts between the two languages as she drifts between youth and age; she is a woman at 'the hour between dog and wolf, as they say' (*After Leaving Mr Mackenzie*, p.136). She remembers a young Russian who came to her for English conversation lessons when she was living in Paris with Enno; he read from *Lady Windermere's Fan*: '"The laughter, the horrible laughter of the world – a thing more tragic than all the tears the world has ever shed."' It is this laughter that becomes a nightmare sound in Sasha's head during her stay in Paris in 1937. In many ways, *Good Morning, Midnight* is Jean Rhys's darkest novel. Very little colour or relief punctuates Sasha's grey despair or the monotony of her rented room existence. More and more she seeks refuge in oblivion, either through drink or through luminal which brings sleep: 'I got so that I could sleep fifteen hours out of the twenty-four' (p.72).

Sasha's marginal and dispossessed status within the European society of the 1930s is echoed by several episodes in the novel which, although superfluous in terms of plot, emphasise metaphorically her vulnerability and dependency. At one stage, for example, Sasha remembers with some guilt how she inadvertently caused the death of a stray kitten, upon which she had clearly projected her own personality: 'The kitten had an inferiority complex and persecution mania and nostalgie de la boue and all the rest' (p.47). The misery of exile, of poverty, and of loneliness – evident not only in Sasha's experience but also in that of minor characters such as the 'mulatto woman' of Notting Hill Gate and Lise the embroiderer – is summed up in the picture which Sasha buys from the artist, Serge, on her return to Paris. It is of a Jewish banjo player, 'standing in the gutter . . . gentle, humble, resigned, mocking, a little mad' (p.91). Her own precarious situation, moving from one rented room to another in a downward social spiral is, of course, given further significance by these episodes.

Her situation is precarious because, having chosen to play the game of 'feminine' dependence upon men, her only asset is an ephemeral one: that of physical beauty. Her attempts to earn her own living are futile, partly because her notions of what constitutes 'feminine' behaviour prevent her from exploiting her best asset, her brain. She is influenced on the one hand by René's idea that a good mind in a woman is a 'sale cerveau' (p.158); on the other hand, she has to endure the insulting epithet, 'Vache! Sale vache!', from the man in the next room who clearly thinks that she is at best a loose living woman and at worst a prostitute. Steering a difficult path between using her brain and using her body in order to survive, Sasha allows herself to be swallowed up by a charade in which the right dress and the right hat take on the power to change her life. The importance of the self as beautiful object is extended to the dress which would have transformed her personality if only she could have had it: 'If I had been wearing it I should never have stammered or been stupid' (p.25); later she nurses a belief that a blonde *cendré* hair dye will change her life. At one stage in the novel, the buying of a hat is described with ironic detachment as an 'extraordinary ritual' (p.59); later the narrator bitterly charts her attempt to be conventional:

> Please, please, monsieur et madame, mister, missis and miss, I am trying so hard to be like you. I know I don't succeed, but look how hard I try. Three hours to choose a hat; every morning an hour and a half trying to make myself look like everybody else... (p.88)

Inside, however, she knows that this way of life is a meaningless charade and that she wears a mask in order to survive. In this, she is like the narrator of the short story, 'Vienne', who, with the dreamy cynicism typical of Rhys's heroines, sees that the behaviour desired of women is merely a prostration of the self before the male: 'Oh, abomination of desolation, to sit for two hours being massaged, to stand for hours choosing a dress. All to delight the eyes of the gentleman with the toothpick' (*Tigers Are Better Looking*, p.204).

Masks are a constant motif in Rhys's work; Julia Martin in *After Leaving Mr Mackenzie*, for example, is 'frightened and fascinated' by them (p.90). In Serge's studio there are some 'hideous' masks, which he has made himself from a West African design. He takes one down and shows it to Sasha; she immediately sees it as emblematic of the sneering cruelty a woman like her faces in a city like Paris: 'That's the way they look when they are saying: "Why didn't you drown yourself in the Seine?"' (p.76). Elsewhere, however, the mask is used to express her deep alienation from society and to suggest that the Sasha Jansen whom other people see is only a composition of socially acceptable parts. Beneath the mask lies a more authentic 'self' or 'face': 'it isn't my face, this tortured and tormented mask. I can take it off when I like and hang it up on a nail' (p.76). The tragedy of all Rhys's heroines is that this more authentic 'self' can only ever be glimpsed and never realised. Instead, the mask becomes the true expression of 'self' with the consequence that Sasha, like many other Rhys women, comes to feel ghost-like and unreal: 'I am empty of everything. I am empty of everything but the thin, frail trunks of the trees and the thin, frail ghosts in my room, "La tristesse vaut mieux que la joie"' (p.48). Even language itself comes to seem a mask which conceals the truth: 'Everything is born out of a cliché, rests on a cliché, survives by a cliché. And they believe in the clichés – there's no hope' (p.36). Memories of her time as writer-up of fairy stories for a very rich woman are soured by the fact that the agent demanded a more elaborate style: '"He says it gets monotonous, and don't you know any long words, and if you do, would you please use them?"' (p.139). Lacking faith in her own creative talents, she has been reduced to decorating verbally the stock myths of her culture in which the fairy tale princess is the archetype of femininity. In this, she is like the heroine of Margaret Atwood's *Surfacing* who, influenced by her lover's opinion that 'there have never been any important women artists' (*Surfacing*, p.52), becomes an illustrator instead. Atwood's nameless narrator finds herself dealing in the visual clichés of commercial art – 'I outline a princess, an ordinary one, emaciated fashion-model torso and infantile face, like those I did for *Favorite Fairy Tales*' (*Surfacing*, p.53); Sasha similarly finds that everything 'rests on a cliché'.

Thrown into a state of despair and alienation by these endless charades, Sasha Jansen desperately tries to hang on to her sanity by masquerading as a conventional citizen: 'I am a respectable woman, une femme convenable, on her way to the nearest cinema. Faites comme les autres – that's been my motto all my life. Faites comme les autres, damn you' (p.88). However, this mask of respectability only just hides a mind deeply critical of the predatory nature of society. The price Sasha pays for her overt conformity is a recurrent feeling of desolation which occasionally manifests itself physically in fits of panic (p.22), crying (pp.78, 152) and, most significantly, a constriction of the throat:

> My throat shuts up, my eyes sting. This is awful. Now I am going to cry. This is the worst . . . If I do that I shall really have to walk under a bus when I get outside. (p.44)

> I drink. Something in his voice has hurt me. I can't say anything. My throat hurts and I can't say anything. (p.144)

In so far as this particular symptom lacks any obvious physical cause, it is clearly an emotional reaction to a situation. An hysterical response, it conveys the information that there is a problem and, simultaneously, the fear of facing it. Like the heroine of *Surfacing* who frequently experiences a 'strangling feeling, paralysis of the throat' (*Surfacing*, p.19), Sasha's repression of her misery engenders a physical symptom of dis-ease. Antoinette Cosway in *Wide Sargasso Sea* announces that 'words are no use, I know that now' (*Wide Sargasso Sea*, p.111); similarly, Sasha's hysterical symptoms suggest metaphorically that the discourse within which she moves and defines herself provides no language for the expression of her deepest desires. In a sense, then, Sasha both knows the desperate nature of her plight and wishes not to know it, just as Rhys wrote novels exposing the coercive nature of patriarchy whilst firmly denying any interest in feminism.[5]

Although neither Sasha nor her creator ever assume anything other than a merely fatalistic attitude to her situation, a more critical and sceptical analysis of society can be found in the metaphorical structure of the novel. Central to this is the role of the room which, in its various guises, is a constant presence in the text. Occasionally it appears to be human – 'Now the room springs out at me, laughing, triumphant' (p.149) and several times it actually 'speaks', as if it were a character: 'The room says: "Quite like old times. Yes? . . . No? . . . Yes"' (p.120). The phrase 'always the same room' resounds through the text, despite the different geographical locations of the rooms Sasha inhabits, as far apart as London and Amsterdam. Her reflections on this life of living in rented spaces result in an insight which is only half articulated: 'But never tell the truth about this business of rooms, because it would bust the roof off everything and undermine the whole social system' (p.32).

What is this 'truth' about the 'business of rooms'? We have to deduce it for ourselves from the metaphors of the novel. Central to our creation of such a 'truth' is the fundamental ambiguity with which 'the room' is presented in the text. On the one hand, the room is a place of safety and retreat; in Sasha's fantasies it is associated with comfort, luxurious withdrawal from the world and the power which derives from having money:

> A room. A nice room. A beautiful room. A beautiful room with bath. A very beautiful room with bath. A bedroom and sitting-room with bath. Up to the dizzy heights of the suite. Two bedrooms, sitting-room, bath and vestibule . . . Anything you want brought up on the dinner-wagon. (p.29)

> That's my idea of luxury – to have the sheets changed every day and twice on Sundays. That's my idea of the power of money.
>
> Yes, I'll have the sheets changed. I'll lie in bed all day, pull the curtains and shut the damned world out. (p.68)

Sasha, however, only dreams of 'the dizzy heights of the suite'; in reality, she moves from one small and rather dingy room to another with 'nothing in it but the bed, the stove and the looking-glass' (p.83). Even such an inadequate room can, however, act as a refuge from the world: 'What do I care about anything when I can lie on the bed and pull the past over me like a blanket? Back, back, back' (p.49). As a place of retreat, the room offers the chance of withdrawal from society into a state of isolation, oblivion and regression. This sense of the room as an escape from life is, however, far outweighed by more abstract and oblique images which present it as a place of constraint, imprisonment and coercion, of which the following is an example:

> Now the room springs out at me, laughing, triumphant. The big bed, the little bed, the table with the tube of luminal, the glass and the bottle of Evian, the two books, the clock ticking on the ledge, the menu – 'T'as compris? Si, j'ai compris. . . .' Four walls, a roof and a bed. *Les Hommes en Cage* . . . Exactly. (p.149)

In this scenario of the room, the door takes on a metaphoric meaning to do with boundary, escape and enclosure. Usually the image is used negatively: 'The passages will never lead anywhere, the doors will always be shut' (p.28); 'I never think of what it will be like to have this baby or, if I think, it's as if a door shuts in my head. Awful, terrible! And then a door shuts in your head' (p.114). Occasionally, however, it suggests the possibility of happiness or escape: 'And the dreams that you have, alone in an empty room, waiting for the door that will open, the thing that is bound to happen' (p.83); 'I've never been so happy in my life. I'm alive, eating ravioli and drinking wine. I've escaped. A door has opened and let me out into the sun. What more do I want?' (p.104). Significantly, perhaps, a rare lyrical moment in the novel is evoked by the sight of the room's curtains being gently stirred by the wind:

> The curtains are thin, and when they are drawn the light comes through softly. There are flowers on the window-sill and I can see their shadows on the curtains. The child downstairs is screaming.
>
> There is a wind, and the flowers on the window-sill, and their shadows on the curtains, are waving. Like swans dipping their beaks in water. Like the incalculable raising its head, uselessly and wildly, for one moment before it sinks down, beaten into the darkness. Like skulls on long, thin necks. Plunging wildly when

> the wind blows, to the end of the curtain, which is their nothingness. Distorting themselves as they plunge.
>
> The musty smell, the bugs, the loneliness, this room, which is part of the street outside – this is all I want from life. (p.109)

Strangely reminiscent of Clarissa Dalloway's bird of paradise curtains which blow into her party room (see page 107), these curtains carry a similar metaphorical meaning. The flowers, suggestive perhaps of a growth and change denied to Sasha, cast their shadows in swan shapes on the curtains. Traditionally associated with death, swans are here emblematic of flight and a frenetic escape into 'nothingness'; the bobbing flower heads become horribly transformed into 'skulls on long, thin necks'. They are also transmuted into the abstraction of 'the incalculable' in Sasha's mind. If we read the room as an image for the constraints imposed by discourse and ideology, then Sasha's overt acceptance of her role as woman in the European society of the 1930s (expressed by her statement that the room 'which is part of the street outside . . . is all I want from life') is qualified, metaphorically, by her intuitive awareness that beyond the boundaries imposed by such constraints there is another way of being and defining oneself. This awareness expresses itself as a sense of 'the incalculable' but the association of this with drowning and annihilation in the passage suggests that for Sasha the notion of being able to move beyond the social construction of the self is too terrifying to contemplate. Like the swans who exist only in so far as the curtain creates their shadows from the flowers, and who are constrained by 'the end of the curtain, which is their nothingness', she fears complete loss of identity if she moves beyond the boundaries of discourse and ideology which both constrain and give definition. Significantly, then, water in this text, as in Wharton's *The House of Mirth*, usually carries negative associations:

> It doesn't matter, there I am, like one of those straws which floats round the edge of a whirlpool and is gradually sucked into the centre, the dead centre, where everything is stagnant, everything is calm. Two-pound-ten a week and a room just off the Gray's Inn Road. (p.38)

> And, after all, the agitation is only on the surface. Underneath I'm indifferent. Underneath there is always stagnant water, calm, indifferent – the bitter peace that is very near to death, to hate. (p.128)

The sense of stasis communicated by 'the dead centre' of the whirlpool and the stagnant water is one which will be developed in the trope of being 'marooned' which informs Rhys's later novel, *Wide Sargasso Sea*. Here, it metaphorically represents the emotional impasse faced by the woman who intuitively senses the nature of the boundaries society and its discourses have imposed upon her, but who represses those intuitions. Only twice in the novel does water carry positive associations (pp.77 and 116); significantly, these derive from memories of another land and a younger, pre-pubertal self.

It is in this metaphorical context that we should read the final episode in the novel when Sasha allows the gigolo and the *commis voyageur* (the travelling salesman) from next door to have sexual intercourse with her in quick succession in her dingy room. Sasha's story closes in a dramatic and deeply disturbing manner. She returns with René, the gigolo, to her room late at night; they struggle on the bed together, her resentful anger expressing itself in barbed remarks whilst he brags of his participation in a gang rape in Morocco. The 'love-making' is unsuccessful and Sasha feels a mixture of physical and emotional pain: 'I feel his hard knee between my knees. My mouth hurts, my breasts hurt, because it hurts, when you have been dead, to come alive' (p.153). She tells him to take his money and go, but finds after he has left that he has gone without it. Surprised by this courteous gesture, her ambivalent feelings about René express themselves as a dialogue between two voices in her head. Fantasising about his return, Sasha crawls into bed, leaving the door open in case he should return. Instead, the man in the room next door, the travelling salesman, who has several times addressed her as 'Vache! Sale vache!', appears. He is someone she has always tried to avoid and whom she finds physically repulsive, yet the novel closes with the *commis* in his white dressing gown, which makes him look 'like a priest, the priest of some obscene, half-understood religion' (p.30), being tacitly invited to have sexual intercourse with her:

> I don't need to look. I know.
> I think: 'Is it the blue dressing-gown, or the white one? That's very important. I must find that out – it's very important.'
> I take my arm away from my eyes. It is the white dressing-gown.
> He stands there, looking down at me. Not sure of himself, his mean eyes flickering.
> He doesn't say anything. Thank God, he doesn't say anything. I look straight into his eyes and despise another poor devil of a human being for the last time. For the last time . . .
> Then I put my arms round him and pull him down on to the bed, saying: 'Yes – yes – yes. . . .' (p.159)

With no narrative comment or guidance on the moral implications of Sasha's act, we are left to judge for ourselves whether this is a negative or a positive moment for Sasha. This narrative abstention reflects, in part, Rhys's refusal to collude with conventional society's judgement of women's sexual behaviour, a refusal which finds voice in the narrator's comment in 'Vienne': 'For God knows, if there's one hypocrisy I loathe more than another, it's the fiction of the "good" woman and the "bad" one' (*Tigers Are Better Looking*, p.194). Rhys deliberately leaves us puzzled. Is Sasha's behaviour to be seen as an act of generosity towards another *misérable*? Is it a desperate attempt to break through the numbing indifference she feels towards humanity – a move towards feeling again? Or does it indicate complete loss of hope and pride and become a grim validation of her sense of self as an object to be used by men? Readers have come to very different conclusions in interpreting Sasha's behaviour: Elgin W. Mellown sees it as an act of 'compassion' in which the repetition of 'yes' recalls Molly Bloom's affirmation of life;[6] Peter Wolfe sees the *commis*' advance as providing both punishment (because Sasha rejected the gigolo) and resurrection ('the lovemaking affirms a dedication to commitment on Sasha's part');[7] Rosalind Miles, however, argues that 'the man who offers sex also offers death and in full awareness Sasha embraces the two experiences, which for her have always been one.'[8] The difference between these responses is no doubt partly explained by gender; it is interesting that both Mellown and Wolfe construe Sasha's surrender to the *commis* positively, whereas Miles sees it negatively. However, any speculation about the true 'meaning' of Sasha's act is futile, since there is no way we can 'know' any more about Sasha's feelings and motives than Rhys chooses to give us; Sasha is, after all, a purely fictional character. What Rhys gives us is a puzzle unless we are aware of the metaphorical implications of Sasha's surroundings. It is significant that the episode opens with a fantasy running through Sasha's 'film-mind' of a room and a man:

> I am in a little whitewashed room. The sun is hot outside. A man is standing with his back to me, whistling that tune and cleaning his shoes. I am wearing a black dress, very short, and heel-less slippers. My legs are bare. I am watching for the expression on the man's face when he turns round. Now he ill-treats me, now he betrays me. He often brings home other women and I have to wait on them, and I don't like that. But as long as he is alive and near me I am not unhappy. If he were to die I should kill myself. (p.147)

This fantasy darkly presages her surrender to the gigolo and the *commis*, both of whom enter her room uninvited. Sasha says goodnight to René at the door of the hotel but finds, when she is groping for the light on the landing, that he is there, waiting for her in the dark. She is strangely happy to see him and allows him into her room which, like a character, springs out at her, 'laughing, triumphant' (p.149). It is at this point that the phrase '*Les Hommes en Cage*' floats through her mind. After a drink of whisky, Sasha suddenly feels irritated by René's presence and asks him to leave. He and the room seem to collude against her, however, the 'damned room grinning at me' (p.150), the gigolo threatening to make a scene if she will not let him stay. The result is a struggle on the bed which culminates in the grim 'game' (p.151) of sexual intercourse. The 'lovemaking' as Peter Wolfe calls it, with Sasha keeping her knees 'clamped together' (p.151) and her eyes shut throughout, is bleakly reminiscent of the act of rape in

Morocco so cheerfully recalled by René. After he has left, Sasha huddles up in the foetal position and cries 'in the way that hurts right down, that hurts your heart and your stomach' (p.154). Only the realisation that the *commis* next door can hear her sobs stops her crying. Her conflicting feelings about René make her wish that he would return and she imagines him walking along the street saying to himself, '"You don't like men, and you don't like women either. You like nothing, nobody. Sauf ton sale cerveau. Alors, je te laisse avec ton sale cerveau"' (p.157). She leaves the door a little open in case he returns and climbs back into bed, realising that she cried not simply because he went away, but also because 'I'll never sing again, because the light in my sale cerveau has gone out' (p.158). It is at this point that the *commis* enters her room and that she allows him to have sexual intercourse with her. It is significant that both men violate her autonomy by intruding upon her in her room: Sasha, like all Rhys's heroines, has no proper room, or space of her own. Her ambivalent feelings about their penetration of her room and her body suggest that, despite her repressed anger, she has capitulated to the demands of a discourse which renders women as spaces within which men may define themselves. This space is the space of the body and there is no room here for that of the mind, or the brain; hence her sorrow at the finally extinguished light in her 'sale cerveau'. This is the darkness at the heart of the novel and its title: Sasha's voyage, like the voyages of all Rhys's heroines, is into the darkness. The title, *Good Morning, Midnight*, intimates loss of youth, hope and freedom; it comes, as Rhys's epigraph indicates, from Emily Dickinson's poem:

> Good morning, Midnight!
> I'm coming home,
> Day got tired of me –
> How could I of him?
>
> Sunshine was a sweet place,
> I liked to stay –
> But Morn didn't want me – now –
> So good night, Day!

Voyage in the Dark

Anna Morgan, the heroine of an earlier novel published in 1934 and set in the London of 1912–14, makes much the same journey. *Voyage in the Dark* gives us a younger woman of 18 who has been living in England for only two years. Brought up in Dominica, she sailed for England after the death of her father, of whom she was very fond. She left behind her in Dominica her English stepmother, a mean, sexually repressed woman called Hester who has since returned to England and is now living in Ilkley, Yorkshire. Their communications during the novel are brief and unsatisfactory, Hester showing no real interest in Anna's welfare, and concerned only that she should remain respectable. Anna works as a chorus girl touring the provincial towns of England, all drearily the same:

> After a while I got used to England and I liked it all right; I got used to everything except the cold and that the towns we went to always looked so exactly alike. You were perpetually moving to another place which was perpetually the same. There was always a little grey street leading to the stage-door of the theatre and another little grey street where your lodgings were, and rows of little houses with chimneys like the funnels of dusty steamers and smoke the same colour as the sky; and a grey stone promenade running hard, naked and straight by the side of the grey-brown or grey-green sea; or a Corporation Street or High Street or Duke Street or Lord Street where you walked about and looked at the shops. (p.8)[9]

As in Woolf's *Mrs Dalloway*, the all-pervasiveness of grey here is associated with a specifically English respectability and conformity which mask hidden deeds and desires.

When the novel opens, Anna is living with another chorus girl, called Maudie, in rooms in Southsea. Anna and Maudie are picked up by two men whilst shopping for stockings in the town; one of them, Walter Jeffries who lives in London, asks Anna to contact him when she comes to Holloway with the show. At the beginning of the cold English winter of 1912, the company moves to London, a city yet to experience the pain of the First World War and one in which characters pursue eating, drinking and sexual liaisons with a languid enthusiasm. She and Walter Jeffries meet again; he seduces her in his Green Street home and she becomes his mistress. Rich, well-connected and charmed by her youth and naiveté, Walter gives Anna money and moves her from her cold Judd Street room which is like 'a small, dark box' (p.22) to more comfortable rooms in Adelaide Road, near Chalk Farm Tube station. After a year or so, however, he tires of her and, returning from a trip to New York, arranges for his cousin, Vincent Jeffries, to end the relationship by letter. The letter contains a cheque for £20 and the promise of a small allowance so that Anna will 'not have to worry about money (for a time at any rate)' (p.80). No longer in work, Anna arranges to leave her Adelaide Road rooms in order to look for cheaper accommodation; she finds a room in a house where the landlady has 'bulging eyes, dark blobs in a long, pink face, like a prawn' (p.89). Here she is befriended by Ethel Matthews, a woman who 'had her own cunning' (p.92) and who quickly notices Anna's fur coat. Ethel has a flat (which is being 'done up') in a road 'just off Oxford Street' (p.96) where she claims to earn her living as 'a Swedish masseuse' (p.95). Through characters such as Laurie Gaynor, who are more experienced than Anna, the reader comes to realise before Anna does, that Ethel is, in fact, a prostitute. Ethel persuades Anna to move her flat and to train as a manicurist; Anna gradually becomes absorbed into Ethel's world and the respectable front of being a manicurist gives way to that of earning her living by prostitution. She soon realises that she is pregnant, announcing to Vincent Jeffries that she does not 'know whose it is' (p.146). Laurie persuades her to write to Walter Jeffries in the hope that he will provide money for the abortion. Walter replies from Paris and arranges that she meet Vincent in London, who agrees, on Walter's behalf, to provide the money. A Mrs Robinson performs the necessary operation and Anna returns to her flat in Langham Street, financed by Walter. The novel closes with a very short section which charts Anna's experience of abortion in a mixture of dream, realism and nightmare. Anna Morgan's 'fall' at the end of *Voyage in the Dark* refers not only to the lie she tells the doctor about her 'miscarriage' and her childhood memories of falling from a mule (pp.129, 158), but also to conventional society's perception of her as a 'fallen' woman. The young chorus girl who was reading Zola's *Nana* at the beginning of the novel has translated herself into a more truthful rendering of the slide into prostitution and Maudie's judgement – 'I bet you a man writing a book about a tart tells a lot of lies one way and another' (p.9) – has been completely vindicated. This fall into a state of destitution is present as a dark abyss at the centre of the text; it lends Rhys's novels a profoundly pessimistic air.

In much of Rhys's work, however, the darkness offered by the future and the greyness of England are offset to a certain extent by another more inviting landscape for which the heroine often longs. The West Indies evoke warmth, sensual lushness and a black race who seem to be passionate, 'alive' (*Wide Sargasso Sea*, p.28) and free:

> Also there wasn't for them, as there was for us, what I thought of as the worry of getting married . . .
>
> Black girls on the contrary seemed to be perfectly free. Children swarmed but negro marriages that I knew of were comparatively rare. Marriage didn't seem a duty with them as it was with us.
>
> All this perhaps was part of my envy which rose to a fever pitch at carnival time. (*Smile Please*, p.51)

Significantly, Anna Morgan of *Voyage in the Dark* wishes to be black: 'I wanted to be black. I always wanted to be black . . . Being black is warm and gay, being white is cold and sad' (p.27). She also identifies strongly with the Caribs, the indigenous population of the West Indies, who came to be despised by the negro population and ignored by the whites. Whilst singing a song containing the line 'Oceans away from despair', she dreams of this race and idealises the Caribs as fierce and noble warriors. As Lucy Wilson has noted, the distinction between the Caribs and the West Indians is a significant one in relation to Rhys's heroines:

> Although they identify with the black West Indians, their destinies more closely parallel the fate of the Caribs who, Anna recalls, 'are now practically exterminated'. Antoinette *is* exterminated, and Anna's abortion symbolizes the end of her line of descent.[10]

Anna's identification with this dying tribe also suggests, however, that she perceives them as somehow emblematic of a 'real self' which has been denied existence in European, and even West Indian, culture. The exotic distance of this tribe from the life she actually leads suggests how remote are the chances of any such 'real self' surviving. It also suggests how impossible it is to imagine any alternative, more authentic 'self' without reference to another social reality or culture; Anna's metaphorical 'real self' is essentially a nostalgic fantasy awash with primitivism.

Haunted, then, by memories of the warm West Indies, Anna moves from one room to another in a cold and grey England. She feels a sense of deep dislocation: 'Sometimes it was as if I were back there and as if England were a dream. At other times England was the real thing and out there was the dream, but I could never fit them together' (p.8). Because of her West Indian background, she is known derisively as the 'Hottentot' by the girls with whom she works. Anna's final protector figure, Ethel Matthews, turns out to be a false Samaritan (like the Heidlers in *Quartet*), and someone who constantly parades her dislike of 'foreigners'. In this implictly racist society, Anna moves from pride in her background – 'I'm a real West Indian . . . I'm the fifth generation on my mother's side', she boasts to Walter Jeffries (p.47) – to an exasperated lie about her origins to Joe, Laurie's friend: '"You're a liar . . . You didn't know my father. Because my real name isn't Morgan and I'll never tell you my real name and I was born in Manchester and I'll never tell you anything real about myself"' (p.107). Her procession of minor illnesses – colds, sore throats, influenza – mirror a deep malaise of the spirit. As in *Good Morning, Midnight*, certain symptoms suggest an hysterical reaction to a social reality from which she feels alienated. She suffers frequently from discomfort in the throat (pp.10, 18, 82, 109) and feelings of asphyxiation: 'I wanted to pretend it was like the night before, but it wasn't any use. Being afraid is cold like ice, and it's like when you can't breathe. "Afraid of what?" I thought' (p.76).

Anna is afraid of 'the dark'; it is left to the reader, however, to deduce the metaphorical meaning of that phrase. Anna herself does not understand the nature of her alienation and fear; she knows, however, *what* she fears. She comes to loathe England with its 'dark streets round the theatre (which) made me think of murders' (p.16) and its inhabitants whose 'faces are the colour of woodlice' (p.23). She takes refuge from the world, like other Rhys heroines, in her rented room. After her lover, Walter Jeffries, breaks with her, she retreats more and more into a seedy seclusion:

> I stopped wanting to go out. That happens very easily. It's as if you had always done that – lived in a few rooms and gone from one to the other . . . Really all you want is night, and to lie in the dark and pull the sheet over your head and sleep, and before you know where you are it is night – that's one good thing. (p.120)

However, against this sense of the room as ambiguous sanctuary there is, once again, the image of the room as prison:

> I lay down and started thinking about the time when I was ill in Newcastle, and the room I had there, and that story about the walls of a room getting smaller and smaller until they crush you to death. *The Iron Shroud*, it was called. It wasn't Poe's story; it was more frightening than that. 'I believe this damned room's getting smaller and smaller', I thought. And about the rows of houses outside, gimcrack, rotten-looking, and all exactly alike. (p.26)

Conversely, when Walter arrives at her cold Judd Street room with money and presents, the 'room looked different, as if it had grown bigger' (p.29). Anna passes through a series of rented rooms and hotel rooms in the novel and her perception of them changes according to her own situation. Although these rooms are all different in scale and furnishing, they – and the streets of which they are part – seem eventually to blur into one same street and room:

> all the houses outside in the street were the same – all alike, all hideously stuck together – and the streets going north, east, south, west, all exactly the same. (p.89)

> I . . . slid off into thinking of all the bedrooms I had slept in and how exactly alike they were, bedrooms on tour. Always a high, dark wardrobe and something dirty red in the room; and through the window the feeling of a small street would come in. (p.128)

Sensing intuitively that the room is a place of constraint as well as refuge, Anna is able to perceive that 'something about the darkness of the streets has a meaning' (p.49) although she is unable to articulate what it is. It is left to the reader to make a 'meaning' out of the 'darkness of the streets' and the insistent presence of the room and its boundaries. For the reader these boundaries suggest those of a post-Edwardian culture which, reticent about female sexuality, sharply categorises women as 'good' and 'bad' according to their sexual behaviour. Vincent Jeffries, who constantly strikes up casual sexual liaisons with women such as Germaine, nevertheless has an ideal of womanhood which is based on the Victorian notion that modesty, chastity and self-sacrifice are 'feminine' virtues. Rhys brilliantly and economically evokes his archaic value system by making him comment on *The Rosary* as 'a damned fine book. When I read it I thought, "The man who wrote this should be knighted"' (p.73). *The Rosary* was a best-selling novel published in 1909. The heroine, Jane, is plain and is a tamed and domesticated version of Jane Eyre; she refuses to marry a young artist who loves her since she fears that his passion for physical beauty will lead him to regret the marriage later. However, when he is blinded in an accident she goes to look after him as 'Nurse Gray' and wins his love again.[11] Vincent assumes that the book was written by a man, but Walter points out that the author was a woman (Florence Barclay, in fact). The quaint Victorianism of Vincent's view is mocked by Germaine, with whom he is spending a weekend in the country: '"He ought to be put in a glass case, oughtn't he?"' (p.73). Through this brief reference to a popular novel, Rhys pinpoints the hypocritical attitudes of the English male on the eve of the First World War. These 'mystic boundaries' constrain woman's sense of herself and effect containment, just like the parameters of the room. They also result in a terrible hypocrisy about relations between the sexes: '*This is England, and I'm in a nice, clean English room with all the dirt swept under the bed*' (p.27). Women themselves, however, frequently collude with the maintenance of this hypocrisy as the female authorship of *The Rosary* demonstrates.

Despite the bleak containment of these rooms and their metaphoric significance, however, *Voyage in the Dark* is a less grey novel than *Good Morning, Midnight*. The hypocrisy and misogyny of England is counterpointed throughout the text by Anna's memories of Dominica, a landscape of colour and warmth. This landscape has two important metaphoric functions: it allows a less inhibited expression of desire than the discourse of England in 1914 (or 1934, when the book was first published) permitted and it enables Rhys to present an oblique but sharp critique of European ideas about sexuality. For example, the loss of Anna's virginity to Walter Jeffries and her affair with him are presented through a mixture of dialogue and internal monologue in which images of death and slavery bleakly counterpoint European notions of the romantic seduction. As Anna sits with Walter in his dark and uninviting house in Green Street 'thinking about when he would start kissing me and about when we would go upstairs' (p.43), memories of the lush Constance Estate where she grew up, its garden full of roses, orchids, ferns and honeysuckle evoke an erotic sensuality. Almost immediately, however, she recollects 'an old slave-list' (p.45) that she once saw there and during intercourse in the bedroom the memory of one name on the list 'Maillotte Boyd, aged 18, mulatto, house servant' (p.46), haunts her. These words alternate with memories of those uttered by a nun who taught her when she was a child:

> 'Children, every night before you go to sleep you should lie straight down with your arms by your sides and your eyes shut and say: "One day I shall be dead. One day I shall lie like this with my eyes closed and I shall be dead."' (p.48)

Anna's sexual initiation is thus presented in language which becomes redolent of death and ambiguous submission:

> Lying down with your arms by your sides and your eyes shut.
> 'Walter, will you put the light out? I don't like it in my eyes.'
> *Maillotte Boyd, aged 18. Maillotte Boyd, aged 18 . . . But I like it like this. I don't want it any other way but this.*
> 'Are you asleep?'
> 'You were lying so still,' he said.
> *Lying so still afterwards. That's what they call the Little Death.*
> 'I must go now,' I said. 'It's getting late.'
> I got up and dressed. (p.48)

On the way home from Green Street Anna continues to dwell nostalgically on her childhood, remembering the 'acrid-sweet' smell of Francine, the black woman who brought her up, and the colour of the hibiscus: 'it was so red, so proud, and its long gold tongue hung out. It was so red that even the sky was just a background for it' (p.49). (Significantly, perhaps, Antoinette Cosway in *Wide Sargasso Sea* decides that she will write her name in 'fire red' underneath the green, blue and purple roses she has just embroidered (p.44) and Atwood's heroine is denied the use of red in her illustrations (*Surfacing*, p.54).) Inhibited by English cultural constraints, Anna can come to terms with sensuality and eroticism only through images of the landscape which belong to her childhood: there is no equivalent language or landscape of desire in the England of 1914. The English countryside leaves her unmoved ('the wildness had gone out of it', (p.67)) and English hypocrisy stifles her. It is as if her desire has been left in Dominica whilst her body moves mechanically within England; as if she is divided. Behind her, of course, she has also left Francine, the caring and uninhibited mother-figure who dominated her childhood. Francine stands in obvious opposition to Hester, who, Anna remembers, never felt at ease in the Dominican landscape: 'We used to sit on the verandah with the night coming in, huge. And the way it smelt of flowers. ("This place gives me the creeps at night", Hester would say)' (p.71). Francine's joyous sensuality is celebrated and her latent eroticism contrasts very vividly with Hester's puritanism. Significantly, Hester has no honest language with which to explain the onset of menstruation to Anna:

> when I was unwell for the first time it was she [Francine] who explained to me, so that it seemed quite all right and I thought it was all in the day's work like eating or drinking. But then she went off and told Hester, and Hester came and jawed away at me, her eyes wandering all over the place. I kept saying, 'no, rather not. . . . Yes, I see. . . . Oh yes, of course . . . .' But I began to feel awfully miserable, as if everything were shutting up around me and I couldn't breathe. I wanted to die. (p.59)

As Anna gradually drifts into prostitution in England, so her memories of the West Indies become darker – as if these internal landscapes present a truer barometer of her sexual predicament and despair than any overt analysis can give. Cameos of suffering and horror present themselves involuntarily so that, as the book charts her pregnancy, slide into prostitution and abortion, this landscape of the mind takes on a nightmarish hue. The woman with yaws, a contagious disease characterised by raspberry-like growths on the face, acts as an epilogue to a daydream about the road that led to the Constance Estate: 'I suppose she was begging but I couldn't understand because her nose and mouth were eaten away; it seemed as though she were laughing at me' (p.130). The nausea of her pregnancy drives Anna to hit an old client's bandaged wrist, in order to make him release her; the fitful sleep which follows is full of strange dreams of home presented in a stream of consciousness which abandons orthodox punctuation altogether. Dream memories of Miss Jackson, 'Colonel Jackson's illegitimate daughter' (p.139), give way to a dream vision of the blue mountains of the island, one of which was said to be haunted:

> Obeah zombis soucriants – lying in the dark frightened of the dark frightened of soucriants that fly in through the window and suck your blood – they fan you to sleep with their wings and then they suck your blood – you know them in the day-time – they look like people but their eyes are red and staring and they're

> soucriants at night – looking in the glass and thinking sometimes my eyes look like a soucriant's eyes. (pp.139–40)

The distinctly gothic element of *Voyage in the Dark* which comes to play such an important part in *Wide Sargasso Sea* is not simply gratuitous; it acts metaphorically, conveying through dream what Leslie Fiedler has described as our 'deepest fears and guilts'.[12] The state of death-in-life, that the 'zombis' metaphorically represent in the novel, suggests an emotional numbness in Anna which prevents her from recognising the predators who surround her: the various men who prey on her sexually and women such as Ethel who wish to exploit her for their own purposes. Their worst qualities are, however, frankly faced in the metamorphosis which Dominica provides through the imagery of Anna's dreams. A similar transformation, which allows Anna intuitively to glimpse the truth about the English who surround her, occurs as she struggles back to her flat after the abortion; here an image of Meta and the masquerade flashes upon her mind. In *Voyage in the Dark*, Meta is Francine's malignant opposite:

> most of all I was afraid of the people passing because I was dying; and, just because I was dying, any one of them, any minute might stop and approach me and knock me down, or put their tongues out as far as they would go. Like that time at home with Meta, when it was Masquerade and she came to see me and put out her tongue at me through the slit in her mask. (p.151)

Meta is a character based on a nurse who terrified Jean Rhys as a child: 'It was Meta who talked so much about zombies, soucriants, and loups-garoux . . . Meta had shown me a world of fear and distrust, and I am still in that world' (*Smile Please*, pp.30 and 31). Laurie Gaynor, who helps Anna and stays with her throughout the abortion – and who represents the 'golden-hearted tart' of Britain's post-Edwardian sexual mythology – is a Francine character. Ethel Matthews who preys on Anna and lures her into prostitution – and who represents the prostitute as scheming parasite in that same sexual mythology – is a Meta character. Anna's dreams allow the reader to perceive the nature of her social identity in relation to these paradigmatic points of reference. It is Dominica which provides the visual images through which we come to understand the nature of the people who surround her and their implication in a specific discourse of sexuality.

The last, short section of the novel, which deals with Anna's near-fatal haemorrhage as she aborts her unwanted child, brings this metaphoric use of landscape to a vivid climax. In the original version of the novel Anna died, but her publishers persuaded Rhys to change it; it is clear, however, from a letter to Selma Vaz Dias written in 1963 that Rhys felt the original ending to be more fitting.[13] Anna's delirious imaginings revolve around the three-day masquerade which she used to watch from between the slats of the blinds at home in Dominica; these hallucinatory, dream-like scenes both vie with, and obliquely continue, the more realist narrative in which Laurie and the charwoman, Mrs Polo, resort to calling a doctor who stems Anna's bleeding. The two modes of narrative are skilfully woven together by phrases which contain the word 'stop'. 'It's bound to stop in a minute' says Laurie of the bleeding, and Anna remembers saying 'Stop, please stop' to an elderly client (p.156). She then dreams of the masquerade, recollections of the lascivious old man merging with memories of 'the slobbering tongue of an idiot' which protruded from a carnival mask:

> A pretty useful mask that white one watch it and the slobbering tongue of an idiot will stick out – a mask Father said with an idiot behind it I believe the whole damned business is like that – Hester said Gerald the child's listening – oh no she isn't Father said she's looking out of the window and quite right too – it ought to be stopped somebody said it's not a decent and respectable way to go on it ought to be stopped – Aunt Jane said I don't see why they should stop the Masquerade they've always had their three days Masquerade ever since I can remember why should they want to stop it some people want to stop everything. (p.157)

The white onlookers are themselves divided in their response to the masquerade and there is an unpleasant mixture of racism, puritanism and voyeurism implicit in Uncle Bo's condemnation: 'you can't expect niggers to behave like white people all the time . . . it's asking too much of human nature' (p.157). At one point 'the whole damned business' of sexuality is made very clearly in the rhythms and images of the writing:

> The concertina-man was very black – he sat sweating and the concertina went forwards and backwards backwards and forwards one two three one two three pourquoi ne pas aimer bonheur supreme – the triangle-man kept time on his triangle and with his foot tapping and the little man who played the chak-chak smiled with his eyes fixed. (p.157)

Through this internal monologue of dream and hallucination Rhys seems to break down authorial control (although this itself is, of course, an illusion); as at the close of *Good Morning, Midnight*, there is no narrative judgement to guide the reader's response. Any coherent understanding of the text must derive from an attempt to deduce the metaphorical meaning of the masquerade. The masquerade, like the Dominican landscape, allows a franker appraisal of the forces of aggression, sexuality and coercion than the hypocritical society of England permits, with its advertisements for 'Venus Carnis' cream on the one hand and its prostitution trade on the other. Unlike the invisible mask of respectability which Sasha Jansen feels constrained to wear, the masks of the carnival bring about a temporary freedom and dislocation from cultural hierarchies: blacks can put out their tongues at the whites who employ them and sexual desires can be expressed and acted out. As Edward Brathwaite has pointed out, the masquerades which took place in Jamaica during the late eighteenth and early nineteenth centuries – to which the late nineteenth-century masquerade on the island of Dominica is clearly related – derived 'their energy and motifs, not from Catholicism in Protestant Jamaica, but from Africa'.[14] Many aspects of public entertainment during this earlier period, including street performances by African or Afro-Creole bands, 'continued to dramatize or satirize aspects of the slave society – their and their masters' condition'.[15] The music of the masquerades and carnivals therefore clearly originally had a political as well as a recreational function:

> because this music and dance was so misunderstood, and since the music was based on tonal scales and the dancing on choreographic traditions entirely outside the white observers' experience – not forgetting the necessary assumption that slaves, since they were brutes could produce no philosophy that 'reached above the navel' – their music was dismissed as 'noise', their dancing as a way of (or to) sexual misconduct and debauchery. On the other hand, the 'political' function of the slaves' music was quickly recognized by their masters – hence the banning of drumming or gatherings where drumming took place – often on the excuse that it disturbed the (white) neighbours.[16]

This sense of the masquerade as threatening to, and subversive of, white European values is also conveyed by Rhys's description of the masquerade in *Voyage in the Dark*. Further, the conflation of the masquerade with Anna's experience of abortion allows her to half-perceive the parallel between the hierarchical and oppressive social system of the West Indies, based on colour and deriving from a slave society, with that of England in the years 1912–14 in which women are exploited and constrained in a less obvious manner: '*you look at everything and you don't see it only sometimes you see it like now I see*' (p.158). The motley carnival reveals, both by implicit parallel and contrast, how English society is itself a masquerade in that its very 'civilised' modes of behaviour merely mask what are essentially predatory and coercive inclinations. Such an insight is, of course, dangerous; its challenge to the boundaries of discourse and ideology is metaphorically suggested by the fact that in her delirium Anna sees the masquerade through the window, 'from between the slats of the jalousies' (p.156). Unable to take part in the singing and dancing outside and constrained by the 'mystic boundaries' of white respectability, Anna nevertheless glimpses through the slats of the blind a critique of the cultural assumptions in whose terms she is defined. As in *Good Morning, Midnight*, however, there is fear and pessimism concerning the construction of the self beyond those boundaries and expectations. This is communicated in the novel by the use of ambiguous sea and water imagery:

> It was like letting go and falling back into the water and seeing

> yourself grinning up through the water, your face like a mask, and seeing the bubbles coming up as if you were trying to speak from under the water. And how do you know what it's like to try to speak from under water when you're drowned? (p.84)

When Ethel Matthews becomes irritated by Anna's lack of hospitality to her clients (and all that that implies) she shouts at her, '"Who wants you here anyway? Why don't you clear out?"' Anna oddly replies, 'I can't swim well enough, that's one reason' (p.124), an answer that makes no sense at all unless we are aware of the metaphoric dimensions of the text. In a strange dream which seems to presage her abortion, Anna imagines herself on board a ship, about to kiss the hand of a small dwarf who is dressed as a priest, sitting up in a coffin. In the dream she is desperately trying to reach the shore and on waking she notes that 'It was funny how, after that, I kept on dreaming about the sea' (p.141). Her ambivalence towards water and sea suggests a desire to escape from the constraints of cultural expectations and a terror of so doing; both desire and terror are repressed and lead to a numb passivity and mild hysteria. Anna, then, will stay within the confines of the room and all that it metaphorically represents; she will, as the closing words of the novel make clear, soon start 'all over again, all over again' (p.159). In this respect, her journey is a voyage into, not out of, the dark.

Wide Sargasso Sea

Antoinette Cosway of *Wide Sargasso Sea*, published in 1966, also makes that same voyage into the dark. As she leaves her homeland of Jamaica for life in England with the unnamed man who is based on Charlotte Brontë's Rochester, he recalls a snatch of song which does not seem to augur well for her future:

> Blot out the moon,
> Pull down the stars.
> Love in the dark, for we're for the dark,
> So soon, soon
>
> (p.139)[17]

In order to reach England, they must cross the Sargasso Sea, but exactly what Jean Rhys meant to convey by the title of her novel is still a mystery to most readers. The sea is mentioned by name in neither Charlotte Brontë's novel, *Jane Eyre*, nor Rhys's own work which tells the story of Bertha Mason before her marriage to Edward Rochester. Yet clearly the title was important to Rhys and she took enormous care in choosing it:

> I have no title yet. 'The First Mrs Rochester' is not right. Nor, of course, is 'Creole'. That has a different meaning now. I hope I'll get one soon, for titles mean a lot to me. Almost half the battle. I thought of 'Sargasso Sea' or 'Wide Sargasso Sea' but nobody knew what I meant. (*Jean Rhys: Letters 1931–66*, p.154)

The Sargasso Sea takes its name from *Sargassam natans*, a floating brown seaweed brought to the area by ocean currents; at the centre of a warm maelstrom of North Atlantic waters it forms a clockwise gyre of seaweed-logged waters: a calm and stagnant surface within an immense whirlpool. Presumably any merchant ship, carrying slaves or cargo, travelling from the West Indies to England, or vice versa, would have had to cross the Sargasso Sea and presumably it thereby ran the risk of being becalmed or marooned. In this novel, Antoinette finds herself marooned between the two cultures of England and the West Indies; more generally, the word seems to suggest metaphorically the powerlessness of women within a nineteenth-century imperialist culture.

Jean Rhys's last novel vividly dramatises this sense of destructive inertia in the fate of Antoinette who finally emerges from a state of apathy and despair into a dream-like frenzy of death and hatred. This despair is also shared at different times by her mother and the benign Aunt Cora who, having failed to secure any justice for Antoinette, finally 'turned her face to the wall' (p.95). Their apathy is not the result – as the malicious Daniel Cosway claims – of inherited insanity; it is their enforced helplessness as women which finally drives them mad. Annette Cosway, Antoinette's Creole mother, has her horse poisoned by resentful blacks who find themselves still oppressed and deprived five years after the passing of the Emancipation Act in 1834; the horse's death leaves the small family literally stranded: '"Now we are marooned," my mother said, "now what will become of us?"' (p.16). 'Marooned' in this context also carries other metaphorical meanings. Annette is marooned between two cultures: neither really Jamaican nor European, she is only a Creole, a 'white cockroach' (p.20); she is marooned between servants and masters because as a middle-class woman in 1839 she supervises servants but must be subservient to her husband. Annette grows 'thin and silent' (p.16) after the doctor's diagnosis of her infant son's sickly condition; the reader remains ignorant of the doctor's words but it seems likely – given her first husband's promiscuous sexual behaviour – that the child is a victim of congenital syphilis. She loses the will to live ('To die and be forgotten and at peace' (p.19)) and becomes increasingly distant from those around her: 'My mother walked over to the window. ("Marooned," said her straight narrow back, her carefully coiled hair. "Marooned")' (p.22). However, Antoinette's 'running wild' with the little black girl, Tia, who both cheats her and steals her clothes despite the love between them, shocks Annette out of her apathy into a course of action. Widowed for five years and facing poverty, she resolves to marry a Mr Mason in order to secure money for herself and Antoinette; in telling Rochester about this period of her life, Antoinette blames herself for her mother's subsequent slide into misery and 'madness':

> Then there was that day when she saw I was growing up like a white nigger and she was ashamed of me, it was after that day that everything changed. Yes, it was my fault, it was my fault that she started to plan and work in a frenzy, in a fever to change our lives. (p.109)

It is perhaps ironically significant that 1834 marks not only the Emancipation Act but also the death of Annette's first husband. However, any freedom for Annette is illusory since, like the negroes of Jamaica, she lives within a colonial system which discriminates against the weak, the female and the black. She therefore has no choice but to marry to secure economic means. Soon after her marriage to Mr Mason, Annette's house on the Coulibri estate in Jamaica is burnt to the ground by blacks who have become deeply resentful of the whites and their economic power and frustrated by their own lack of autonomy; this act, of course, presages the dream of burning down Thornfield at the end of the novel which expresses a similar rage and despair. At the heart of this deed of revenge is not only anger at exploitation but also a clash of cultures: Myra, a black serving-girl, has overheard Mr Mason threatening to import 'coolies' from the East Indies to work on the Coulibri Estate because the West Indians are, in his eyes, lazy.[18] Defending them, his wife Annette insists that he does not understand the black people: '"You don't like, or even recognize, the good in them," she said, "and you won't believe in the other side"' (p.28).

This lack of understanding runs through private relationships as well as cultural ones: '"I don't always understand what they say or sing"', says Rochester of the black people (p.85) and, of course, he does not understand Antoinette either. Nor does Antoinette understand him: '"I don't understand you. I know nothing about you, and I cannot speak for you"' (p.141), she says as they leave for England. More seriously, Rochester, coming from a culture which has placed a taboo on woman's expression of sexual desire, cannot understand Antoinette's frank eroticism. Adrienne Rich, in her essay 'Jane Eyre: The temptations of a motherless woman', recognises this aspect of their relationship as an important element in Brontë's novel: 'Rochester's story is part Byronic romance, but it is based on a social and psychological reality: the nineteenth-century loose woman might have sexual feelings, but the nineteenth-century *wife* did not and must not.'[19] In writing *Wide Sargasso Sea* Rhys set herself the task of presenting 'the other side' (p.106) of Charlotte Brontë's story:

> That unfortunate death of a Creole! I'm fighting mad to write *her* story . . .
>
> Of course Charlotte Brontë makes her own world, of course she convinces you, and that makes the poor Creole lunatic all the

more dreadful. I remember being quite shocked, and when I re-read it rather annoyed. 'That's only one side – the English side' sort of thing. (*Letters*, pp.157 and 297)

In a novel in which there is no authoritative narrator and which consists of two often conflicting narratives, Rochester is also allowed to tell his side of the story. In Rhys's version of *Jane Eyre*, he is the product of an imperialist and mysogynist culture; the clash between this culture's values and those of the West Indies affect him deeply. The change it effects in him is presented to us through the words of Mrs Eff in Antoinette's last narrative: '*I knew him as a boy. I knew him as a young man. He was gentle, generous, brave. His stay in the West Indies has changed him out of all knowledge. He has grey in his hair and misery in his eyes*' (p.145). Letting him tell his own tale, however, Rhys makes it clear that Rochester is victim as well as victimiser; he is not quite the 'unmitigated villain' of Barbara Hill Rigney's *Madness and Sexual Politics in the Feminist Novel.*[20] The second son in a culture which favours first sons, he has been manipulated into marriage with Antoinette by a father from whom he is emotionally estranged:

Dear Father. The thirty thousand pounds have been paid to me without question or condition. No provision made for her (that must be seen to). I have a modest competence now. I will never be a disgrace to you or to my dear brother you love. No begging letters, or mean requests. None of the furtive shabby manoeuvres of a younger son. (p.59)

Vainly trying to explain her own story to Rochester, Antoinette tells him of her mother's life. She reveals how, traumatised by the death of her small son in the fire, she became ill and alienated from her second husband, who 'bought her a house and hired a coloured man and woman to look after her' (p.110); Antoinette's own incarceration at Thornfield is here grimly presaged. She tells Rochester how, one day, she went secretly to visit her mother, only to find her being made drunk and being sexually abused by 'a fat black man':

I saw the man lift her up out of the chair and kiss her. I saw his

> mouth fasten on hers and she went all soft and limp in his arms and he laughed. The woman laughed too, but she was angry. When I saw that I ran away. (p.111)

Annette Cosway dies, presumably in these unsavoury circumstances, whilst Antoinette is an adolescent girl at convent school. Her story has close parallels with the story of her daughter's life, which charts the metamorphosis of Antoinette Cosway, a 'Creole girl . . . [with] the sun in her' in Christophine's words (p.130) into a madwoman locked up in a cold English attic. Christophine, a wise and dignified woman from Martinique, who was herself given as 'a wedding-gift' to Annette by Antoinette's father, knows that Annette's breakdown was the result of suffering, not madness. The deepest insights allowed to any character are given to Christophine, whose opinions Rochester disdains and even Antoinette occasionally rejects, because she is only a black, female, newly emancipated slave. She comes from a culture, as Edward Brathwaite notes, which had little regard for the conventions of marriage[21] and this allows her to take a justly cynical view of arranged marriages between Creoles and Europeans:

> She spat over her shoulder. 'All women, all colours, nothing but fools. Three children I have. One living in this world, each a different father, but no husband, I thank my God. I keep my money. I don't give it to no worthless man.' (p.91)

She is also quick to see through the new age of emancipation and equality, realising that the old brutal slave system has merely been replaced by more subtle forms of constraint:

> No more slavery! She had to laugh! 'These new ones have Letter of the Law. Same thing. They got magistrate. They got fine. They got jail house and chain gang. They got tread machine to mash up people's feet. New ones worse than old ones – more cunning, that's all.' (pp.22–3)

Indeed, it is through the law that Rochester finally subdues Christophine: he threatens to have her arrested on a charge of practising obeah. In the culture of the West Indies the obeah-man held much power and was regarded as doctor, philosopher and priest.[22] However, after the Tacky slave rebellion of 1760 in Jamaica – said to have been inspired by obeah men and women – the Europeans on the island perceived the practice of obeah as a dangerous threat to the white power structure.[23] Christophine's presence in the novel is therefore suggestive of political subversion, however, ineffectual. Indeed, Christophine's political shrewdness enables her to understand exactly the manner in which white women, as well as black, are culturally constrained:

> 'They drive her to it. When she lose her son she lose herself for a while and they shut her away. They tell her she is mad, they act like she is mad. Question, question. But no kind word, no friends, and her husban' he go off, he leave her.' (p.129)

She also realises that Antoinette's life is about to repeat the pattern, accusing Rochester: '"You think you fool me? You want her money but you don't want her. It is in your mind to pretend she is mad. I know it . . . you wicked like Satan self!"' (p.132). As Christophine predicts, Annette's marriage, to which she submitted in order to secure economic freedom for her daughter, ironically brings about a repetition of her own fate. It is an irony that Antoinette seems unconsciously to recognise in her conversation with Rochester: '"I have tried to make you understand. But nothing has changed"' (p.111).

Antoinette and Rochester do not understand each other and they do not understand each other's land. The landscapes of *Wide Sargasso Sea* are heavily charged with meaning; the West Indies and England become irreconcilable opposites, with the greyness and coldness of the latter becoming predominant over the colour and warmth of Jamaica and the Windward Islands as the narrative progresses. Rochester enters the West Indies as a despoiler enters paradise – albeit a postlapsarian one. The Coulibri estate is beautiful but it is also a garden of Eden in which anarchy holds sway:

> Our garden was large and beautiful as that garden in the Bible – the tree of life grew there. But it had gone wild. The paths were overgrown and a smell of dead flowers mixed with the fresh living smell. Underneath the tree ferns, tall as forest tree ferns, the light

> was green. Orchids flourished out of reach or for some reason not to be touched. One was snaky looking, another like an octopus with long thin brown tentacles bare of leaves hanging from a twisted root. Twice a year the octopus orchid flowered – then not an inch of tentacle showed. It was a bell-shaped mass of white, mauve, deep purples, wonderful to see. The scent was very sweet and strong. I never went near it. (p.17)

These colours – 'white, mauve, deep purples' – are Antoinette's colours; later, at the convent, she chooses to colour her roses within the same spectrum: 'We can colour the roses as we choose and mine are green, blue and purple' (p.44). They are colours which Rochester comes to hate: 'Everything is too much, I felt as I rode wearily after her. Too much blue, too much purple, too much green' (p.59).

The orchid, with its suggestively vulval flower, is her flower, and increasingly the landscape of the West Indies comes to represent her female sexuality and desire. Rochester and Antoinette leave Jamaica to honeymoon in the Windward Islands with its wilder terrain: 'a beautiful place – wild, untouched, above all untouched, with an alien, disturbing, secret loveliness' (p.73) in Rochester's eyes. The heavy scents of the indigenous flowers and trees become suggestive of Antoinette's female sensuality and, as Rochester becomes more and more estranged from his wife, he begins to despoil the vegetation with secret rage. The first time is an accident – he treads on the frangipani wreath that Christophine has made as a welcome garland: 'The room was full of the scent of the crushed flowers' (p.62). Later, however, the destruction is deliberate:

> I passed an orchid with long sprays of golden-brown flowers. One of them touched my cheek and I remembered picking some for her one day. 'They are like you,' I told her. Now I stopped, broke a spray off and trampled it in the mud. (p.82)

The colour, warmth and passion of the West Indies landscape express Antoinette's desires. The lush beauty of the land is something she loves and responds to: 'The sky was dark blue through the dark green mango leaves, and I thought, "This is my place and this is where I belong and this is where I wish to stay"' (p.90). As their relationship deteriorates, Antoinette's misery infects even her love of the West Indies: '"But I loved this place and you have made it into a place I hate"' (p.121).

For Rochester, the West Indies become a nightmare: he finds that the scent of the flowers begins to cloy and makes him feel giddy; everything around him becomes menacing: 'it seemed to me that everything round me was hostile . . . The trees were threatening and the shadows of the trees moving slowly over the floor menaced me' (p.123). The darkness of the tropical forest becomes a deeply disturbing presence and suggests forces beyond his control. Eventually his hatred of the place becomes inseparable from his hatred of his wife and suggests a profound anxiety about her sexuality and his own desires. Like Antoinette's, his pain revolves around the sense of a lost paradise, never to be regained:

> I hated the mountains and the hills, the rivers and the rain. I hated the sunsets of whatever colour, I hated its beauty and its magic and the secret I would never know. I hated its indifference and the cruelty which was part of its loveliness. Above all I hated her. For she belonged to the magic and the loveliness. She had left me thirsty and all my life would be thirst and longing for what I had lost before I found it. (p.141)

Significantly, the word 'thirst' in the novel is used to express sexual desire: 'I was thirsty for her, but that is not love' (p.78) says Rochester of the early days of their marriage; later, before they leave for England, he thinks to himself, 'Sneer to the last, Devil. Do you think that I don't know? She thirsts for *anyone* – not for me' (p.135). Entering the postlapsarian paradise of the West Indies, Rochester falls from innocence: he discovers the nature of female sexuality and finds to his horror that, like the forest, it is beyond his control. Oblique hints suggest that although he arouses Antoinette's desire, he is not sexually very experienced. He becomes defensive and oddly anxious when he is served, or thinks of, the drink entitled 'Bull's Blood'. His attitude to black women is distastefully racist and reveals an intense inner conflict in which his own sexual desires can be acknowledged only by projecting them upon a race supposedly less 'civilised'. As Lee Erwin rightly points out, 'for Rochester, Antoinette's sexuality itself is an index of racial contamination . . . Both fear of some unspeakable taint and an inadmissible desire are suggested here.'[24] He is revolted by Antoinette's hugging Christophine, yet he seduces Amélie shortly after his wedding – only to find himself repelled by her the next morning: 'And her skin was darker, her lips thicker than I had thought' (p.115). His seduction of Amélie is a deliberate act of revenge: both Amélie and Daniel Cosway have implied that Antoinette and Sandi, her coloured cousin and the son of her own father's illegitimate offspring, have long been lovers. Antoinette's memories of Sandi in Part Three seem to confirm this ('He had found out that Sandi had been to the house and that I went to see him. I never knew who told' (p.152)). Rochester's need to control and contain her sexuality[25] at first takes the form of brutality; Christophine, noticing the marks on Antoinette's body, comments, '"I see you very rough with her eh?"' (p.124). Initially aroused by her passion, he is later repelled by it when he discovers that he is not its only recipient: 'She'll loosen her black hair, and laugh and coax and flatter (a mad girl. She'll not care who she's loving). She'll moan and cry and give herself as no sane woman would – or could. *Or could*' (pp.135–6).

Rochester's judgement that such sexual appetite in a woman suggests insanity derives from the discourse of English nineteenth-century pathology. Elaine Showalter's discussion of British nineteenth-century attitudes to 'nymphomania', in *The Female Malady: Women, madness and English culture, 1830–1980*, sheds much light on the sexual struggle within *Wide Sargasso Sea*:

> Psychiatrists wrote frequently about the problem of nymphomania. John Millar, the medical superintendent at Bethnal House Asylum in London, observed that nymphomanic symptoms were 'constantly present' when young women were insane . . . The most extreme and nightmarish effort to manage women's minds by regulating their bodies was Dr Isaac Baker Brown's surgical practice of clitoridectomy as a cure for female insanity . . . Brown

> carried out his sexual surgery in his private clinic in London for seven years, between 1859 and 1866 . . . Although Brown did not treat a great number of patients, clitoridectomy has a symbolic meaning that makes it central to our understanding of sexual difference in the Victorian treatment of insanity. Clitoridectomy is the surgical enforcement of an ideology that restricts female sexuality to reproduction. The removal of the clitoris eliminates the woman's sexual pleasure, and it is indeed this autonomous sexual pleasure that Brown defined as the symptom, perhaps the essence, of female insanity.[26]

Showalter's discussion of the ideological function of clitoridectomy accords precisely with Gayatri Spivak's argument that the practice is metonymic of how women are less violently, but none the less appallingly, constrained within civilised, first world patriarchies: 'it is this ideologico-material repression of the clitoris as the signifier of the sexed subject that operates the specific oppression of women.'[27] Seen in this light, Antoinette's frank sexuality politically subverts the code by which Rochester lives, just as Edna Pontellier's eroticism threatens the values which Robert Lebrun embraces uncritically. Not surprisingly, then, for Rochester the final confirmation of Antoinette's 'madness' occurs during the voyage to England when, 'lost' on the way to England – perhaps becalmed on the Sargasso Sea – he witnesses what he sees as her attempt to seduce the steward who brings her food. Interestingly, the episode is told from Antoinette's point of view during her incarceration at Thornfield:

> We lost our way to England. When? Where? I don't remember, but we lost it. Was it that evening in the cabin when he found me talking to the young man who brought me my food? I put my arms round his neck and asked him to help me. He said, 'I don't know what to do, sir.' I smashed the glasses and plates against the porthole. I hoped it would break and the sea come in. (p.148)

Typically, Rhys abstains from any narrative judgement as to whether Antoinette is, in fact, attempting to seduce the steward or whether she is a 'good' or a 'bad' woman. Conversely, Elgin Mellown's description of her as a 'frustrated nymphomaniac'[28] clearly betrays his position as a male reader; no doubt Rhys would have been alive to the irony that there is no corresponding pathological term with which to describe such behaviour in men. Antoinette's desires, unconstrained by English convention, express themselves as a wish to be merged with the sea, but for Rochester such behaviour goes beyond the bounds of what is normal in a woman and is seen as madness. He intends to 'civilise' her, just as the Europeans 'civilised' Jamaica. Significantly, Rochester obliquely expresses his need to control Antoinette's desires by drawing a house in which she is contained:

> I drank some more rum and, drinking, I drew a house surrounded by trees. A large house. I divided the third floor into rooms and in one room I drew a standing woman – a child's scribble, a dot for a head, a larger one for the body, a triangle for a skirt, slanting lines for arms and feet. But it was an English house. (p.135)

If Antoinette's desires cannot be confined to marriage and monogamy, then she will be more literally contained in the house: shut up in the attic on the third floor. This is something of which Antoinette herself has already had a visionary glimpse: 'I must know more than I know already. For I know that house where I will be cold and not belonging, the bed I shall lie in has red curtains and I have slept there many times before, long ago' (p.92). This is the dark side of her dream of England, which is otherwise built out of pictures like that of 'The Miller's Daughter' and 'chandeliers and dancing . . . swans and roses and snow. And snow' (p.92). (Christophine's appraisal of England is, of course, much more sceptical: '"I hear it cold to freeze your bones and they thief your money, clever like the devil"' (p.92).)

Thus, in *Wide Sargasso Sea*, the control of woman in the private house is implicitly linked to authoritarianism in the political sphere, as it is in Woolf's *Three Guineas*. For Rhys, heterosexual relationships are always a battle ground. The relationship between man and woman is a power struggle in which one term is privileged at the expense of the other; as such it is implicitly linked with the wider political scenario of colonisation and imperialism.[29] The marriage between Rochester and Antoinette becomes, then, a fight to the death in which neither can comprehend the other's physical and mental landscapes. Rochester's decision to return to England suggests both a desire to escape from a land which breathes sensuality like Antoinette's body and a need to control and contain an eroticism which suggests autonomous pleasure and political subversion. Here, Rochester – with the law on his side – is determined to make Antoinette his subject, even if it means destroying her identity. And indeed, as her narrative progresses, Antoinette becomes more and more like a doll – a 'marionetta' (p.127) as Rochester calls her – or a ghost; unreal, insubstantial, without identity: 'Names matter, like when he wouldn't call me Antoinette, and I saw Antoinette drifting out of the window with her scents, her pretty clothes and her looking-glass' (p.147). Winning the battle, Rochester himself also comes to see her in this light:

> I saw the hate go out of her eyes. I forced it out. And with the hate her beauty. She was only a ghost. A ghost in the grey daylight. Nothing left but hopelessness. *Say die and I will die. Say die and watch me die.* (p.140)

(Rochester's victory here is, of course obliquely undermined by the fact that in Rhys's text he has no name; he may, or may not, be Rochester.) As the struggle between them becomes more bitter, their misconceptions about each other's land intensify:

> 'Is it true,' she said, 'that England is like a dream? Because one of my friends who married an Englishman wrote and told me so. She said this place London is like a cold dark dream sometimes. I want to wake up.'
>
> 'Well,' I answered annoyed, 'that is precisely how your beautiful island seems to me, quite unreal and like a dream.' (p.67)

However, for the reader, Antoinette's incarceration at Thornfield is an appropriate metaphor for the less tangible oppressions she has formerly experienced; similarly the reader learns much about Rochester's psychology through his relationship with the exotic landscape of the West Indies. Presumably because of his socialisation, Rochester can only function competently within certain tightly defined relationships; the anarchic quality of human intercourse which he encounters in the West Indies renders him both emotionally numb and savage. His brusque rejection of the young servant boy's loyalty and affection, for example, suggests that he feels threatened by unconditional love: 'That stupid boy followed us, the basket balanced on his head. He used the back of his hand to wipe away his tears. Who would have thought that any boy would cry like that. For nothing. Nothing' (p.142). Suspicious of West Indian culture, Rochester views it as primitive and pagan. Yet, according to a definition he finds in a book on the area, he has become perilously like a zombi himself: 'A zombi is a dead person who seems to be alive or a living person who is dead' (p.88). Indeed, twice he is closely associated with zombis: at one point Amélie announces to Antoinette '"Your husban' he outside the door and he look like he see zombi"' (p.83); shortly after this a small girl in the forest actually mistakes Rochester for one: 'to my astonishment she screamed loudly, threw up her arms and ran' (p.87). 'There are always two deaths, the real one and the one people know about' (p.106) according to Antoinette; the nightmare figure of the zombi in *Wide Sargasso Sea* is a projection of Rochester's deepest subconscious fears. He is fearful of the landscape of Antoinette's body which, like the landscape of Jamaica, threatens his socially constructed 'masculine' self. The sensuality of both Antoinette's body and her land disrupt and undermine the binary opposition which equates active sexual desire with 'masculinity' and sexual passivity with the 'feminine' in Victorian England. Thus Rochester's own identity is undermined by his experiences in the West Indies since they threaten a sexual polarity essential to his sense of self. Having unconsciously glimpsed what he has lost by being socialised in a particular way ('all my life would be . . . longing for what I had lost before I found it' (p.141)), he nevertheless forecloses on that longing and desire by a return to England, which will reinstate and reaffirm his 'masculine' sense of self. The figure of the zombi thus suggests not only his deepest fears, but also the death of such desires.

Antoinette experiences a similar state of internal numbness and despair which represents the destruction of her longings and desires. Her misery transforms her: 'Her hair hung uncombed and dull into her eyes which were inflamed and staring, her face was very flushed and looked swollen. Her feet were bare. However when she spoke her voice was low, almost inaudible' (p.120). This is the stasis – or Sargasso Sea – on Antoinette's voyage in the dark. Numb with pain, she withdraws into a state of autism and blank indifference: 'She was there in the *ajoupa*; carefully dressed for the journey, I noticed, but her face blank, no expression at all' (p.137). She is 'marooned' between life and death; powerless to move, caught in a state of stasis in which outside forces control and manoeuvre her. Here, in her final novel, Rhys has translated the symptoms of hysterical passivity and muteness, which themselves act as metaphors for a state of alienation in her earlier novels, into a metaphor of place. There is thus a double metaphor at work in the notion of being 'marooned' in the Sargasso Sea: woman's sense of alienation is expressed through physical dis-ease, which is then caught up in a metaphor of topography. The result is the conflation of the body's desires with the landscape itself. The archetypal image of the voyage as quest and fulfilment is therefore ironically subverted in this novel; the Sargasso Sea, 'dangerous to navigation' (*The Voyage Out*, p.38), becomes an image for the denial of desire. The several distinctive threads of metaphor which run through Rhys's work are thus here brought to a subtle and triumphant conclusion.

The novel closes with Antoinette, now the mad wife of Charlotte Brontë's Rochester, confined to a room at the top of Thornfield in a cold and grey England. For the women servants of the household, Grace Poole, Mrs Eff and Leah, 'the house is big and safe, a shelter from the world outside which, say what you like, can be a black and cruel world to a woman' (p.146). Not only do these women accept the constraints which rooms and houses – metaphors for discourse and ideology – inflict upon them, they collude with them and are shown, like the women who guard over Rachel Vinrace during her illness, as being the jailers of the young heroine.

For Antoinette, however, who still craves another way of being, the house is a prison and the room deprives her of her proper identity:

> There is one window high up – you cannot see out of it. My bed had doors but they have been taken away. There is not much else in the room . . .
>
> There is no looking-glass here and I don't know what I am like now . . . What am I doing in this place and who am I? (p.147)

Deprived of light and reflection, Antoinette 'lives in her own darkness' (p.146), a phrase which suggests, as Kathy Mezei has noted, that 'Her attic is not England, a place, but a configuration of her mind, an enclosure.'[30] All she has to remind her of her past self is the red dress which, 'the colour of fire and sunset' and smelling 'of vetivert and frangipanni, of cinnamon and dust and lime trees when they are flowering' (p.151), suggests another landscape; it also, significantly, evokes memories of her love and sexual desire for Sandi: 'I was wearing a dress of that colour when Sandi came to see me for the last time' (p.151); 'I took the red dress down and put it against myself. "Does it make me look intemperate and unchaste?" I said' (p.152).

Antoinette's 'other self' has been destroyed by Rochester and England; she is now merely a ghost who haunts a house filled with ghosts; in her turn she becomes a destroyer and asserts a terrible autonomy. It is a logical culmination to all the agonies and oppressions suffered by Julia, Anna and Sasha; by Aunt Cora and Antoinette's mother; by the black people of the West Indies; by all those ghostly women of Thornfield. The narrative, which becomes dream-like and conflates past and future, subverts linear sequence: Antoinette dreams of the fire which she will start as Bertha Mason yet it is also the fire that burnt down her mother's house. Her scream as she wakes becomes, for Grace Poole, a scream she must have dreamt she heard. The line between past and present, waking and dreaming, has been erased. Antoinette, having been marooned between light and dark, life and death, has escaped the still waters and is on the last lap of her journey. Suddenly her purpose is clear:

> Now at last I know why I was brought here and what I have to do. There must have been a draught for the flame flickered and I thought it was out. But I shielded it with my hand and it burned up again to light me along the dark passage. (pp.155–6)

The fire at Thornfield will be a recreation of the colour and the heat which was once a part of herself; more importantly, it allows her metaphorically to reclaim the landscape of the West Indies as her proper terrain:

> Then I turned round and saw the sky. It was red and all my life was in it. I saw the grandfather clock and Aunt Cora's patchwork, all colours, I saw the orchids and the stephanotis and the jasmine and the tree of life in flames. (p.155)

The fire will also destroy the boundaries which have separated her from Tia and Christophine, so that, in her dream, she calls 'Tia!' before she jumps. These boundaries are metaphorically represented by Thornfield itself; in burning it down she will, as Sue Roe points out, burn down 'all the partitions in her head which have prevented her from seeing herself, and from recognising the implications of her own desires'.[31] This moment of insight and triumph is, however, also the final leap into the dark abyss of death and madness; to burn down 'all the partitions' in the head is also to destroy oneself – at least that is the case for the Bertha Mason of Charlotte Brontë's novel. Significantly, in Jean Rhys's work, what we have is not the act of burning down Thornfield (although it is often read as if this were the case) but the *dream* of that act. The actual fire, like the sea of the title, is absent from the text; we have only a dream of the fire and the presence of absence for the sea: '"The sea was not far off but we never heard it, we always heard the river. No sea"' (p.108) says Antoinette of her childhood home. The critique of discourse and ideology which both fire and sea metaphorically represent in this text is, therefore, the text's 'secret'.[32] Rhys's alienation from patriarchy, like that of her heroines, is repressed: in her heroines such alienation manifests itself in symptoms of hysteria; in her novels it emerges in the cipher of metaphor which itself speaks of repression. Significantly, then, the figure of the woman as artist is excluded from Rhys's work as part of that same pattern of repression. In contrast with Woolf's work, which affirms the emergence of the woman artist and implicitly endorses Woolf's own vision, Rhys's novels express a fundamental dis-ease with the notion of herself as both woman and writer. In a letter to Peggy Kirkaldy, Rhys confessed: 'I never wanted to write. I wished to be happy and peaceful and obscure. I was *dragged* into writing by a series of coincidences – Mrs. Adam, Ford, Paris – need for money.'[33] This sense of dis-ease with herself as a writing woman is echoed by the narrator of the short story, 'The day they burned the books', who conjures up Caribbean society's attitude to the woman artist in a blackly humorous manner: 'by a flicker in Mrs Sawyer's eyes I knew that worse than men who wrote books were women who wrote books – infinitely worse. Men could be mercifully shot; women must be tortured' (*Tigers Are Better Looking*, p.41).

An internal dialogue in the unfinished autobiography, *Smile Please*, betrays Rhys's fear that to write as a woman is necessarily to pose a political threat to the established order and to risk being diagnosed as 'mad':

> *You are aware of course that what you are writing is childish, has been said before. Also it is dangerous under the circumstances.* Yes, most of it is childish. But I have not written for so long that all I can force myself to do is to write, to write. I must trust that out of that will come the pattern, the clue that can be followed.
> *Why is all this dangerous?*
> Because I have been accused of madness. But if everything is in me, good, evil and so on, so must strength be in me if I know how to get at it.
> *This is the way?*
> I think so.
> *All right, but be damned careful not to leave this book about.* (*Smile Please*, pp.163–4)

'Madness' is not here celebrated as a psychic rite of passage, as it is in Margaret Atwood's *Surfacing*; it is, instead, perceived more in the spirit of *The Yellow Wallpaper* and *Mrs Dalloway* as an ambiguous state of pain and insight. Rhys's fear that her writing will lead her into 'madness' is, of course, linked to her characters' experience of hysteria. Adrienne Rich, in her book *On Lies, Secrets and Silence*, neatly sums up the 'double jeopardy' resulting from this state of psychic alienation within patriarchy:

> In all societies women are in double jeopardy; on the one hand we are expected to conform to certain emotional standards in our relationships with others, at the penalty of being declared mad or insane; on the other, our political perceptions can be labeled 'irrational' and 'hysterical'.

> I go on believing in the power of literature, and also in the politics of literature . . . it is the subjects, the conversations, the facts we shy away from, which claim us in the form of writer's block, as mere rhetoric, as hysteria, insomnia, and constriction of the throat.[34]

The terrible difficulty of documenting honestly these 'subjects' and 'conversations' and of exposing the 'mystic boundaries' which constrain woman's sense of self is reflected in the malaise of her heroines and in Rhys's own attitude to writing. In all her works, heterosexual relationships, far from satisfying woman's desire, lead to pain and/or death; this suggests that in her fictional relationships between the sexes, sexual desire and its fulfilment are metonymic of man's cultural supremacy. Rhys offers no political solution to this situation and presumably would not have seen it as the role of the novelist so to do; hence the pessimism and sense of impasse in her work. Hence also the pain, guilt, fear – and hysteria – which surround the act of writing. This, however, according to Juliet Mitchell, is endemic to the experience of writing as a woman within a patriarchal society: 'The woman novelist must be an hysteric. Hysteria . . . is simultaneously what a woman can do both to be feminine and to refuse femininity, within patriarchal discourse.'[35] Recent work by feminist theorists on the cultural meaning of 'hysteria' clearly illuminates both Rhys's fiction and her attitude to herself as writing woman. However, as in Gilman's *The Yellow Wallpaper*, we must carefully distinguish between the female narrator as hysteric (and indicative of woman's dis-ease in a patriarchal society) and the woman writer who, although she may embrace a notional hysteria concerning her art, controls the text in a manner which defies the mute powerlessness so often associated with hysteria as a clinically diagnosed condition.

4
Beyond boundaries and back again: Margaret Atwood's *Surfacing*

Margaret Atwood's *Surfacing* presents us, like Charlotte Perkins Gilman's novella, with a nameless narrator. This narrator is free to be an artist but is shown as compromising her artistic gifts in her career as an illustrator. Although no obvious external barriers hinder the fulfilment of her creative potential she has internalised the judgement of the male world, expressed by a previous lover, that 'there have never been any important woman artists' (p.52)[1] and has conformed accordingly. Like Jean Rhys's marooned women, she feels dislocated from the culture in which she grew up. The daughter of rather eccentric, avowedly pacifist, English-speaking parents who chose to live on the margins of society in rural French Canada, she remembers her family as being 'by reputation, peculiar as well as *anglais*' (p.20). With her lover, Joe, and two married friends, Anna and David, she returns to her home – a log house, or cabin, on an island in one of the large lakes of Northern Quebec – in order to search for her father who seems to have 'simply disappeared' (p.24) into the landscape. Convinced at first that he is still alive and merely away 'on a sort of trip' (p.95), she pursues every clue to his whereabouts. His drawings of Indian rock paintings lead her to dive into the lake: since the flooding of the lake these paintings are now 'twenty feet below water' (p.127). Encountering 'a dead thing', 'a dark oval trailing limbs' (p.142) in the depths of the lake, she surfaces, choking and terrified. This grotesque confrontation with her father's corpse[2] forces her to come to terms not only with his death but with the death she delivered to her own child when, under pressure from her lover, she agreed to have an abortion. Returning to the cabin, she searches for her mother's 'legacy' (p.140) which, unlike her father's, 'had to be inside the house' (p.156) and finds it in one of the scrapbooks: it is the drawing of a pregnant woman 'with a round moon stomach: the baby was sitting up inside her gazing out' (p.158). She then takes Joe outside the cabin where they make love on the ground; she knows that the act has made her pregnant and she feels the 'lost child surfacing within me, forgiving me, rising from the lake' (pp.161–2). When the others return to the mainland for the journey home, she hides and regresses to a state of 'natural' woman, living off berries and feels herself merge with the landscape: 'I am a tree leaning . . . I am a place' (p.181). Only after this period of withdrawal and mystic contemplation does she decide to return to civilisation and her relationship with Joe.

With its wasteland-like scenario (the white birches along the lake are dying from pollution and 'the lake's fished out' (p.28)) and its predilection for religious symbolism (a dead heron is linked to the crucifixion of Christ and the Indian paintings are associated with 'sacred places', 'salvation' and 'truth' (p.145)), Atwood's *Surfacing* is often read as an essentially theological quest.[3] Implicit in this reading is the feminist notion that in a late twentieth-century world which has been almost destroyed by man, only woman can effect the much-needed spiritual transformation whereby harmony, both between man and woman and nature and humanity, can be re-established. Atwood's work thus seems to accord with the views of Adrienne Rich who similarly sees spiritual salvation as the duty and prerogative of women alone, and who urges women to face up to the 'knowledge that men we have nurtured, supported, and done time for were not our spiritual and emotional equals, and that our selfhood, our womanhood itself, has been contemptible or terrifying to them.'[4] Olive Banks argues that this notion of women's spiritual superiority is a characteristic element of the evangelical tradition in feminism which, descending from the temperance movement in England and the United States, claims an innate moral goodness for women.[5] Such a tradition tends also to link women very closely with celebration of the female body, childbirth, and nature; it places responsibility for the next generation with women since they are seen to possess a more sharply defined moral sensibility than men. As such, of course, it is profoundly different from that variety of feminism which concerns itself primarily with the legal and material reformation of society and which derives from Enlightenment thinking (specifically the work of Mary Wollstonecraft) and the suffragettes; this latter type of feminism can be found today in the struggle for equal rights and responsibilities both at work and at home. It is, perhaps, both more pragmatic and accommodating to men and less visionary and uncompromising than radical feminism which in the case of Adrienne Rich, for example, leads to the belief that female psychology is essentially lesbian[6] and to the practice of lesbianism as a form of political commitment.

From our point of view, however, Atwood's book is particularly interesting in that its plot embraces madness, enclosure (the cabin) and immersion in water; significantly, however, this water is not the uncharted space of the sea, but a lake in which floats the dead body of the father. Linked with language and sight as ways of seeing, this configuration comes to take on a metaphoric significance which again probes how the constraints of ideology might seem to create a mutation of a more authentic 'self'. As in the other works examined, however, this sense of another self is the *ignis fatuus* of the text which lures the reader beyond the ending of the novel. The narrator's return to society and the implementation of her new values and vision are left in a wordless future which exists beyond the plot.

Carefully charted in the novel, however, is the spiritual change which takes place in the narrator during her quest for the father. Central to this is her understanding of his drawings which itself results in a re-assessment of her father's refusal to conform. At first, she thinks of him as 'a voluntary recluse' (p.11), a botanist who, 'working for the paper company or the government' (p.79), wanted to 'recreate not the settled farm life of his own father but that of the earliest ones who arrived when there was nothing but forest and no ideologies but the ones they brought with them' (p.59). However, her tendency at this stage to see him through the eyes of others – 'They must find it strange, a man his age staying alone the whole winter in a cabin ten miles from nowhere' (p.58) – suggests that she initially harbours only a very superficial understanding of his quest. This is confirmed by her readiness to label his strange drawings as 'unintelligible' (p.60), and 'lunatic' (p.101). In fact, she privately thinks of him as mad:

> we're leaving tomorrow. My father will have the island to himself: madness is private, I respect that, however he may be living it's better than an institution. (p.67)

> Total derangement. I wondered when it had started; it must have been the snow and the loneliness, he'd pushed himself too far . . . The drawing was something he saw, a hallucination; or it might have been himself, what he thought he was turning into. (p.101)

However, she comes across some correspondence and an article by an academic which indicate that her father's drawings are meticulous copies of Indian rock paintings. The creators of these paintings, the academic article argues, '*were interested exclusively in symbolic content, at the expense of expressiveness and form*' (p.102). The implication is that her father's quest involved deciphering the artistic codes of another race who had 'no ideologies but the ones they brought with them'. We learn later that the weight of his camera pulled him down in the water to his death and this obliquely suggests that the sense of vision demanded by such a quest is not to be found in anything mechanical, but in the mind's eye. The discovery of the 'meaning' of her father's drawings produces a peculiar moment of insight in the narrator who now realises that not only was her father completely sane, but that her knowledge of his sanity has killed him: 'I shouldn't have tried to find out, it's killed him. I had the proof now, indisputable, of sanity and therefore of death' (p.103). A strangely condensed and illogical process leads her to feel guilt for her father's death. She now realises that two options existed: either her father was alive and mad, wandering alone in the area; or, he was sane and dead. The logical explanation for his strange drawings proves her father's sanity, forces her to face up to his death and simultaneously implicates her in it through her earlier denial of his vision. This irrational sense of guilt the narrator feels for her father's death is later followed by an acknowledgement of her complicity in both the death of the heron ('I felt a sickening complicity, sticky as glue, blood on my hands' (p.130)) and that of her unborn child ('Whatever it is, part of myself or a separate creature, I killed it' (p.143)).

It is no accident, then, that during her retreat into nature, the narrator associates the transubstantiation of the heron with the changes taking place inside her own pregnant body: 'I remember the heron; by now it will be insects, frogs, fish, other herons. My body also changes, the creature in me, plant-animal, sends out filaments in me; I ferry it secure between death and life, I multiply' (p.168). Both bird and child are offered the possibility of resurrection through her retreat from sanity and civilisation into a state of 'madness' and nature. At the same moment that she understands the nature of her father's disappearance, the narrator realises that she is dead inside – 'I didn't feel much of anything, I hadn't for a long time' (p.105) – and his death triggers an awareness of her own state of numbness and alientation: 'It was no longer his death but my own that concerned me' (p.107). Like Antoinette Cosway, she has come to realise that 'There are always two deaths, the real one and the one people know about' (*Wide Sargasso Sea*, p.106). His drawings now become the map of a quest which will restore her to life so that she can 'surface' into feeling and being again; the implication is that only by following her father's footsteps into isolation will she be able to emerge from this state of autism and numbness. In this, her quest resembles the voyage of Antoinette Cosway, whose journey across the Sargasso Sea is also a voyage through and out of a state of mute misery. The many references in *Surfacing* to crossing water in canoes or by portages suggest, as does Antoinette's own name (Cosway evokes causeway[7]), that the journey is not simply a physical one but constitutes a rite of passage. The fear of facing and understanding the nature of her own guilt is suggested by the narrator's persistent fear of her father (pp.62, 78, 142), from whom she wishes to protect her friends in order to 'save all of them from knowledge' (p.83). Only gradually does the reader come to understand how the narrator's sense of guilt is linked to her gender and society's attitude to gender.

Crossing the water is, however, not enough, as Antoinette Cosway's tragic end seems to imply. Nor is simply wading at the water's edge (p.75): the narrator has to plumb the lake's depths in her watery quest for another way of seeing. Increasingly, this quest for an alternative perspective is associated with a rejection of narratives and representations that come to seem false. History at school she remembers as an evasion of the truth: 'a long list of wars and treaties and alliances, people taking and losing power over other people; but nobody would ever go into the motives, why they wanted it, whether it was good or bad' (p.97). It did not bear close scrutiny as an accurate narrative of the human condition: 'If you put your eye down close to the photograph (of the 'generals' and 'the historic moments') they disintegrated into grey dots' (p.98).

More important, the narrator comes to realise that her own social conditioning has involved a cultural inscription of the 'feminine' which distorts woman into something artificial, a doll for men to play with. She looks with distaste at a photograph of herself as a 1950s teenager: 'myself in the stiff dresses, crinolines and tulle, layered like store birthday cakes; I was civilized at last, the finished product' (p.108). Anna, with her terror of being seen without her make-up, is a typical product of this period which, after the stringencies and equalities brought by the Second World War, returned women to the kitchen whilst elevating Marilyn Monroe as the archetype of the desirable woman. The narrator recognises how such a fantasy keeps women child-like; she sees Anna as mirroring her own behaviour 'at sixteen' (p.51) and thinks of her friend as frozen in a state of constant adolescence. Describing Anna as 'a seamed and folded imitation of a magazine picture that is itself an imitation of a woman who is also an imitation' (p.165) she comes to realise that her friend is 'locked into' this fantasy which a man controls 'at the other end of the room' (p.165). Looking at her childhood drawings of 'Ladies in exotic costumes, sausage rolls of hair across their foreheads, with puffed red mouths and eyelashes like toothbrush bristles' (p.42) she acknowledges that she also once believed that life should be 'a slavery of pleasure' (p.43). She comes to see that she has colluded with that fantasy in her own work as an illustrator of children's fairy stories. She regularly produces drawings in which the princess has an 'emaciated fashion-model torso and infantile face' (p.53); struggling to illustrate *The Tale of the Golden Phoenix*, however, she finds that this fantasy refuses to materialise under her fingers and, instead, the princess is 'crosseyed and has one breast bigger than the other' (p.54). A further attempt results in a princess 'sprouting an enormous rear' who turns into a werewolf on the page (p.57). Her growing iconoclasm refuses to let her subscribe to these cultural stereotypes any longer; like Edna Pontellier in *The Awakening*, she rejects an art that seems to lie and destroys it. Caught up in a process of spiritual transformation herself, she now sees that the metamorphosis in *The Tale of the Golden Phoenix* changes and challenges nothing but merely preserves the status quo:

> I snap the catches on my case and take out the drawings and the typescript, *Quebec Folk Tales*, it's easily replaceable for them in the city, and my bungled princesses, the Gold Phoenix awkward and dead as a mummified parrot. The pages bunch in my hands; I add them one by one so the fire will not be smothered, then the paint tubes and the brushes, this is no longer my future. (p.176)

The influence of these false social narratives are obliquely linked with poor vision and inappropriate language: 'I was seeing poorly, translating badly, a dialect problem, I should have used my own' (p.76). Significantly, being on the pill (which produces a false pattern of menstruation) interfered with her sight: 'It was like having vaseline on my eyes' (p.79). One of the most mendacious narratives in the novel is the film sequence, *Random Samples*, being made by David and Joe. Supposedly catching 'real' life spontaneously by juxtaposing shots of disparate events and things in a random manner, it actually charts their manipulation of women (Anna is forced to strip for one sequence) and their fascination with the bizarre and the absurd. This film is destroyed by the narrator who unwinds it and lets it fall into the lake, so that 'hundreds of tiny naked Annas [are] no longer bottled and shelved' (p.166); this image recalls the aborted foetus and also suggests Anna's stunted emotional and spiritual growth. The film sequence is false for the narrator partly because it contains a male inscription of female sexuality which sees women as creatures whose function is to assuage men's lust.

Further cultural inscriptions of this nature are to be found in her memories of the drawings in the abandoned tugboat which, she now realises, like cave paintings, carried their own kind of magic: 'You draw on the wall what's important to you, what you're hunting' (p.120). What is being hunted in contemporary Canadian culture is woman herself; her sexual organs have become, for men, something both obscene and to be relished:

> I thought they were plants or fish, some of them were shaped by clams, but my brother laughed, which meant he knew something I didn't; I nagged at him until he explained. I was shocked, not by those parts of the body, we'd been told about those, but that they should be cut off like that from the bodies that ought to have gone with them, as though they could detach themselves and crawl around on their own like snails. (p.119)

Her early ignorance here is reflected later in her blankness at David's joke about the split beaver replacing the maple leaf as Canada's emblem on the national flag:

> He looked exasperated. 'It's a joke', he said; and when I still didn't laugh, 'Where've you been living? It's slang for cunt. The Maple Beaver for ever, that would be neat.' He lowered his line into the water and began to sing, off-key:
>
> In days of yore, from Britain's shore
> Wolfe, the gallant hero, came;

> It spread all o'er the hooerhouse floor
> On Canada's fair domain.
> (p.119)

In this masculine vision of things, then, the landscape itself becomes an iconography of male desire so that plants, fish and beavers become disembodied representations of the female genitalia. Further, the dead heron itself becomes suggestive of the mutilation of the female principle: 'A part of the body, a dead animal. I wondered what part of them the heron was, that they needed so much to kill it' (p.119). Not surprisingly, then, a main feature of the narrator's sense of alienation is her feeling that she exists only as a collection of disparate parts:

> I'd allowed myself to be cut in two. Woman sawn apart in a wooden crate, wearing a bathing suit, smiling, a trick done with mirrors, I read it in a comic book; only with me there had been an accident and I came apart. The other half, the one locked away, was the only one that could live; I was the wrong half, detached, terminal. I was nothing but a head, or no, something minor like a severed thumb; numb. (p.108)

Against these false narratives are other narratives – pictorial sequences which help the narrator towards a resurrection of this 'other half, the one locked away' so that finally the dead heron can be reintegrated into the landscape of her own body with the changes that pregnancy brings. One of the most important of these is the scrapbooks which, appearing to be genuinely 'random' collections of memorabilia, in fact constitute a narrative which both illumines her past and guides her future. Through them she comes to re-assess her brother's drawings which are full of 'weapons' and 'disintegrating soldiers' as a 'more accurate' picture of the world than her own wishful fantasies illustrated by 'rabbits with their coloured egg houses, sun and moon orderly above the flat earth, summer always, I wanted everyone to be happy' (p.131). Having nearly drowned in childhood, this brother has metaphorically plumbed the same depths as her dead father and is ready to face up to his own complicity in a violent world. His pictures, which ambiguously both celebrate the world of masculine aggression and record its all-pervasiveness, force her to face her own passivity in that world. She now undoes the lies that she invented to make her life easier – including the fantasy of having been married, divorced and having abandoned her child. The truth lies in the more murky reality of an affair with a married man who persuaded her to have an abortion. Now she sees that fiction as a 'faked album, the memories fraudulent as passports'; a 'paper house' (p.144) in which she had lived rather than face the reality of her situation. As she re-assesses her own life in this way, the narrator also comes to realise that the warfare and conflict that pervade her brother's childhood drawings are present not only in the mythical war with the Americans about which David constantly fantasises (and in which Canada is the victimised woman writ large) but in every relationship between man and woman:

> Anna was more than sad, she was desperate, her body her only weapon and she was fighting for her life, he was her life, her life was the fight: she was fighting him because if she ever surrendered the balance of power would be broken and he would go elsewhere. To continue the war. (pp.153–4)

Like the narrators of Jean Rhys's novels, the narrator in *Surfacing* comes to see that the relationship between man and woman in the twentieth century has become a power struggle in which one term is privileged at the expense of the other: 'Prove your love, they say. You really want to marry me, let me fuck you instead. You really want to fuck, let me marry you instead. As long as there's a victory, some flag I can wave, parade I can have in my head' (p.87). As well as revealing this disturbing truth, however, the scrapbooks also offer a way out of this cultural impasse. Turning through the pages of one of them, she finds her mother's 'gift' and legacy, one of her own childhood drawings in which man and woman have iconic significance:

> On the left was a woman with a round moon stomach: the baby was sitting up inside her gazing out. Opposite her was a man with horns on his head like cow horns and a barbed tail.

The picture was mine, I had made it. The baby was myself before I was born, the man was God, I'd drawn him when my brother learned in the winter about the Devil and God: if the Devil was allowed a tail and horns, God needed them also, they were advantages.

That was what the picture had meant then but their first meaning was lost now like the meanings of the rock paintings. They were my guides, she had saved them for me, pictographs. I had to read their new meaning with the help of the power. The gods, their likenesses: to see them in their true shape is fatal. While you are human; but after the transformation they could be reached. First I had to immerse myself in the other language. (p.158)

This 'other language' is the language of nature and in order to become fluent in it, she has to divest herself of the language in which she has grown up. She will thereby also be able to shed the cultural inscriptions of masculinity and femininity which patriarchal ideology has constructed through that language. In *Surfacing* films and photographs, which seem so accurate a representation of reality, are revealed as part of the process of ideological interpellation and their fictions exposed as pernicious; the pictographs of the cave paintings and drawings, however, because they are divorced from the conventions of realism, illuminate the mythology through which a culture sustains itself. The meaning of the cave paintings might be lost but as the legacy of an Indian culture, the paintings implicitly suggest a people who lived in harmony with nature; their absence from the text (no one ever sees the actual paintings in the novel) speaks of the annihilation of that culture by a modern and rapacious world. Indeed, as the narrator comes to 'make sense' of her father's drawings, she realises that:

There was no painting at White Birch Lake and none here, because his later drawings weren't copies from things on the rocks. He had discovered new places, new oracles, they were things he was seeing the way I had seen, true vision; at the end, after the failure of logic. When it happened the first time he must have been terrified, it would be like stepping through a usual door

> and finding yourself in a different galaxy, purple trees and red moons and a green sun. (p.145)

The scrapbook drawing will lead the narrator through this same door; she will undergo a transformation in which words will play no part and in which the boundaries effected through language will be broken down. Like the king 'who learnt to speak with animals' in the fairy tale (p.84), she will find a new tongue. A language 'is everything you do' (p.129) comments the narrator; she comes to see that in this culture, 'Language divides us into fragments' (p.146). The narrator believes that by immersing herself in the 'other language' of nature she will thereby be made spiritually 'whole' (p.146). Her own tongue comes to seem strange to her – 'I had to concentrate in order to talk to [David], the English words seemed imported, foreign' (p.150) – as the time for her withdrawal from society comes closer. Later, during her retreat into nature, she overhears some men on the island talking but their language sounds foreign to her: 'It must be either English or French but I can't recognize it as any language I've ever heard or known' (p.184). At the moment of her child's conception, she vows that she 'will never teach it any words' (p.162).

Intimations of the change that the 'other language' can bring about were given to her in childhood; she remembers how, playing hide and seek

> in the semi-dark after supper, it was different from playing in a house, the space to hide in was endless; even when we knew which tree he had gone behind there was the fear that what would come out when you called would be someone else. (p.50)

Frightened of such transformations and associating them at this age with local tales of the *loup-garou*, she comes to realise as she faces her father's death in adulthood that the most profound change is to do with the landscape of the mind: 'it gets in through your eyes, the thin black cold of mid-winter night, the white days dense with sunlight, outer space melting and freezing into different shapes, your mind starts doing the same thing' (p.101). This is the change that she must now brace herself to face. Realising that leaving with Joe will take her back to the metaphoric house of convention ('he will lead me back to the city and tie me to fences, doorknobs' (p.163)), she decides to stay by the lake, although she goes through the charade of packing her 'own . . . caseful of alien words and failed pictures' (p.164) for the trip. Disappearing into the landscape at the moment of departure, she hears the others call her name but 'It's too late, I no longer have a name. I tried for all those years to be civilized but I'm not and I'm through pretending' (p.168). She realises that 'from any rational point of view I am absurd' (p.169) but since her father's death has taught her that 'madness is only an amplification of what you already are' (p.101) this no longer concerns her; what does concern her is the pursuit of 'true vision . . . after the failure of logic' (p.145). As she stands alone, outside the locked cabin, she realises that 'the truth is here' (p.170).

Significantly, the pursuit of this vision also involves both destruction of the cabin and reclamation of its 'space'. As her friends have left it locked up, she has to break in through a window; one of the first things she notices as she climbs in is her mother's leather jacket which, by this stage of the novel, has assumed talismanic qualities. Indeed, at first she regresses to a state of infantile rage at the fact that her parents have died and left her alone: 'They didn't consider how I would feel, who would take care of me' (p.172). Invoking their spirits to 'come out, from wherever it is they are hiding' (p.173), her behaviour begins to suggest the beliefs and mythology of a lost Indian tribe, who learnt wisdom and insight through the presence of their ancestors in nature. Like a shaman figure, however, she must effect a deep transformation of the self before she can achieve contact with these spirit figures. This transformation involves a destruction of the cabin's contents, and all that they metaphorically represent, followed by an immersion in water. As the rain falls heavily during the night the narrator feels that 'the house unmoored and floating like a boat, rocking and rocking' (p.174) has become a vessel for the first part of her spiritual voyage. The next day her first task is to 'clear a space' within the cabin; the most important dimension of this 'space' is, of course, its psychic element. Her task takes on the quality of ritual, again suggesting a culture fundamentaily different from the secular Canadian civilisation in which she has grown up: 'If I do everything in the right order, if I think of nothing else. What sacrifice, what do they want?' (p.176). The awareness that her own culture has provided her with faulty spiritual vision is expressed in her rejection of the cabin's windows and its mirror: 'There are too many windows . . . I must stop being in the mirror . . . Not to see myself but to see' (p.175). Further, this desire 'to see' results in a destruction of everything which presents a barrier between the narrator and her spirit parents. First she burns her recent drawings, next her false wedding ring, then the scrapbooks of her childhood with their pictures of moons, rabbits and eggs, 'my false peace' (p.176). She then destroys her guide – the drawing of 'the miraculous double woman and the god with horns', the pictures of 'ladies on the wall . . . with their watermelon breasts and lampshade skirts', her father's rock paintings and the photograph album (p.177).

As the photographic representations of herself and her parents all curl into the same ashy blackness, she realises that 'It is time that separates us, I was a coward, I would not let them into my age, my place. Now I must enter theirs' (p.177). The final task is to destroy symbolically both clothes, which separate the self from nature and metaphorically suggest role-playing, and language, which enacts ideology through discourse. To this end, the narrator tears one page from each book in the cabin, since 'to burn through all the words would take too long' and, with a big kitchen knife, rips through the bedclothes, her father's felt hat and the beloved grey leather jacket which belonged to her mother: 'these husks are not needed any longer' (p.177). She is now ready to become 'a natural woman' (p.190); she steps over the many psychological boundaries that the cabin represents as she steps over its threshold, taking with her only a blanket: 'I will need it until the fur grows' (p.177). Like Edna Pontellier in *The Awakening*, her rejection of such boundaries is expressed by a stripping away of all clothes and an embrace of water. For this heroine, however, immersion in water does not mean physical death, only the death of the old self; she arises from the water as from a ceremony of baptism:

> I untie my feet from the shoes and walk down to the shore; the earth is damp, cold, pockmarked with raindrops. I pile the blanket on the rock and step into the water and lie down. When every part of me is wet I take off my clothes, peeling them away from my flesh like wallpaper. They sway beside me, inflated, the sleeves bladders of air.
>
> My back is on the sand, my head rests against the rock, innocent as plankton; my hair spreads out, moving and fluid in the water. The earth rotates, holding my body down to it as it holds the moon; the sun pounds in the sky, red flames and rays pulsing from it, searing away the wrong form that encases me, dry rain soaking through me, warming the blood egg I carry. I dip my head beneath the water, washing my eyes.
>
> When I am clean I come up out of the lake, leaving my false body floated on the surface, a cloth decoy; it jiggles in the waves I make, nudges gently against the rock. (p.178)

Committing herself to a psychic state of animism, in which even the slashed blanket is described as 'wounded' (p.177), the narrator gives herself up entirely to nature and leaves the world of the cabin behind her: 'The food in the cabin is forbidden, I'm not allowed to go back into that cage, wooden rectangle' (p.178). Indeed, the very next day she finds that 'they' have also forbidden her entry to the garden, 'where the food is' (p.179) since land so marked out stands metaphorically for borders and boundaries:

> The garden is a stunt, a trick. It could not exist without the fence.
>
> Now I understand the rule. They can't be anywhere that's marked out, enclosed: even if I opened the doors and fences they could not pass in, to houses and cages, they can move only in the spaces between them, they are against borders. (p.180)

Sleeping on dry leaves and eating vegetables and berries, she begins to take the wildness of the land into herself so that it comes to express her as yet unarticulated desires: 'Around me the space rustles; owl sound, across the lake or inside me, distance contracts. A light wind, the small waves talking against the shore, multilingual water' (p.178). Free from the constraints of one language and all that it carries with it in terms of ideology, the water is many-tongued and suggests a dissolution of the boundaries effected by culture and discourse. Gradually even the landscape itself seems imbued by water and its 'other language': 'everything is made of water, even the rocks. In one of the languages there are no nouns, only verbs held for a longer moment. The animals have no need for speech, why talk when you are a word' (p.180).

Only when she has reached this other level of consciousness is the narrator allowed contact with her spirit parents; in a vision she sees her mother 'wearing her grey leather jacket . . . her hair . . . down to her shoulders in the style of thirty years ago' standing in front of the cabin feeding the birds as she did in her life (p.182). As the narrator approaches, her mother vanishes, seeming simply to disappear into the landscape, becoming one of the jays cawing from the nearby trees. The next day, having evaded capture by a boatload of men visiting the island, she sees her father. Somehow she knows that he now accepts his own complicity with a culture that has over-valued logic and has become divisive; this is metaphorically expressed by his rejection of fences and borders:

> He is standing near the fence with his back to me, looking in at the garden . . .
>
> He has realized that he was an intruder; the cabin, the fences, the fires and paths were violations; now his own fence excludes him, as logic excludes love. He wants it ended, the borders abolished, he wants the forest to flow back into the places his mind cleared: reparation. (p.186)

As he turns towards her, however, she sees that it is not her father, but 'what my father saw, the thing you meet when you've stayed here too long alone' (p.187). What she sees is the *loup-garou* which has haunted the text as a gothic inscription of repressed fear and insight: 'it gazes at me for a time with its yellow eyes, wolf's eyes' (p.187). Like her mother who is now part of the landscape as a jay, her father has become absorbed into the natural world as a wolf-figure. Her ancestors, like those of the Indians, have never left her but live on around her in the natural world: 'I see now that although it isn't my father it is what my father has become. I knew he wasn't dead' (p.187). These two visitations are followed by a mystical awareness of how a fish in the lake can be not only itself, but can also live in the abstract idea of fish as well as in the representation which art affords. Finally the fish returns to itself: 'It hangs in the air suspended, flesh turned to icon, he has changed again, returned to the water. How many shapes can he take' (p.187). Together with her visions of her parents, this mystical experience breaks down the boundaries of a culture which, through language and the language of logic, seeks to divide and fragment experience. Carrying overtones of the Christian religion with its fish symbolism and the Eucharistic nature of Christ, it merges the animist philosophy of the Indians with the beliefs of Christianity in a mystic vision of harmony and transubstantiation.

The following night the narrator dreams of her parents and, realising that they 'have gone finally, back into the earth, the air, the water, wherever they were when I summoned them' (p.188), she now senses that she can return to the paths offered by civilisation: 'The rules are over. I can go anywhere now, into the cabin, into the garden, I can walk on the paths' (p.188). She has had her vision; her parents have spoken to her 'in the other language' (p.188) and she must now return to normal life, albeit profoundly changed. She accepts full responsibility for her own behaviour and puts transcendentalism and mysticism behind her; she now also fully understands the nature of her guilt. She has come to realise that her vision of the world, rooted first in sentimentality and later in passive nonconformity, has led to her own victimisation: 'This above all, to refuse to be a victim. Unless I can do that I can do nothing. I have to recant, give up the old belief that I am powerless and because of it nothing I can do will ever hurt anyone' (p.191).

Realising that the mirror shows her appearance to match the stereotype of the madwoman, 'straws in the hair, talking nonsense or not talking at all' (p.190), she puts her own clothes back on and re-enters her own time. At that moment Paul's boat carrying Joe back to the island arrives and, hearing Joe call her name, she re-assesses their relationship in the light of her recent experiences. Seeing him as a kind of mediator, and knowing that he will take her back to 'captivity in any of its forms' or perhaps a 'new freedom' (p.192) the narrator vows that they will try for change and growth. The metaphorical boundaries suggested by the room and the house are to be rejected, although she foresees that the culture in which they move offers little hope for alternative lifestyles beyond those boundaries:

> If I go with him we will have to talk, wooden houses are obsolete, we can no longer live in spurious peace by avoiding each other, the way it was before, we will have to begin. For us it's necessary, the intercession of words; and we will probably fail, sooner or later, more or less painfully. That's normal, it's the way it happens now. (p.192)

Against this pessimism about the relationships between men and women lies the real hope for the future: her unborn child whose consciousness, in its watery fluidity, is as yet unfixed by language and culture:

> But I bring with me from the distant past five nights ago the time-traveller, the primaeval one who will have to learn, shape of a goldfish now in my belly, undergoing its watery changes. Word furrows potential already in its proto-brain, untravelled paths. No god and perhaps not real, even that is uncertain; I can't know yet, it's too early. But I assume it; if I die it dies, if I starve it starves with me. It might be the first one, the first true human; it must be born, allowed. (p.191)

Atwood's *Surfacing* has, therefore, the same configuration of metaphor as its structuring principle as the other works discussed in *Landscapes of Desire*. The novel can thus be seen as part of the continuing quest by women writers for an alternative vision of society through which the fixity of the dominant discourse is questioned. However, although the novel attempts to dissolve contemporary cultural inscriptions of womanhood and leave the reconstruction of the self open for future generations, it implicitly looks backwards to a previous generation and the Indian culture in order to find models as guidelines for this reconstruction. In this sense it resurrects and positively re-affirms previous cultural inscriptions of the feminine and the 'natural'. In so doing, it limits the sense of openness that the sea metaphorically carries in other texts and closes off certain other possible constructions of the self; the past, like the lake, is dredged for new templates of being. *Surfacing* offers an alternative construct of woman which can be embraced by contemporary women; it is therefore a more overtly political and didactic work than the other texts examined in *Landscapes of Desire*. The use of the parents as avatars connects the narrator to both the Indian culture and a vision of woman as 'naturally' good because she lives in an harmonious relationship with nature. The animism of the Indian culture, which is perhaps the hidden meaning of the rock paintings, suggests in the novel a people who lived in a rich and spiritually rewarding relationship with nature. Able to inscribe their own fears and beliefs on the landscape around them, they exist in the text as shadowy polar opposites to the men of the modern world who have overvalued the importance of logic as a way of understanding; even her own father was a very logical man and we learn that he admired 'the eighteenth century rationalists' (p.38). Men have therefore degenerated spiritually so that now they are 'halfway to machine' (p.184). The meaning of this textual opposition seems to be that 'logic excludes love' (p.186), a principle which implicitly affirms the value of emotion over intellect and that of the female above the male.

This principle, however, resurrects a cultural inscription of woman which ultimately limits possibilities for women; indeed, it is one that has been used in the past to justify male supremacy. It is a principle which was revived by radical feminism in the 1960s and 1970s and it has left its mark on Atwood's text. This type of radical feminism, as Olive Banks has pointed out, derives from the evangelical temperance women's movement of the nineteenth century and, as such, it tends to glorify 'woman in her maternal role' and look to her 'in her specifically feminine attributes to reform the world'.[8] If we examine the narrator's mother as an exemplar of this philosophy, we can see that she stands as a polar opposite to Anna in the text. Associated always with her dusty old leather jacket she is oblivious to her appearance and devoid of vanity, unlike Anna who defines herself by male response to her beauty. Brave and dignified in the face of death, she 'hated hospitals and doctors' – and, by implication, all modern technology. In this, she both echoes and influences her daughter's attitudes; the narrator rejects technological interference in childbirth ('you might as well be a dead pig, your legs are up in a metal frame, they bend over you, technicians, mechanics, butchers' (p.80)) and vows that when she gives birth, she will 'do it by myself, squatting, on old newspapers in a corner alone; or on leaves, dry leaves, a heap of them, that's cleaner. The baby will slip out easily as an egg' (p.162). Once again, Atwood's work accords with that of Adrienne Rich, who has analysed motherhood as a political institution and who states that: 'medical technology has . . . become a means of alienating women from the act of giving birth, hence from their own bodies, their own procreative powers, and of keeping birth itself so far as possible in male control.'[9]

The mother, then, is associated with what is 'natural', unlike Anna who is always linked with the artificial. She is seen frequently as a female St Francis figure, feeding the jays which she has tamed; in her death she is likened to a bird, 'hands on the sheet curled like bird claws clinging to a perch' (p.22) and after her death she exists as a bird spirit for the narrator. We learn that she kept sunflower seeds in the pockets of her leather jacket (p.43), that she compared the advent of the seasons in her diary (p.22), and that she would on some days 'simply vanish' into the forest (p.52). Initially rejecting her mother's affinity with nature – 'Impossible to be like my mother, it would need a time warp' (p.52) – the narrator comes to identify with her values and way of life as she begins to assess the values and lifestyle of her own contemporaries. The mother's closeness to nature has, it is implied, resulted in a benign philosophy of life which 'prohibited cruelty' (p.132). Such a philosophy also, however, involves a reclamation of power which, in the words of Adrienne Rich, 'will begin to speak in us more and more as we repossess our own bodies, including the decision to mother or not to mother, and how, and with whom, and when'.[10] Thus, although she states that Joe is 'good in bed' (p.42), the narrator comes to see him as representative of all men and therefore often rejects his sexual advances: 'I didn't want him in me, sacrilege, he was one of the killers' (p.147). Only when she manipulates him into impregnating her by the light of the moon does she seem to enjoy fully the sexual act. When she hears Anna's orgasmic noises through the walls of the cabin, she equates them with the noise an animal makes when it is caught in a trap and thinks of death. The subtext therefore suggests that heterosexual intercourse is hallowed only by the reproductive function, without which it is degenerate and meaningless. In the narrator's vision of the relationship between the sexes, man comes to be merely the instrument through which woman can effect a matriarchy. Such a vision, of course, endows woman with a 'maternal mystique'[11] which, while offering her an exclusive spirituality, nevertheless ties that spirituality to her reproductive functions and seems to come dangerously close to biological essentialism, despite Carol Christ's claim that the narrator 'transcends the limitations'[12] of both sexes. The problem for many women readers of Atwood's novel is that it seems simply to invert the values of the old sexual mystique. Jan Montefiore has queried the nature of this inversion in recent radical feminist poetry:

> there is something worrying in all these poems about the opposition implied between a bedrock female nature on the one hand, persisting through and in spite of patriarchal culture on the other. This is paradoxically similar to D. H. Lawrence's ideas of 'blood-consciousness': womb and vulva symbolism get privileged instead of the phallus, and his Etruscans are replaced by the women of Dahomey, but the basic notions of eternal sexual principles are very similar.[13]

In its distrust of objects and language, the whole novel

moves towards endorsing symbolism as a form of metaphysical essentialism; the Indian rock paintings within the novel metaphorically communicate this through their creators who were 'interested exclusively in symbolic content, at the expense of expressiveness and form' (p.102). The implication is that there is a 'truth' to be discovered about woman; the narrator has a 'real self' which is restored to her only through a wordless immersion in water and nature. However, if the philosopher Richard Rorty is correct in maintaining that 'the human self is *created* by the use of a vocabulary rather than being adequately or inadequately *expressed* in a vocabulary' (our italics),[14] then the pursuit of a 'real self' outside the realm of language is a false quest and is doomed to failure. In this sense, the death of the heroine in several other texts we have examined is quite logical: the metaphorical meaning of water (the inexpressible) as non-being leads her to choose death rather than continue to be confined within the boundaries of discourse and ideology. In the case of *Surfacing*, the quest for a 'real self' *seems* to lead the narrator into the realm of the inexpressible, metaphorically imaged in so many texts by the sea, but in fact it does not do so. Instead, it leads her to a lake which contains the dead father, metaphorically the pool of history and past meanings. The recovery of the dead father, as well as the dead mother, could be read as a metaphoric embrace of androgyny. This reading is itself undermined, however, by the identification of each parent with a fixed gender identity rendered as metaphysical 'truth' through a mystic epiphany: the father becomes a source of vision whilst the mother embodies the giving and nurturing of life. Such an epiphany actually endorses previous cultural inscriptions of woman, unlike the work of Gilman, Chopin and Woolf. *Surfacing* was therefore a contribution to the woman's movement which looked to the past for inspiration. The most recent text examined in *Landscapes of Desire*, it is also the most nostalgic.

Conclusion

We have seen that the ways in which women writers use the room/sea configuration of metaphor are variable and may not be reduced to a formula. The historical placing of texts is one element which seems to determine the pattern. Atwood's novel appears to be very much the product of the early 1970s which saw a huge revival of feminism in the women's movement. This movement itself contained many types of feminism, including the radical feminism which seems to inform the vision of Atwood's narrator and which goes unchallenged by any ironic perspective. At a period when women were actively seeking new ways to live their lives and writing fictions which attempted to change lives,[1] *Surfacing* offered a way into the future. Atwood's novel springs from a precise historical moment and her use of the metaphorical configuration of room, house/landscape, water has been influenced accordingly. This is also true, of course, of the other works we have discussed in *Landscapes of Desire*. The American novels of the 1890s derive from a decade of great change in the status of women, marked particularly by the energetic fight for women's suffrage; as such they are the products of a time which fiercely questioned the social, political and economic constraints placed upon women. Woolf's *Mrs Dalloway* and her *To the Lighthouse* were written during the 1920s; Jean Rhys's *Voyage in the Dark* and *Good Morning, Midnight*, during the 1930s. These were lean years for feminism, as Olive Banks explains:

> in the years between 1920 and the 1950s many of the issues that had been of central concern to nineteenth-century feminists had

> almost disappeared from view. In part this was because the success of many equal rights campaigns led a lot of feminists to believe that the battle was over. By the 1920s not only was the vote won, or virtually won, but women had succeeded in opening most of the doors not only to higher education but to professional associations . . . The unemployment of the 1930s, which certainly harmed women's opportunities . . . had the effect of depressing feminist aspirations, and these were years in which feminism as both an ideology and a movement began seriously to decline.[2]

Deirdre Beddoe's more recent work, *Back to Home and Duty: Women between the wars, 1918–1939*, confirms Banks's findings. She notes that 'it is important to distinguish between the 1920s and the 1930s: feminism in the 1920s, though diminished from its mass suffrage campaign days, was still alive and kicking: by the 1930s it is hard to find traces of it.'[3]

Woolf's fictional treatment of women's aspirations probes the more insidious and less obvious boundaries which deny women true autonomy. Her novels, eschewing the complacency which followed votes for women, therefore articulate feminist concerns in a particularly subtle manner. Her sophisticated use of the metaphorical configuration of room, house/landscape, sea is an essential element in that subtlety of style and structure. Conversely, writing in the 1930s, Jean Rhys seems to repress feminist notions in her novels just as society at large was doing in its political and social discourses – only for them to emerge metaphorically in her use of room, landscape and sea. As we have seen, symptoms of hysteria in her female characters suggest their dis-ease in society, and the rooms which they inhabit, the constraints which face them. Only in *Wide Sargasso Sea*, significantly published much later in 1966, does she resolve the metaphoric impasse reached in the earlier novels; she does so by translating the hysteria of her women characters into the stasis of the Sargasso Sea, so that finally the landscape itself expresses metaphorically the repressed desires of woman's mind and body. Atwood's novel, published in 1972, springs out of what Banks describes as 'the heady optimism of the early 1970s'[4] and embraces a radical feminism which seemed, at that time, to offer a spiritual direction to women of the late twentieth century; since then, however, the biological essentialism enshrined in such a vision has been seen by many women as limiting rather than liberating.

We can see, then, that the configuration of room, house/landscape, sea has been used differently by the different writers whose works are discussed in *Landscapes of Desire*. What is striking, however, is the constancy with which that configuration recurs in writing by women as a structuring principle of the text; *Landscapes of Desire* has presented only a small sample of numerous works shaped in this way. The value of this configuration has been to probe metaphorically the limits of ideology and the way it expresses itself through discourse; in this sense it embraces what Richard Rorty describes as 'a willingness to face up to the *contingency* of the language we use'.[5] Going on to argue that this contingency leads to 'a recognition of the contingency of conscience', he suggests that both recognitions 'lead to a picture of intellectual and moral progress as a history of increasingly useful metaphors rather than of increasing understanding of how things really are'.[6] We do not, however, subscribe to Rorty's sense of language as a self-sufficient medium; rather, we would argue that the room/sea configuration of metaphor has contributed to a profound 'understanding of how things really are' by questioning the fixity of the dominant discourse which has sought to render femininity as natural and unproblematic. In order to understand this metaphorical dimension of women's writing we need to draw on both what Janet Todd calls the 'presence of history' for author and work and on our own experience as women and women readers in the late twentieth century.

It has been the thesis of this book that the landscape of desire mapped out in the binary opposition of room, house/landscape, sea has become 'an increasingly useful' metaphor in modern women's fiction. In representing the opposition between fixity and fluidity, it foregrounds the way in which metaphor itself is unstable; thus 'the contingency of language' is a recurrent theme in all the texts we have examined. Far from detracting from a notional aesthetic unity, however, the accommodating nature of metaphor gives these texts a richness and complexity which we, as women readers, are now beginning to appreciate more fully.

Notes

Introduction

1. Patrocinio P. Schweickart, 'Toward a feminist theory of reading' in *Gender and Reading: Essays on readers texts and contexts*, edited E. A. Flynn and P. P. Schweickart (Baltimore, 1986).
2. Jean E. Kennard, 'Convention coverage or how to read your own life', *New Literary History* (Autumn 1981), vol. 13, no.1, Autumn 1981, quoted in Mary Jacobus, *Reading Woman: Essays in feminist criticism* (London, 1986), p.233.
3. See Sara Mills, 'Authentic realism' in *Feminist Readings/Feminists Reading*, edited Sara Mills, Lynne Pearce, Sue Spaull and Elaine Millard (Hemel Hempstead, 1989) for a full description of this method of working.
4. Janet Todd, *Feminist Literary History: A defence* (Oxford, 1988), p.84.
5. *ibid.*, p.84.
6. Shoshana Felman, 'To open the question', Introduction to no. 55/6, *Yale French Studies*, 'Literature and psychoanalysis – the question of reading: otherwise', 1977, p.6.
7. *ibid.*, pp.9 and 10.
8. *ibid.*, p.8.
9. Alan Singer, *A Metaphorics of Fiction* (Florida, 1983), p.14.
10. Don Cupitt, *The Long-Legged Fly: A theology of language and desire* (London, 1987), p.114.
11. Patricia Parker, 'The metaphorical plot' in *Metaphor: Problems and perspectives*, edited David Miall (Hemel Hempstead, 1982), pp.133 and 155.
12. Sandra M. Gilbert and Susan Gubar, *The Madwoman in the Attic: The woman writer and the nineteenth-century literary imagination* (New Haven and London, 1979); Elaine Showalter, *A Literature of Their Own: British women novelists from Brontë to Lessing* (London, 1982); Jennifer Gribble, *The Lady of Shalott in the Victorian Novel* (London, 1983).
13. Elaine Showalter, 'Feminist criticism in the wilderness' in *The New*

Feminist Criticism: Essays on women, literature and theory, edited Elaine Showalter (London, 1986), p.262.
14. *ibid.*, p.264.
15. For examples of work in this field, see Griselda Pollock, *Vision and Difference: Femininity, feminism and the histories of art* (London and New York, 1988) and Sandra M. Gilbert and Susan Gubar, *No Man's Land: The place of the woman writer in the twentieth century, Vol. 1: The war of the words* (1988) and *Vol. 2: Sexchanges* (1989) (New Haven and London).
16. Quentin Bell, *Virginia Woolf: A biography, Vol. II* (London, 1972; 1987), p.7.
17. Janet Sayers, *Sexual Contradictions: Psychology, psychoanalysis and feminism* (1986) quoted in Patricia Waugh, *Feminine Fictions: Revisiting the postmodern* (London, 1989), p.59.
18. Jane Austen, *Mansfield Park* (London, 1814; Harmondsworth, 1984), p.127.
19. Jane Austen, *Persuasion* (London, 1818; Harmondsworth, 1977), p.237.
20. Jennifer Dawson, *The Ha-Ha* (1961) (Harmondsworth, 1962), p.50.
21. Virginia Woolf in *Virginia Woolf: Women and writing*, edited Michèle Barrett (London, 1979), p.63.

1 Awakenings

1. Kate Chopin, *The Awakening and Selected Stories*, edited Sandra M. Gilbert (Harmondsworth, 1985), p.151.
2. Susan J. Rosowski, 'The novel of awakening' in *The Voyage In: Fictions of female development*, edited Elizabeth Abel, Marianne Hirsch and Elizabeth Langland (Hanover and London, 1983), p.49.
3. Mary Jacobus, *Reading Woman: Essays in feminist criticism* (London, 1986, 1987), p.37.
4. Edith Wharton, *The House of Mirth*, edited Cynthia Griffin Wolff (Harmondsworth, 1985), p.5.
5. Sandra M. Gilbert and Susan Gubar, *No Man's Land: The place of the woman writer in the twentieth century, Vol. 2: Sexchanges* (New Haven and London, 1989), p.129.
6. Edith Wharton quoted in Cynthia Griffin Wolff's Introduction to *The House of Mirth*, p.xi.
7. Rachel Blau DuPlessis, *Writing Beyond the Ending: Narrative strategies of twentieth-century women writers* (Bloomington, 1985), p.17.
8. Cynthia Griffin Wolff, Introduction to *The House of Mirth*, p.xv. See also Gilbert and Gubar, *Sexchanges*, pp.123–68 for an interesting reading of Wharton's work which links her fiction to her life and times.
9. Gilbert and Gubar, *Sexchanges*, p.133.
10. Judith Fryer, *Felicitous Space: The imaginative structures of Edith Wharton and Willa Cather* (Chapel Hill, 1986), p.58.

11. This quotation and the previous information concerning the painting are taken from Cynthia Griffin Wolff's notes to the Penguin edition of *The House of Mirth* p.335. The portrait by Reynolds can be found reproduced in Ellis K. Waterhouse, *Reynolds* (London, 1941), p.177.
12. Mary Webster, 'The eighteenth century' in *The Genius of British Painting*, edited David Piper (London, 1975), pp.163–4.
13. We owe this point to an artist friend, Patricia Linnell.
14. Griselda Pollock, *Vision and Difference: Femininity, feminism and the histories of art* (London and New York, 1988), pp.86 and 87.
15. Cynthia Griffin Wolff, *A Feast of Words: The triumph of Edith Wharton* (Oxford, 1978), p.132.
16. Virginia Woolf, *Moments of Being: Unpublished autobiographic writings*, edited Jeanne Schulkind (1976) (London, 1978), p.157.
17. Mary Jacobus, *Reading Woman*, pp.240–1.
18. All references are to Charlotte Perkins Gilman, *The Yellow Wallpaper*, with Afterword by Elaine R. Hedges (London, 1981).
19. Virginia Woolf, *Collected Essays Vol. 2* (London, 1966–7), pp.145–6.
20. Weir Mitchell's ideas concerning the treatment of 'neurasthenia' in intelligent women were highly influential at this time. His famous rest cure, which he first described in America in 1873, was introduced to England in the 1880s. It involved separation from friends and family, enforced idleness in one of his special clinics and a bovine passivity brought about by lack of stimulation and over-feeding. Elaine Showalter, in her account of Weir Mitchell's influence, notes that a neurasthetic patient 'was expected to gain as much as fifty pounds on a diet that began with milk and gradually built up to several substantial meals a day' (*The Female Malady: Women, madness and English culture, 1830–1980*, (London, 1987), pp.138–9). Edith Wharton was treated by him 1898 (see Gilbert and Gubar, *Sexchanges*, p.135) and Sir George Savage prescribed rest cures based on his theories for Virginia Woolf. There was much speculation in both America and England during the last two decades of the century as to how far 'neurasthenia' was related to women's ambitions for social, intellectual and political freedom (see Showalter, *The Female Malady*, pp.136–7).
21. Showalter, *The Female Malady*, p.141.
22. Annette Kolodny, 'A map for rereading: gender and the interpretation of literary texts' in *The New Feminist Criticism: Essays on women, literature and theory*, edited Elaine Showalter (New York, 1985; London, 1986), p.50.
23. Charlotte Brontë, *Jane Eyre* (Oxford, 1969), pp.131–2.
24. Jacobus, *Reading Woman*, p.238.
25. *ibid.*, p.234.
26. *ibid.*, pp.243,242.
27. *ibid.*, p.244.
28. R. K. R. Thornton (ed.), *Poetry of the 'Nineties* (Harmondsworth, 1970), pp.16–17.

29. Katherine Lyon Mix, *A Study in Yellow: 'The Yellow Book' and its contributors* (London, 1960), pp.2–3.
30. *The Yellow Book: An illustrated quarterly.* An anthology edited by Fraser Harrison (London, 1974), pp.27–8.
31. *ibid.*, pp.32–3.
32. Virginia Woolf, *The Waves* (London, 1985), p.77.
33. Judith Fetterley, 'Reading about reading' in *Gender and Reading: Essays on readers texts and contexts*, edited E. A. Flynn and P. P. Schweickart (Baltimore, 1986), pp.163 and 160.
34. Virginia Woolf, *A Room of One's Own* (Harmondsworth, 1972), p.87.
35. Michael T. Gilmore, 'Revolt against nature: The problematic modernism of *The Awakening*' in *New Essays on 'The Awakening'*, edited Wendy Martin (Cambridge, 1988), p.60.
36. Cristina Giorcelli, 'Edna's wisdom: a transitional and numinous merging' in Martin, *New Essays*, p.136.
37. Andrew Delbanco, 'The half-life of Edna Pontellier' in Martin, *New Essays*, p.95.
38. Elaine Showalter, 'Tradition and the female talent: *The Awakening* as a solitary book' in Martin, *New Essays*, p.43.
39. Michael T. Gilmore in Martin, *New Essays*, p.79.
40. Elaine Showalter in Martin, *New Essays*, pp.46–7.
41. Jacobus, *Reading Woman*, p.79.
42. Cf. Willa Cather:

> The parrot, Father Jesus said, had always been the bird of wonder and desire to the pueblo Indians. In ancient times its feathers were more valued than wampum and turquoises. Even before the Spaniards came, the pueblos of northern New Mexico used to send explorers along the dangerous and difficult trade routes down into tropical Mexico to bring back upon their bodies a cargo of parrot feathers. To purchase these the trader carried pouches full of turquoises from the Cerrillos hills near Sante Fé. When, very rarely, a trader succeeded in bringing back a live bird to his people, it was paid divine honours, and its death threw the whole village into the deepest gloom. Even the bones were piously preserved. (*Death Comes for the Archbishop* (1926), (New York, 1928), pp.86–7)

43. Sandra Gilbert, Introduction to Chopin, *The Awakening*, p.20.
44. Extract from Leonard Woolf, *Sowing: An autobiography of the years 1880–1904* (1960) entitled 'Cambridge friends and influences' in S. P. Rosenbaum, *The Bloomsbury Group: A collection of memoirs, commentary and criticism* (Toronto, 1975), p.106.
45. Linda Dowling, 'The decadent and the new woman in the 1890s', *Nineteenth-Century Fiction*, vol.33, no.4, March 1979, p.435.
46. Shirley Foster, 'The open cage: freedom, marriage and the heroine in early twentieth-century American women's novels' in *Women's Writing:*

A challenge to theory, edited Moira Monteith (Hemel Hempstead, 1986), p.166.
47. Gilbert and Gubar, *Sexchanges*, p.110.
48. Elaine Showalter in Martin, *New Essays*, p.52.
49. Suzanne Wolkenfeld quoted in Gilbert and Gubar, *Sexchanges*, p.109.
50. *ibid.*, pp.96,102.
51. *ibid.*, p.109.
52. Michael T. Gilmore in Martin, *New Essays*, p.84.
53. Cristina Giorcelli in Martin, *New Essays*, p.125.
54. Toril Moi, *Sexual/Textual Politics: Feminist literary theory* (London and New York, 1985), p.117.
55. Hélène Cixous, 'The laugh of the Medusa' in *New French Feminisms: An anthology*, edited and introduced by Elaine Marks and Isabelle de Courtivron (Hemel Hempstead, 1981), p.260.
56. Catherine Clément in Hélène Cixous and Catherine Clément, *The Newly Born Woman*, translated Betsy Wing (Manchester, 1986), p.6.
57. D. Davidson, 'What metaphors mean', *Critical Inquiry*, 5, (1978) quoted in Eva Feder Kittay, *Metaphor: Its cognitive force and linguistic structure* (Oxford, 1987), p.117.
58. Cristina Giorcelli in Martin, *New Essays*, p.138.
59. Quoted in Fryer, *Felicitous Space*, p.289.

2 Virginia Woolf's 'mystic boundaries'

1. Virginia Woolf, *Three Guineas* (London, 1986), p.21.
2. Virginia Woolf, *A Writer's Diary* (London, 1978), p.293.
3. Theodora Bosanquet, review from *Tide and Tide*, 4 June, 1938, reprinted in *Virginia Woolf: The critical heritage*, edited Robin Majumdar and Allen McLaurin (London, 1975), p.402.
4. Unsigned review from *The Times Literary Supplement*, 4 June 1938, reprinted in *Virginia Woolf*, edited Majumdar and McLaurin, p.400.
5. Virginia Woolf, 'Professions for women' in *Virginia Woolf: Women and writing*, edited Michèle Barrett (London, 1979), pp.57–63.
6. *ibid.*, p.59.
7. Elaine Showalter, *A Literature of Their Own: British women novelists from Brontë to Lessing*, (London, 1982), p.283.
8. Virginia Woolf, *A Room of One's Own* (London, 1977), p.5.
9. Showalter, *A Literature of Their Own*, p.297.
10. Woolf, *A Writer's Diary*, pp.31–2.
11. See Louise DeSalvo, *Virginia Woolf's First Voyage* (London, 1980).
12. Stephen Trombley, *'All That Summer She Was Mad: Virginia Woolf and her doctors*, (London, 1981) and Roger Poole, *The Unknown Virginia Woolf* (Hemel Hempstead, 1987).

13. See, for example, W. H. Hudson's letter to Edward Garnett, 12 June 1915, reprinted in *Virginia Woolf* edited Majumdar and McLaurin, p.61 and David Dowling, *Bloomsbury Aesthetics and the Novels of Forster and Woolf* (London, 1985) pp.108–16.
14. Cf. Virginia Woolf: '[Meredith] has been, it is plain, at great pains to destroy the conventional form of the novel. He makes no attempt to preserve the sober reality of Trollope and Jane Austen; he has destroyed all the usual staircases by which we have learnt to climb' (*The Common Reader, Vol. 2* (London, 1986), p.228).
15. Virginia Woolf, *The Voyage Out* (London, 1978), p.21.
16. Is this word perhaps an echo of 'Duckworth', associating it with the half-brothers who subjected Virginia to sexual abuse? (see Poole, *The Unknown Virginia Woolf*).
17. Trombley, *All That Summer She Was Mad*, p.20; Poole, *The Unknown Virginia Woolf*, pp.35–6.
18. The image of the vault echoes the reference to *Antigone* earlier in the novel (p.41). Cf. also Woolf's use of the vault in *Antigone* as an image of patriarchal oppression in *Three Guineas* (p.161).
19. In the tradition of Jane Austen, who is discussed earlier in the novel by Helen, Rachel and the Dalloways, the public room and more particularly the dance, may be seen as representing the fabric of relationships within society.
20. Terence is reading Milton's *Comus*. For an interesting reading of the *Comus* allusion in *The Voyage Out*, see Beverly Ann Schlack, *Continuing Presences: Virginia Woolf's use of literary allusion* (Pennsylvania and London, 1979) pp.20–8.
21. Trombley, *All That Summer She Was Mad*, p.33.
22. E. M. Forster, review in *Daily News and Leader*, reprinted in *Virginia Woolf*, edited Majumdar and McLaurin, p.54.
23. E. M. Forster, *A Room with a View* (1908) (Harmondsworth, 1955), p.36.
24. James Hafley, *The Glass Roof* (New York, 1963), p.70.
25. Jeremy Tambling, 'Repression in Mrs Dalloway's London' in *Essays in Criticism*, vol.32, no.2, April 1989.
26. Hafley, *The Glass Roof*, p.23.
27. Kate Millett, *Sexual Politics* (London, 1977), p.139.
28. See respectively Suzette Hencke, '*Mrs Dalloway*: the communion of saints' in *New Feminist Essays on Virginia Woolf*, edited Jane Marcus (London, 1981); Barbara Hill Rigney, *Madness and Sexual Politics in the Feminist Novel: Studies in Brontë, Woolf, Lessing and Atwood* (Wisconsin, 1978); Makiko Minow-Pinkney, *Virginia Woolf and the Problem of the Subject: Feminine writing in the major novels* (Hemel Hempstead, 1987) and Jeremy Hawthorn, *Virginia Woolf's 'Mrs Dalloway': A study in alienation* (Brighton, 1975).
29. Woolf, *A Writer's Diary* p.66.
30. Rachel Bowlby, *Virginia Woolf: Feminist destinations* (Oxford, 1988), p.93.

31. Hawthorn, *Virginia Woolf's 'Mrs Dalloway'*, p.94.
32. Virginia Woolf, *Mrs Dalloway* (London, 1976), p.109.
33. Hencke, in *New Feminist Essays*, edited Marcus, p.128.
34. Minow-Pinkney, *Virginia Woolf and the Problem of the Subject*, p.67.
35. *ibid.*, p.67.
36. Schlack, *Continuing Presences* p.166, note 41.
37. *ibid.*, p.63.
38. *ibid.*, p.62.
39. *ibid.*, p.62.
40. See, for example, Hawthorn, *Virginia Woolf's 'Mrs Dalloway'*, pp.55–6.
41. Cf. Patricia Waugh:

> The colonel in *Between the Acts* (1941) may sit back bemused at Miss La Trobe's pageant, protesting 'What's history without the Army?' (p.115) but the novel suggests that history is not simply winning wars, it is also the 'between', the 'no man's' land largely inhabited by women.
>
> This 'between' involves the daily domestic duties, attention to human feelings, and maintenance of connection, often expressed in Woolf's work (as in later writers such as Alice Walker) through the images of knitting, stitching, or weaving. (*Feminine Fictions: Revisiting the postmodern* (London, 1989), p.93)

42. Hencke in Marcus, *New Feminist Essays*, p.138.
43. Woolf, *A Writer's Diary*, p.58.
44. See, for example, Rigney, *Madness and Sexual Politics in the Feminist Novel*; Hawthorn, *Virginia Woolf's 'Mrs Dalloway'* and Schlack, *Continuing Presences*.
45. Schlack, *Continuing Presences*, p.73.
46. Miss Isabel Pole, although a peripheral figure in the novel, is one of the ways in which a connection is established between Clarissa and Septimus. Her green dress links her with Clarissa at a literal level and in this context suggests fertility, her name Pole evoking the maypole of 'Merrie England', ironically contrasted with the celibacy of Clarissa's attic room and the sterility of Septimus's marriage to Rezia.
47. Virginia Woolf would have been 12 when the first issue of *The Yellow Book* appeared and 15 when the last issue was published. In a household as literary as that of the Stephens, some discussion of *The Yellow Book* would surely have taken place. It is quite possible, therefore, that her use as an adult novelist of yellow as suggestive of social change, non-conformity and a hopefulness for the future – held in opposition with grey as the colour of Victorian social respectability and conformity – derives, perhaps unconsciously, from this period of her life. (Cf. Fraser Harrison on the metamorphosis of *The Yellow Book* from yellow to grey:

> The fifth volume was at the printers, but, after a day or two of hesitation, Chapman recalled it and expunged all traces of Beardsley.

Two weeks late, on 30th April 1895, the new, emasculated version was published. 'It turned grey overnight,' E. F. Benson remarked. (*The Yellow Book: An illustrated quarterly* introduced and edited by Fraser Harrison (London: 1974), p.13)

48. Virginia Woolf, *Night and Day* (1919) (London, 1960), pp.417–18.
49. Letter to Roger Fry, quoted in Quentin Bell, *Virginia Woolf* (1972) (London, 1987), p.129.
50. Woolf, *A Writer's Diary*, p.81.
51. Virginia Woolf, *To the Lighthouse* (London, 1977), p.39.
52. Woolf, 'Professions for Women' in *Virginia Woolf*, edited Barrett, p.59.
53. Hafley, *The Glass Roof*, p.82.
54. Toril Moi, *Sexual/Textual Politics: Feminist literary theory* (London and New York, 1985), p.13.
55. Griselda Pollock, *Vision and Difference: Feminity, feminism and histories of art* (London, 1988) p.87.

3 '...marooned...': Jean Rhys's desolate women

1. Carole Angier, *Jean Rhys* (Harmondsworth, 1985), p.121.
2. Catherine Belsey, *Critical Practice* (London, 1980), p.65.
3. All references are to Jean Rhys, *Good Morning, Midnight* (Harmondsworth, 1984).
4. France Bhattacharya and Marie-Claudette Kirpalani, 'The French women – aspirations and achievements' in *Women of the World: Illusion and reality*, edited Urmila Phadnis and Indira Malani (New Delhi, 1978), pp.186–7.
5. It seems to us that Rhys's heroines are closer to the hysteric of Hélène Cixous's and Catherine Clément's debate than to Elizabeth Abel's description of the schizophrenic. (See, respectively, Hélène Cixous and Catherine Clément, *The Newly Born Woman* (Manchester, 1986) especially pp.95, 99, 107, 147 ff., 154 ff. and 165–6, and Elizabeth Abel, 'Women and schizophrenia: the fiction of Jean Rhys', *Contemporary Literature*, vol.20, 1979, pp.155–77.) It is particularly interesting to compare and contrast Hélène Cixous's celebratory reading of hysterics as 'wonderful' (p.95) and powerful (p.154) with Catherine Clément's more circumspect rendering of them as powerless because marginalised: 'Ethnologists, analysts, or anyone naively able to say this, at the same time recognize in them an exceptional capacity for language and an *exclusion correlative to it*' (p.155). One could argue that Rhys's early and ineffectual heroines fit Clément's analysis, whereas Antoinette Cosway exemplifies the destructive power accorded to the hysteric in Cixous's poetic and mythic celebration of her.

6. Elgin W. Mellown, 'Character and themes in the novels of Jean Rhys', *Contemporary Literature*, vol.13, no.4, Autumn 1972, pp. 462 and 467.
7. Peter Wolfe, *Jean Rhys* (Boston, 1980), pp.134–5.
8. Rosalind Miles, *The Fiction of Sex: Themes and functions of sex differences in the modern novel* (London, 1974), p.101.
9. All references are to Jean Rhys, *Voyage in the Dark* (Harmondsworth: Penguin Books, 1984).
10. Lucy Wilson, '"Women must have spunks": Jean Rhys's West Indian outcasts', *Modern Fiction Studies*, vol.32, no.3, Autumn 1986, p.442.
11. Plot summary taken from William Rose Benét, *The Reader's Encyclopedia, Second Edition* (London, 1972), p.876.
12. Leslie Fielder quoted in Anthony A. Luengo, '*Wide Sargasso Sea* and the gothic mode', *World Literature in English*, vol.15, no.1, April 1976, p.231.
13. Francis Wyndham and Diana Melly (eds), *Jean Rhys: Letters 1931–66* (Harmondsworth, 1985), pp.236–7.
14. Edward Brathwaite, *The Development of Creole Society in Jamaica, 1770–1820* (1971) (Oxford, 1978), p.228.
15. *ibid.*, p.232.
16. *ibid.*, p.220.
17. All references are to Jean Rhys, *Wide Sargasso Sea* (Harmondsworth: Penguin Books, 1983).
18. Cf. Edward Brathwaite: 'the general and overwhelming assumption was that slaves, if human, were of a different *genus*; that they were lazy, lying, profligate, promiscuous, cowardly, savage, debased, tyrannical to their own people, ugly, and demonstrably inferior to whites' (*The Development of Creole Society*, p.181).
19. Adrienne Rich, *On Lies, Secrets and Silence: Selected prose 1966–1978* (1979) (London, 1984), p.99.
20. Barbara Hill Rigney, *Madness and Sexual Politics in the Feminist Novel: Studies in Brontë, Woolf, Lessing and Atwood* (Wisconsin, 1978), p.27.
21. Cf. Edward Long, whose *The History of Jamaica* was published in 1774, in Brathwaite: 'They laugh at the idea of marriage, which ties two persons together indissolubly' (*The Development of Creole Society*, p.215).
22. *ibid.*, p.219.
23. *ibid.*, pp.162–3.
24. Lee Erwin, '"Like in a looking-glass": history and narrative in *Wide Sargasso Sea*', *Novel*, vol.22, no.2, Winter 1989, p.147.
25. Cf. Sandra L. Gilman:

   > 'The white *man's* burden' thus becomes his sexuality and its control, and this is transferred into the need to control the sexuality of the Other, the Other as sexualized female. The colonial mentality that sees 'natives' as needing control is easily transferred to 'woman'. (Quoted in Erwin, p.147)

26. Elaine Showalter, *The Female Malady: Women, madness and English culture, 1830–1980* (London, 1987), pp.74–7.

27. Gayatri Chakravorty Spivak, 'French feminism in an international frame' in *Yale French Studies* no.62, 1981, p.183.
28. Mellown, 'Characters and themes in the novels of Jean Rhys', p.464.
29. Cf. Virginia Woolf's suggestion that the desire to colonise is an essential component of masculine behaviour (*A Room of One's Own*, pp.49–50).
30. Kathy Mezei, '"And it kept its secret": narration, memory and madness in Jean Rhys '*Wide Sargasso Sea*', *Critique*, vol.XXVIII, no.4, Summer 1987, p.198.
31. Sue Roe, '"The shadow of light": the symbolic underworld of Jean Rhys' in *Women Reading Women's Writing*, edited Sue Roe (Hemel Hempstead, 1987), p.259.
32. See Kathy Mezei's article for a rather different approach to the 'secret' of *Wide Sargasso Sea* which emphasises the narrative rather than the metaphoric dimension of the text.
33. *Jean Rhys*, edited Wyndham and Melly, p.65.
34. Adrienne Rich, *On Lies, Secrets and Silence: Selected prose 1966–1978* (1979) (London, 1984), pp.118 and 201.
35. Juliet Mitchell, *Women: The longest revolution: Essays in feminism, literature and psychoanalysis* (London, 1984), pp.289–90.

4 Beyond boundaries and back again: Margaret Atwood's *Surfacing*

1. All references to Margaret Atwood, *Surfacing* (1972) (London, 1979).
2. See Carol Christ: 'In a letter to Dan Noel dated December 4, 1974, Atwood stated that "what is *actually* seen during the diving scene is the father's corpse"' (Carol Christ, *Women Writers on Spiritual Quest* (1980) Boston, 1986), p.142).
3. See, for example, Carol Christ's work cited in Note 2.
4. Adrienne Rich, *On Lies, Secrets and Silence: Selected prose 1966–1978* (1979) (London, 1984) pp.308–9.
5. See Olive Banks, *Faces of Feminism* (1981) (Oxford, 1986), in particular chapters 2, 5 and 6.
6. Cf.:

> In a striking essay, the novelist Bertha Harris has written of the silence surrounding the lesbian . . . That reality was nothing so simple and dismissible as the fact that two women might go to bed together. It was a sense of desiring oneself; above all, of choosing oneself; it was also a primary intensity between women, an intensity which in the world at large was trivialized, caricatured, or invested with evil . . . I believe it is the lesbian in every woman who is compelled by female energy, who gravitates towards strong women,

who seeks a literature that will express her energy and strength. It is the lesbian in us who drives us to feel imaginatively, render in language, grasp, the full connection between woman and woman. It is the lesbian in us who is creative, for the dutiful daughter of the fathers in us in only a hack. (Rich, *On Lies, Secrets and Silence*, pp.200–1)

7. Cf. Selma James: 'The name she gives her is Cosway – or causeway, the bridge between the Third World and Europe, between one race and another, a causeway from defeat to victory' (*The Ladies and the Mammies: Jane Austen and Jean Rhys* (Bristol, 1983), p.93)
8. Banks, *Faces of Feminism*, p.243.
9. Rich, *On Lies, Secrets and Silence*, p.268. See also her *Of Woman Born: Motherhood as experience and institution* (New York, 1976).
10. *ibid.*, p.272.
11. Banks, *Faces of Feminism*, p.96.
12. Christ, *Women Writers on Spiritual Quest*, p.47.
13. Jan Montefiore, *Feminism and Poetry: Language, experience, identity in women's writing* (London, 1987), p.84.
14. Richard Rorty, *Contingency, Irony and Solidarity* (Cambridge, 1989), p.7.

Conclusion

1. Cf. Fay Weldon's description of Marilyn French's *The Women's Room* (1977) as 'the kind of book that changes lives' on the cover of the novel (London, 1978).
2. Olive Banks, *Faces of Feminism* (1981) (Oxford, 1986), pp.252, 258.
3. Deirdre Beddoe, *Back to Home and Duty: Women between the wars, 1918–1939* (London, 1989), p.6.
4. Banks, *Faces of Feminism*, p.241.
5. Richard Rorty, *Contingency, Irony and Solidarity*, (Cambridge, 1989), p.9.
6. *ibid.*, p.9.

Bibliography

Abel, Elizabeth, 'Women and schizophrenia: the fiction of Jean Rhys', *Contemporary Literature*, vol. 20, 1979, pp.155–77.
Abel, Elizabeth, (ed.), *Writing and Sexual Difference* (Hemel Hempstead: Harvester Wheatsheaf, 1982).
Abel, Elizabeth, Marianne Hirsch and Elizabeth Langland (eds), *The Voyage In: Fictions of female development* (Hanover and London: University Press of New England, 1983).
Angier, Carole, *Jean Rhys* (Harmondsworth: Penguin Books, 1985).
Atwood, Margaret, *Surfacing* (1972; London: Virago Press, 1979).
Banks, Olive, *Faces of Feminism* (1981; Oxford: Basil Blackwell, 1986).
Barrett, Michèle, (ed.), *Virginia Woolf: Women and writing* (London: The Women's Press, 1979).
Bazin, Nancy Topping, *Virginia Woolf and the Androgynous Vision* (New Brunswick: Rutgers University Press, 1973).
Beddoe, Deirdre, *Back to Home and Duty: Women between the wars, 1918–1939* (London: Pandora Press, 1989).
Beja, Morris, (ed.), *To the Lighthouse: Casebook* (London: Macmillan, 1970).
Bell, Quentin, *Virginia Woolf: A biography* (London: The Hogarth Press, 1972 (2 vols); Triad/Paladin, 1987 (1 vol.))
Belsey, Catherine, *Critical Practice* (London: Methuen, 1980).
Benét, William Rose, *The Reader's Encyclopedia, Second Edition* (London: Book Club Associates, 1972).
Bennett, Joan, *Virginia Woolf: Her art as novelist* (Cambridge: Cambridge University Press, 1964).
Blackstone, Bernard, *Virginia Woolf: A commentary* (London: Hogarth Press, 1949).
Bowlby, Rachel, *Virginia Woolf: Feminist destinations* (Oxford: Basil Blackwell, 1988).
Brathwaite, Edward, *The Development of Creole Society in Jamaica 1770–1820* (1971; Oxford: Clarendon Press, 1978).
Brontë, Charlotte, *Jane Eyre* (Oxford: Clarendon Press, 1969).
Brownstein, Rachel, *Becoming a Heroine* (New York: Viking Press, 1982).

Cather, Willa, *Death Comes for the Archbishop* (1926; New York: Alfred A. Knopf, 1928).

Chopin, Kate, *The Awakening and Selected Stories*, edited by Sandra M. Gilbert (Harmondsworth: Penguin Books, 1985).

Christ, Carol, *Women Writers on Spiritual Quest* (1980; 2nd edn, Boston: Beacon Press, 1986).

Cixous, Hélène, and Catherine Clément, *The Newly Born Woman*, translated by Betsy Wing (Manchester: Manchester University Press, 1986).

Cupitt, Don, *The Long-Legged Fly: A theology of language and desire* (London: SCM Press, 1987).

Dawson, Jennifer, *The Ha-Ha* (Harmondsworth: Penguin Books, 1962).

DeSalvo, Louise, *Virginia Woolf's First Voyage* (Totowa, NJ: Rowman & Littlefield, 1980; London: Macmillan, 1980).

Dowling, David, *Bloomsbury Aesthetics and the Novels of Forster and Woolf* (London: Macmillan, 1985).

Dowling, Linda, 'The decadent and the new woman in the 1890's', *Nineteenth-Century Fiction*, vol.33, no.4, March 1979, pp.435–53.

DuPlessis, Rachel Blau, *Writing Beyond the Ending: Narrative strategies of twentieth-century women writers* (Bloomington: Indiana University Press, 1985).

Erwin, Lee, '"Like in a looking-glass": History and narrative in *Wide Sargasso Sea*', *Novel*, vol.22, no.2, Winter 1989.

Felman, Shoshana, 'To open the question', Introduction to no.55/6, *Yale French Studies*, 'Literature and psychoanalysis – the question of reading: otherwise' (1977).

Fleishman, Avrom, *Virginia Woolf: A critical reading* (Baltimore: Johns Hopkins University Press, 1975).

Flynn, E. A. and P. P. Schweickart (eds), *Gender and Reading: Essays on readers texts and contexts* (Baltimore: Johns Hopkins University Press, 1986).

Forster, E. M., *A Room with a View* (Harmondsworth: Penguin Books, 1955).

Foucault, Michel, *The History of Sexuality*, translated by Robert Hurley (London: Random House, 1978).

French, Marilyn, *The Women's Room* (1977; London: Sphere Books, 1978).

Fryer, Judith, *Felicitous Space: The imaginative structures of Edith Wharton and Willa Cather* (Chapel Hill: University of North Carolina Press, 1986).

Gilbert, Sandra M. and Susan Gubar, *The Madwoman in the Attic: The woman writer and the nineteenth-century literary imagination* (New Haven and London: Yale University Press, 1979).

Gilbert, Sandra M. and Susan Gubar, *No Man's Land: The place of the woman writer in the twentieth century, Vol.1: The war of the words and Vol.2: Sexchanges* (New Haven and London: Yale University Press, 1988 and 1989).

Gilman, Charlotte Perkins, *The Yellow Wallpaper* (London: Virago Press, 1981).

Gordon, Lyndall, *Virginia Woolf: A writer's life* (Oxford: Oxford University Press, 1984).

Gribble, Jennifer, *The Lady of Shalott in the Victorian Novel* (London: Macmillan, 1983).

Hafley, James, *The Glass Roof* (New York: Russell & Russell, 1963).

Harrison, Fraser, (ed.), *The Yellow Book: An illustrated quarterly* (London: Sidgwick and Jackson, 1974).

Hawthorn, Jeremy, *Virginia Woolf's 'Mrs Dalloway': A study in alienation* (Brighton: Chatto & Windus for Sussex University Press, 1975).

Humm, Maggie, *Feminist Criticism: Women as contemporary critics* (Hemel Hempstead: Harvester Wheatsheaf, 1986).

Humm, Maggie, *An Annotated Critical Bibliography of Feminist Criticism* (Hemel Hempstead: Harvester Wheatsheaf, 1989).

Jacobus, Mary, *Reading Woman: Essays in feminist criticism* (New York: Columbia University Press, 1986; London: Methuen, 1986, 1987).

James, Selma, *The Ladies and the Mammies: Jane Austen and Jean Rhys* (Bristol: Falling Wall Press, 1983).

Kaplan, Sydney Janet, *Feminine Consciousness in the Modern British Novel* (Chicago: University of Illinois Press, 1975).

Kiely, Robert, *Beyond Egotism: The fiction of James Joyce, Virginia Woolf and D. H. Lawrence* (Cambridge, Mass.: Harvard University Press, 1980).

Kittay, Eva Feder, *Metaphor: Its cognitive force and linguistic structure* (Oxford: Clarendon Press, 1987).

Leaska, Mitchell Alexander, *Virginia Woolf's Lighthouse: A study in critical method* (London: Hogarth Press, 1970).

Leaska, Mitchell Alexander, 'Virginia Woolf's *The Voyage Out*: Character, deduction and the function of ambiguity' in *Virginia Woolf Quarterly*, vol.1, part 2, 1973.

Little, Judy, *Comedy and the Woman Writer: Woolf, Spark and feminism* (Nebraska: University of Nebraska Press, 1983).

Lodge, David, *The Modes of Modern Writing: Metaphor, metonymy and the typology of modern literature* (London: Edward Arnold, 1977).

Luengo, Anthony A., '*Wide Sargasso Sea* and the gothic mode', *World Literature in English*, vol.15, no.1, April 1976.

Majumdar, Robin and Allen McLaurin (eds), *Virginia Woolf: The critical heritage* (London: Routledge & Kegan Paul, 1975).

Marcus, Jane, (ed.), *New Feminist Essays on Virginia Woolf* (London: Macmillan, 1981).

Marder, Herbert, *Feminism and Art: A study of Virginia Woolf* (Chicago: University of Chicago Press, 1968).

Marks, Elaine and Isabelle de Courtivron (eds), *New French Feminisms: An anthology* (Hemel Hempstead: Harvester Wheatsheaf, 1981).

Martin, Wendy, (ed.), *New Essays on 'The Awakening'* (Cambridge and New York: Cambridge University Press, 1988).

Mellown, Elgin W., 'Character and themes in the novels of Jean Rhys', *Contemporary Literature*, vol.13, no.4, Autumn 1972.

Mezei, Kathy, '"And it kept its secret": narration, memory and madness in Jean Rhys' *Wide Sargasso Sea*', *Critique*, vol.XXVIII, no.4, Summer 1987.

Miall, David, (ed.), *Metaphor: Problems and perspectives* (Hemel Hempstead: Harvester Wheatsheaf, 1982).

Miles, Rosalind, *The Fiction of Sex: Themes and functions of sex differences in the modern novel* (London: Vision Press, 1974).

Millett, Kate, *Sexual Politics* (1969: London: Virago Press, 1977; repr. 1985).

Mills, Sara, Lynne Pearce, Sue Spaull and Elaine Millard (eds), *Feminist Readings/Feminists Reading* (Hemel Hempstead: Harvester Wheatsheaf, 1989).

Minow-Pinkney, Makiko, *Virginia Woolf and the Problem of the Subject: Feminine writing in the major novels* (Hemel Hempstead: Harvester Wheatsheaf, 1987).

Mitchell, Juliet, *Women: The longest revolution: Essays in feminism, literature and psychoanalysis* (London: Virago Press, 1984).

Mix, Katherine Lyon, *A Study in Yellow: The 'Yellow Book' and its contributors* (London: Constable, 1960).

Moers, Ellen, *Literary Women: The great writers* (1976; London: Women's Press, 1978).

Moi, Toril, *Sexual/Textual Politics: Feminist literary theory* (London and New York: Methuen, 1985).

Montefiore, Jan, *Feminism and Poetry: Language, experience, identity in women's writing* (London: Pandora Press, 1987).

Monteith, Moira, *Women's Writing: A challenge to theory* (Hemel Hempstead: Harvester Wheatsheaf, 1986).

Naremore, James, *The World Without a Self: Virginia Woolf and the novel* (New Haven and London: Yale University Press, 1973).

Phadnis, Urmila and Indira Malani (eds), *Women of the World: Illusion and reality* (New Delhi: Vikas Publishing House, PVT, 1978).

Piper, David, (ed.), *The Genius of British Painting* (London: Weidenfeld and Nicolson, 1975).

Pollock, Griselda, *Vision and Difference: Femininity, feminism and the histories of art* (London: Routledge & Kegan Paul, 1988).

Poole, Roger, *The Unknown Virginia Woolf* (Hemel Hempstead: Harvester Wheatsheaf, 1987).

Restuccia, Frances L., 'The name of the lily: Edith Wharton's feminism(s)', *Contemporary Literature*, vol.28, no.2, Summer 1987.

Rhys, Jean, *Quartet* (1928; Harmondsworth: Penguin Books, 1987).

Rhys, Jean, *After Leaving Mr Mackenzie* (1930; Harmondsworth: Penguin Books, 1987).

Rhys, Jean, *Voyage in the Dark* (1934; Harmondsworth: Penguin Books, 1984).

Rhys, Jean, *Good Morning, Midnight* (1939; Harmondsworth: Penguin Books, 1984).

Rhys, Jean, *Wide Sargasso Sea* (1966; Harmondsworth: Penguin Books, 1983).

Rhys, Jean, *Tigers Are Better Looking* (1968; Harmondsworth: Penguin Books, 1987).

Rhys, Jean, *Sleep it off Lady* (1976; Harmondsworth: Penguin Books, 1979).

Rhys, Jean, *Smile Please: An unfinished autobiography* (1979; Harmondsworth: Penguin Books, 1984).

Rich, Adrienne, *Of Woman Born: Motherhood as experience and institution* (New York: W. W. Norton, 1976).

Rich, Adrienne, *On Lies, Secrets and Silence: Selected prose 1966–1978* (New York: W. W. Norton, 1979; London: Virago Press, 1980; repr. 1984).

Rigney, Barbara Hill, *Madness and Sexual Politics in the Feminist Novel: Studies in Brontë, Woolf, Lessing and Atwood* (Wisconsin: The University of Wisconsin Press, 1978).

Roe, Sue, (ed.), *Women Reading Women's Writing* (Hemel Hempstead: Harvester Wheatsheaf, 1987).

Rorty, Richard, *Contingency, Irony and Solidarity* (Cambridge: Cambridge University Press, 1989).

Rosenbaum, S. P., (ed.), *The Bloomsbury Group: A collection of memoirs, commentary and criticism* (Toronto and Buffalo: University of Toronto Press, 1975).

Rosenthal, Michael, *Virginia Woolf* (London: Routledge & Kegan Paul, 1979).

Schlack, Beverly Ann, *Continuing Presences: Virginia Woolf's use of literary allusion* (Pennsylvania and London: The Pennsylvania State University Press, 1979).

Showalter, Elaine, *A Literature of Their Own: British women novelists from Brontë to Lessing* (Princeton and London: Princeton University Press, 1977; Virago Press, 1978; revised edn, 1982).

Showalter, Elaine, *The Female Malady: Women, madness and English culture, 1830–1980* (New York: Pantheon Books, 1985; London: Virago Press, 1987).

Showalter, Elaine, (ed.), *The New Feminist Criticism: Essays on women, literature and theory* (New York: Pantheon Books, 1985; London: Virago Press, 1986).

Singer, Alan, *A Metaphorics of Fiction* (Florida: University of Florida Press, 1983).

Spivak, Gayatri Chakravorty, 'French feminism in an international frame' in *Yale French Studies*, no.62, 1981.

Suleiman, Susan Rubin, (ed.), *The Female Body in Western Culture* (Cambridge, Mass. and London: Harvard University Press, 1986).

Tambling, Jeremy, 'Repression in Mrs Dalloway's London' in *Essays in Criticism*, vol.39, no.2, April 1989.

Thornton, R. K. R., (ed.), *Poetry of the 'Nineties* (Harmondsworth: Penguin Books, 1970).

Todd, Janet, *Feminist Literary History: A defence* (Oxford: Polity Press, 1988).

Trombley, Stephen, *'All That Summer She Was Mad': Virginia Woolf and her doctors* (London: Junction Books, 1981).

Waterhouse, Ellis K., *Reynolds* (London: Routledge & Kegan Paul/Trench Trubner, 1941).

Waugh, Patricia, *Feminine Fictions: Revisiting the postmodern* (London: Routledge & Kegan Paul, 1989).

Wharton, Edith, *The House of Mirth*, edited by Cynthia Griffin Wolff (Harmondsworth: Penguin Books, 1985).

Wilson, Lucy, '"Women must have spunks": Jean Rhys's West Indian outcasts', *Modern Fiction Studies*, vol.32, no.3, Autumn 1986.

Wolfe, Peter, *Jean Rhys* (Boston: Twayne Publishers, 1980).

Wolff, Cynthia Griffin, *A Feast of Words: The triumph of Edith Wharton* (Oxford: Oxford University Press, 1978).

Woolf, Virginia, *The Voyage Out* (1915; London: Grafton, 1978).

Woolf, Virginia, *Night and Day* (1919; London: The Hogarth Press, 1960).

Woolf, Virginia, *The Common Reader, Vol. 1* (1925; London: The Hogarth Press, 1984).

Woolf, Virginia, *Mrs Dalloway* (1925; London: Grafton, 1976).

Woolf, Virginia, *To the Lighthouse* (1927; London: Panther, 1977).

Woolf, Virginia, *A Room of One's Own* (1929; London: Panther, 1977).

Woolf, Virginia, *The Waves* (1931; London; Grafton, 1977).

Woolf, Virginia, *The Common Reader, Vol. 2* (1932; London: The Hogarth Press, 1986).

Woolf, Virginia, *Three Guineas* (1938; London: The Hogarth Press, 1986).

Woolf, Virginia, *Between the Acts* (1941; London: Triad Panther, 1978).

Woolf, Virginia, *A Writer's Diary* (1953; London: Triad Grafton, 1978).

Woolf, Virginia, *Collected Essays Vols. 1 and 2* (London: The Hogarth Press, 1966–7).

Woolf, Virginia, *Moments of Being: Unpublished autobiographic writings*, edited by Jeanne Schulkind (London: Chatto & Windus, 1976; Triad Grafton Books, 1978).

Wyndham, Francis, and Diana Melly (eds), *Jean Rhys: Letters 1931–66* (Harmondsworth: Penguin Books, 1985).

Index

Note: Page references in italics indicate those pages which are most important.